ALAN OF LILLE

ALAN OF LILLE

THE FRONTIERS OF THEOLOGY IN
THE LATER TWELFTH CENTURY

G. R. EVANS

CAMBRIDGE UNIVERSITY PRESS

Cambridge

London   New York   New Rochelle
Melbourne   Sydney

Published by the Press Syndicate of the University of Cambridge
The Pitt Building, Trumpington Street, Cambridge CB2 1RP
32 East 57th Street, New York, NY 10022, USA
296 Beaconsfield Parade, Middle Park, Melbourne 3206, Australia

First published 1983

Printed in Great Britain by
New Western Printing Ltd, Bristol

Library of Congress catalogue card number: 83–1834

British Library Cataloguing in Publication Data
Evans, G. R.
Alan of Lille.
1. Alan of Lille 2. Philosophers,
Medieval–Biography
I. Title
189'.4 B765.A/
ISBN 0 521 24618 0

NWP

CONTENTS

For some good friends

PREFACE

Alan of Lille (d. 1202–3) possessed a richly-stocked and many-sided mind. The range of his learning impressed his contemporaries, to whom he seemed to 'know everything knowable'. He was up-to-the-minute in his understanding of the latest technical developments in the study of the liberal arts in an age when technical skills were advancing rapidly; he was a good Aristotelian in his logic. But he was also greatly influenced by Thierry of Chartres and Gilbert of Poitiers, who had lectured on Boethius' theological treatises in the middle of the century. They, together with William of Conches in his lectures on Calcidius' commentary on Plato's *Timaeus,* had helped to bring about a revival of interest in Platonist ideas. If anything, the Platonist outweighs the Aristotelian in Alan; he saw the technical *minutiae* of his learning as part of a grand plan in which they were transformed into something finer and higher and made to serve a theology in which there was a good deal of Neoplatonic philosophy.

In his *Marriage of Philology and Mercury,* written in the Vandal Carthage of the late fifth century AD, the pagan Martianus Capella describes how the seven liberal arts can elevate the soul to be fit for heaven. That is Alan's view of them, too. With his poetry and his Platonism braced by a sound grasp of Aristotelian logic and Pythagorean mathematics, he set out to lead his readers to the heights of an intellectual heaven, where the divine is all intelligibility. Like Augustine, Alan is a Christian Platonist through and through. But, unlike Augustine, he retained all his life the curiosity about what was new to him in secular and pagan teaching, which was so strong in Augustine before his conversion. Under a literary and ideological influence more Platonist than Aristotelian, Alan composed his famous symbolist epic, the *Anticlaudianus* (or *The Good and Perfect Man*), on Martianus Capella's model; he adopted the form of the *Marriage of Philology and Mercury* in his prosimetric diatribe, *Nature's Complaint,* a dream-like vision in which Alan sees Nature denouncing sodomy and all the other ways in which the intended paths of sexual activity have been perverted.

Yet, free as he felt to employ pagan authors, and wide though his eclecticism was, drawing even upon the Hermetic writings of the second and third centuries, with their teaching about the 'deification' of man through the use of his higher spiritual and rational powers, Alan was a most orthodox Christian theologian. He preached against the heretics in the south of France; he composed manuals for preachers and confessors, a dictionary of theological terms, every possible aid for the priest engaged in pastoral work.

Alan of Lille has not been neglected by modern scholars. His works are too conspicuous – even exotic – a patch of colour in the late twelfth-century scene not to attract attention. His writings present a number of difficulties, however. Because of the circumstances of their composition in the schools, where many of them began as lectures and went through a number of versions, enlargements and abbreviations, it is all but impossible to establish an authentic text for a number of Alan's works. Other pieces present problems of attribution. And Alan is not an easy author. He was fond of rare words; he loved subtlety and complexity and obscurity. His *Anticlaudianus* puzzled his contemporaries as much as it delighted them, and it has remained by far the most famous of his works, attracting a perhaps disproportionate amount of interest. There has been a series of specialised studies, but only M. T. d'Alverny has attempted a general survey. In her masterly assembling of the materials relating to his life and works she has provided a foundation upon which work on the texts can now go forward.

That is a long-term project, and there is no prospect of its advancing far enough in the foreseeable future to make a comprehensive and definitive study a real possibility yet. But a good part of Alan's work is now in print, much of it in modern editions; there is ample manuscript material. There is perhaps something

to be said for making use of the texts we have as a basis for a
consideration of Alan's achievement as a whole. For it does form
a whole – Alan made a synthesis of many branches of contemporary scholarly and literary endeavour, simply by moving about
so energetically among them.

Alan shows us a capacious and dexterous mind at work, a vast
intellectual energy and a poet's passion. He was, above all, an
innovator – not, perhaps, a profoundly original thinker, but an
eclectic with that taste for experimental juxtapositions and new
combinations of familiar notions which is so attractive in a
number of twelfth-century scholars. Alan invented new words,
new modes of expression, new forms and gestures, to try to meet
changing contemporary needs. He was not an introspective, but
a thoroughly extrovert thinker, addressing himself to the problem
of popular heresy, or the student in need of a dictionary, or the
congregation who came to hear him preach, with a sensitivity
which enabled him to adapt what he had to say to their needs.
For all his love of mystery, Alan was always practical; theory and
practice go hand in hand in his writings. He liked to be able to
reveal the existence of depths of truth beyond anything his
readers have envisaged, and then to give them an explanation
which would enable them to grasp something of that truth. He
showed, as perhaps no other writer of the age was able to do, in
exactly what way poetry and the *artes* alike could be made to
serve the purposes of the theologian. It is in the context of his
work as a theologian that his poetry is considered here. Although,
philosophically speaking, it cannot be said to be of permanent
value, his achievement is a very considerable one. Bernard
Silvestris, whose *Cosmographia* showed Alan what might be
done along these lines, cannot match it in magnitude. Peter the
Chanter, who had Alan's range as a teacher, was not a poet.

The possessor of this rich, complex and quite individual mind
remains an obscure figure. He has not attracted a biographer,
largely, perhaps, because the materials for his life are fragmen-
tary. He has little to offer the political historian because, unlike
his contemporary John of Salisbury, he wrote no memoir, no
political commentary (except in an oblique way in his sermons);
he does not describe the famous teachers of his youth; he made no
collection of his letters for publication. So little trace did con-

temporary events leave in his writings that it is only with difficulty that they can be put into any sort of order and dated even provisionally.

Nevertheless, Alan was abundantly a man of his time as a scholar. If John of Salisbury has some claim to be among the most cultivated of his time, a man truly *cultus*, then perhaps we may claim for Alan the glory of being the most widely learned, *doctissimus*. Alan chose to remain a professional scholar rather than to pursue a career in ecclesiastical politics. And so we hear less of him. But, as we shall see, his horizon was in no way narrowed by the choice he had made.

ACKNOWLEDGEMENTS

F. Giusberti's edition of the Prologue to Peter the Chanter's *De Tropis Loquendi* has recently been published in *Materials for a Study on Twelfth Century Scholasticism* (Naples, 1982), pp. 87–109. I should like to thank his widow for permission to make use of his preliminary work on the manuscripts.

Versions of some of the discussions which follow have been published in the following journals. I should like to thank their editors for permission to make fresh use of the material here:

' "The Book of Experience"; Alan of Lille's use of the classical rhetorical topos in his pastoral writings', *Analecta Cisterciensia,* XXXII (1976), 113–21; 'Boethian and Euclidean axiomatic method in the theology of the later twelfth century', *Archives internationales d'histoire des sciences,* CIII (1980), 13–29; 'Alan of Lille and the threshold of theology', *Analecta Cisterciensia,* XXXVI (1980), 129–47; '*Perfectus Homo*: Alan of Lille's new creation', *Paideia* (forthcoming); 'Alan of Lille's *Distinctiones* and the problem of theological language', *Sacris Erudiri,* XXIV (1980), 67–86; 'Peter the Chanter's *De Tropis Loquendi*: the problem of the text', *New Scholasticism,* LV, 1 (1981), 95–103.

I have to thank many friends and colleagues for their advice and interest, especially Professor J. Norton-Smith, who first introduced me to Alan of Lille, Professor C. N. L. Brooke, Dr A. Crombie, Dr D. P. Henry, the late Dr R. W. Hunt, and Sir Richard Southern.

ABBREVIATIONS

AGJ   *Alain de Lille, Gautier de Châtillon, Jakemart Giélée et leur temps,* ed. H. Roussel and F. Suard, *Actes du Colloque de Lille, 1978* (Lille, 1980)

AHDLMA   Archives d'histoire doctrinale et littéraire du moyen âge

An. Cist.   *Analecta Cisterciensia*

Apostles' Creed   N. M. Häring, 'The Commentary of Alan of Lille on the Apostles' Creed', *An. Cist.,* xxx (1974), 7–46

Baldwin   J. W. Baldwin, *Masters, princes and merchants* (2 vols., Princeton, 1970)

Beiträge   *Beiträge zur Geschichte der Philosophie des Mittelalters*

Bossuat   Alan of Lille, *Anticlaudianus,* ed. R. Bossuat (Paris, 1955)

Cahiers   *Cahiers de l'Institut grec et latin du moyen âge,* Copenhagen

Coll.   *Collectanea Cisterciensia*

CCCM   Corpus Christianorum Continuatio Medievalis

CCSL   Corpus Christianorum Series Latina

CSEL   Corpus Scriptorum Ecclesiasticorum Latinorum

De Lage   G. Raynaud de Lage, *Alain de Lille, poète du xiie siècle* (Paris, 1951)

Gilbert of Poitiers   *Commentaries on Boethius by Gilbert of Poitiers,* ed. N. M. Häring (Toronto, 1966)

MGH Quellen   Monumenta Germaniae Historica: Quellen zur Geistesgeschichte der Mittelalters

MGH SS   Monumenta Germaniae Historica: Scriptores Rerum Germanicarum

Nicene Creed   N. M. Häring, 'The Commentary of Alan of Lille on the Creed of the Mass', *An Cist.,* xxx (1974), 281–303

Our Father   N. M. Häring, 'A Commentary on the Our Father
          by Alan of Lille', *An. Cist.*, XXXI (1975), 149–77
PG   Patrologia Graeca, ed. J. P. Migne (Paris, 1841ff)
PL   Patrologia Latina, ed. J. P. Migne (Paris, 1841ff)
Quoniam Homines   'La Somme "Quoniam Homines"',
          AHDLMA, XX (1954), 113–364
RTAM   *Recherches de théologie ancienne et médiévale*
Roberts   P. B. Roberts, *Studies in the Sermons of Stephen
          Langton* (Toronto, 1968)
R. Bén   *Revue Bénédictine*
Sheridan   J. J. Sheridan (tr.), *Anticlaudianus* (Toronto, 1973)
Simon of Tournai,   *Disputationes* Simon of Tournai,
          Disputationes, ed. J. Warichez, SSLov, XII (1932)
SSLov   Spicilegium Sacrum Lovaniense
Stegmüller   F. Stegmüller, *Repertorium Biblicum Medii Aevi*
          (7 vols., Madrid, 1950–71)
Textes   M. T. d'Alverny, *Textes inédits d'Alain de Lille* (Paris,
          1965)
Theological Tractates   Boethius, Theological Tractates, ed.
          H. F. Stewart, E. K. Rand, S. J. Tester (London, 1973)
Thierry   *Commentaries on Boethius by Thierry of Chartres
          and his School,* ed. N. M. Häring (Toronto, 1971)
Two Questions   'Deux questions sur la foi inspirées d'Alain de
          Lille', ed. G. Raynaud de Lage, *AHDLMA*, XIV
          (1943–5), 323–36
Virtues and Vices   O. Lottin (ed.), 'De Virtutibus et de Vitiis et
          de Donis Spiritus Sancti', *Psychologie et Morale aux
          xiie et xiiie siècles,* vol. VI (Gembloux, 1960)
Wright   T. Wright, *Satirical Poets of the Twelfth Century*
          (London, 1872)

BIOGRAPHICAL NOTES

PETER ABELARD (1079–1142) was perhaps the most famous master of the first decades of the twelfth century. A pupil of the logician Roscelin of Compiègne, of William of Champeaux (founder of the house of St Victor in Paris) and of Anselm of Laon, the leading master of Biblical commentary, Abelard moved from logic to theology and was condemned for his opinions first at the Council of Soissons in 1121 and again at Sens in 1141. His offence lay at least as much in the manner of his approach to theological questions as in any doctrinal unorthodoxy of which he may have been guilty.

ADELARD OF BATH taught at Paris and Laon and travelled in Italy and Greece in the first decades of the twelfth century. An English scholar, respected at the Court of Henry I, he helped to bring works of Arabic scientific learning to the West.

ANSELM OF CANTERBURY (1033–1109) wrote as a monastic scholar; he never taught outside the schoolroom at Bec in Normandy where he had been Lanfranc's pupil; he succeeded Lanfranc as archbishop of Canterbury in 1093. His pioneering work in the use of elementary logical techniques in theology was as uncontroversial as it was philosophically profound. His *Proslogion,* the work of his period at Bec, contains a unique argument for the existence of God, the 'ontological' proof. His *Cur Deus Homo,* completed in exile while he was archbishop, puts forward the view that the Incarnation was a necessary act of God for the redemption of the human race.

BERNARD OF CHARTRES, elder brother of Thierry of Chartres (d. *c.* 1130), left no surviving writings. His reputation as a great teacher rests upon the reports of others, especially John of Salisbury, who describes his grammar lectures in detail.

BERNARD OF CLAIRVAUX (1090–1153), abbot of Clairvaux, famous for his preaching and for his activities throughout Europe as a diplomat and papal adviser, had no taste for the academic life, although he was chosen as the Church's protagonist in the trials of Peter Abelard at Sens and of Gilbert of Poitiers at Rheims. He had a profound influence upon Alan as a preacher.

BERNARD SILVESTRIS is one of a group of scholars associated with the teaching of Bernard of Chartres and his brother Thierry. He was especially drawn to Calcidius' commentary, of the late third or early fourth century, on Plato's *Timaeus* and to the 'scientific' approach of the day to the interpretation of Genesis. His *De Mundi Universitate,* written in the 1140s, contains an account of creation which draws on Plato and on the Hermetic tradition.

BURGUNDIO OF PISA (fl. *c.* 1150), like Adelard of Bath, was a translator. His principal interest lay in the eighth-century Greek author John Damascene and his *Source of Knowledge.*

CLAREMBALD OF ARRAS, a pupil of Hugh of St Victor and Thierry of Chartres, made a contribution of his own to the corpus of twelfth-century commentaries on Boethius' *opuscula sacra,* of a modest and cautious kind, avoiding the controversial areas of Gilbert of Poitiers' commentaries.

EADMER, monk of Canterbury and devoted friend of St Anselm, was a historian and biographer, whose *Life* of Anselm is of exceptional intimacy and accuracy among hagiographies of the day.

GEOFFREY OF AUXERRE, student at Paris at the time of Abelard's condemnation at Sens, was converted to the monastic life by a sermon of St Bernard's and became Bernard's secretary. He continued to write, and is the author of polemical and theological works, as well as of the last books of the *Vita Prima* of Bernard himself.

GILBERT CRISPIN (d. 1117), abbot of Westminster from 1805, had been a pupil of Anselm of Canterbury at Bec and remained his friend. He is the author of the *Disputatio Iudei et Christiani*, the most famous and influential of a number of dialogues between Christians and Jews written in the late eleventh and twelfth century.

GILBERT OF POITIERS (1076–1154), bishop of Poitiers, 1142–54, made his name as a master lecturing on Scripture and on the theological tractates of Boethius. His work was difficult and required an advanced knowledge of logic in his listeners. He was tried at Rheims in 1148 for views on the Trinity advanced, it was believed, in his commentaries. It proved impossible to determine exactly what he had intended and the attempted condemnation failed, although he was widely held in suspicion and opprobrium afterwards.

HERMANNUS JUDAEUS was converted to Christianity from Judaism as a result of discussions with several Christian scholars, notably Rupert of Deutz, composing an account of his conversion (*De Conversione Sua*) in which he describes how he was won over by an appeal to his intellectual vanity.

HONORIUS AUGUSTODUNENSIS, a mysterious figure, an eclectic and wandering scholar who can be connected with Ireland and Canterbury and many parts of Europe, is the author of the *Elucidarium,* an attempt to bring all Christian doctrine together in a convenient reference form, with condensed arguments to support the orthodox view. He was an admirer of St Anselm.

HUGH OF ST VICTOR, a kindly and painstaking schoolmaster with a rare capacity for reducing a vast body of material to order and explaining it simply, ran the school at St Victor, after William of Champeaux, throughout the 1120s and much of the 1130s. He taught the use of the *artes* as straightforward aids in Bible Study.

JOHN OF SALISBURY (*c.* 1115–80) spent twelve years in the French schools at the time when Abelard and Thierry of Chartres and Gilbert of Poitiers were teaching there, before entering the

ecclesiastical civil service, where he served as secretary to the archbishop of Canterbury until his elevation to the See of Chartres
shortly before his death. In his *Metalogicon,* written out of twenty
years' reflection upon his days in the schools, he gives portraits of
many of the masters of the time.

PETRUS ALPHONSUS, another converted Jew of a scholarly turn of
mind, made a substantial contribution to the learning of the
English Court of Henry I, especially in mathematics and astronomy.

PETER THE CHANTER (d. 1197), precentor of the cathedral of
Notre Dame in Paris, is the author of a manual of universal
preaching methods, and of a number of advanced study-aids for
his students in the Paris of the second half of the twelfth century.

PETER COMESTOR adopted the approach of Peter Lombard in his
teaching on Holy Scripture and speculative theology, avoiding the
excesses of the use of dialectic to which the followers of Gilbert of
Poitiers seemed to him to be prone.

PETER HELIAS is best known for his lectures on the grammatical
textbooks of Priscian and Donatus in the middle of the century,
which provided a foundation for new work in speculative
grammar and helped to make grammar a subject intellectually
satisfying in the same way as dialectic. Alan of Lille heard his
lectures.

PETER LOMBARD (*c.* 1100–60) taught in Paris about 1139. His
collection of patristic views on doctrinal topics, the *Sentences,*
became the most widely used theological textbook of the Middle
Ages, but he was also a commentator, who enlarged and perfected
the *Glossa Ordinaria.*

PETER OF POITIERS was a pupil of Peter Lombard before 1159,
himself a master by 1167; in 1169 he took Peter Comestor's chair
at Paris. His *Sentences* constitute a *summa theologica* in miniature, analysing the problems of systematic theology in order, by
reason and with the aid of the authorities.

PETER THE VENERABLE, abbot of Cluny, was instrumental in making the first translation of the Koran into Latin. He also took in Peter Abelard when he needed a refuge on his way to Rome to appeal against his condemnation at Sens; Peter the Venerable was able to persuade him to remain at Cluny.

RICHARD OF ST VICTOR (d. 1173), pupil of Hugh of St Victor, was both a scholar and a mystic, writing on the Bible and on the doctrine of the Trinity and on the spiritual life. He was much interested by Anselm of Canterbury's proof for the existence of God, and put forward a modified theory of his own.

ROBERT OF MELUN (d. 1167), ran a school at Melun from 1142–8, and took over Abelard's chair of theology at Paris before becoming bishop of Hereford from 1163–7. John of Salisbury was one of his pupils.

RUPERT OF DEUTZ (1070–c. 1129 or later), abbot of Deutz near Cologne from c. 1120, had previously taught at Liège and Siegburg. His writings include a grand study of the Bible as a whole, the *De Trinitate et Operibus Eius*. He dissociated himself firmly from the work of the dialecticians in Biblical exegesis.

SIMON OF TOURNAI, another of the Paris masters of the middle of the century was the author of a series of *Disputationes* in which he collected together questions raised by his pupils in the course of the lectures he gave on the Bible; it seems that a time was set aside to discuss these each afternoon, in an early form of the later mediaeval *disputatio*.

THIERRY OF CHARTRES, brother of Bernard of Chartres, was author of commentaries on Boethius' theological tractates, and of an attempt to make a scientific reconciliation of Plato's *Timaeus* and the Genesis account of the beginning of the world.

WILLIAM OF CONCHES (c. 1080–c. 1145) was a grammarian and lecturer on Calcidius' commentary on Plato's *Timaeus*; he composed an encyclopaedia, the *De Philosophia Mundi*, containing an account of earlier and contemporary views on the creation and running of the world.

Introduction

'DOCTOR UNIVERSALIS'

Alan of Lille's *Anticlaudianus* made a considerable impact. One of his pupils, Ralph of Longchamps, wrote a commentary on it, to bring out its usefulness to students of the liberal arts. Adam de la Bassée, who was a canon of St Peter, Lille, passed his time during a period of illness, between 1278 and his death in 1296, in composing a *Ludus super Anticlaudianum*. This light musical version of the piece, with songs at intervals, has a serious moral purpose, but it is a popular entertainment, too. During the thirteenth century, Ellebaut turned the *Anticlaudianus* into French, making what changes he thought fit to the details of the plot.[1] There can be no doubt of Alan's popularity as an author. The number of surviving manuscripts, particularly of the *Art of Preaching* and the sermons, demonstrates clearly enough how widely his works were diffused. The *Regulae Theologicae* was one of the first of his works to be printed, at Basle in the 1490s; the *Distinctiones Dictionum Theologicalium* preceded it (Strasbourg, 1475) and the *Parabolae* and *De Sex Alis Cherubim*, too, were in print before 1500. There were fresh editions of several of Alan's works in the sixteenth, seventeenth, eighteenth and nineteenth centuries. C. de Visch printed his *Opera* in 1654, but P. Leyser in 1721 and J. A. Mingarellius in 1756 produced independent versions of single works. He never went entirely out of fashion.

He was evidently memorable as a teacher, too. Ralph of Longchamps says that when he thought of his master he was moved to tears. Nevertheless, remarkably little information about his life and personality has come down to us. His was not an age when a Dr Johnson was likely to find a Boswell, unless perhaps his life was singular in its holiness. Eadmer's *Life of St Anselm* is

I

both biography and hagiography; but it is a rare achievement. The miscellaneous pieces of evidence assembled by M. T. d'Alverny[2] and recently reconsidered by J. J. Sheridan[3] give an account of his life which is perhaps as close to a biography of Alan of Lille as we can hope to come.

In old age, Alan entered the Cistercian Order, as a number of twelfth-century masters had done before him, including Thierry of Chartres. He died at Cîteaux in 1202 or 3. This is the only date about which we can be reasonably confident. If we work backwards from it, it seems, on the face of it, unlikely that Alan could have been in the schools, even as a student, before the late 1140s. John of Salisbury, who was born *c.* 1115–20, does not mention him in his account of his own student days in the *Metalogicon*, although he names many masters.[4] John's period in the schools between 1136 and 1147 was certainly too early for him to have encountered Alan as a teacher. But there is another possibility: that Alan was a fellow-student, an almost exact contemporary of John of Salisbury. This possibility was strongly supported by the results of the exhumation of Alan's body from its grave at Cîteaux in 1960. It appeared that he had been in his late eighties at least when he died.[5]

If that is the case, then Alan, who certainly studied at Paris and Chartres, would have heard the masters of whom John of Salisbury speaks, Peter Abelard and Gilbert of Poitiers and Thierry of Chartres, and the other great teachers of the Paris and Chartres of the late 1130s and 40s whom John describes. Master Thierry, he says, was a most assiduous investigator of the arts;[6] William of Conches was, after Bernard of Chartres, the *grammaticus opulentissimus*.[7] John found Peter Abelard a *clarus doctor et admirabilis,* outstanding above all others. He learned the first rudiments of the arts from him. When he departed, he attached himself to Master Alberic (of Rheims?), who was very thorough and found questions everywhere in the text.[8] Afterwards he became the pupil of Robert of Melun, Abelard's successor at Paris in the chair of theology. Robert had not yet become a theologian, and as a master of the *artes* John found him always ready with an answer to his questions, perspicacious, brief and comprehensive in his replies. When Robert turned to theology and Alberic went to Bologna to 'unlearn' much of what he knew and, on his return, to 'unteach it',[9] John went to Richard l'Evêque. He was a man who 'knew everything'. From him, John learned a good deal more about the mathematical subjects which he had previously studied under Harduin the German. This pursuit of the best masters went on. John became a pupil of Peter Helias, the famous grammarian, so that he could learn more about rhetoric; he heard Adam of the Petit Pont. He himself took a pupil, William of Soissons, and, when he had taught him the first principles of logic, he sent him to Adam to learn more. When he found himself short of money, John reluctantly gave up his studies for three years and did some teaching. As soon as he could afford to, he returned to Paris, heard Gilbert of Poitiers' *in logicis et divinis*, Simon of Poissy, dependable but dull,[10] Robert Pullen the theologian.[11]

If Alan's experiences were anything like John's, we may read the *Metalogicon* as an account of Alan's schooldays too, with the difference that Alan was clearly a great deal more interested in Boethius' theological tractates and the *Timaeus,* and in the newly popular works he uses in his own writings, than John of Salisbury, who enjoyed grammar and logic most. This is an attractive picture, not least because it brings Alan's time in the schools alive at a stroke. But there is a difficulty. Alan was still active as a scholar and preacher in the 1190s. It is likely enough that the possessor of so active a mind should have continued to work in his seventies and eighties, but it is remarkable that he should have produced so many substantial works so late. Anselm of Canterbury's output after the age of sixty was, however, at least equivalent in quantity and quality to all that he had written in middle age, and his curiosity was still very much alive on his death bed. (He wanted to live long enough to solve the problem of the origin of the soul.) Alan of Lille seems to have been made of the same stuff.

If, then, we may place Alan of Lille with John of Salisbury in the Paris and Chartres of the 1130s and 40s, what of his studies there? The principal subjects were normally those of the *trivium*. Alan would have heard Peter Helias on grammar and rhetoric. He was certainly familiar with his commentaries. He may, too, have encountered lectures on Quintilian, as John seems to have done – not the whole of Quintilian, but those parts known before the fifteenth century, which deal principally with the teaching of elementary grammar. For logic, there were evidently many masters to be had. Teaching on the *quadrivium* was rather harder to come by. Peter Abelard remarks in his *Dialectica* that he found it hard to understand William of Champeaux's comments on the arithmetical aspects of the Aristotelian category of 'quantity', and this was no doubt because he had not been instructed in Boethius' *Arithmetica* with the same thoroughness as he had been taught grammar and logic – if indeed he had read it at all. In the decades since Abelard had been a student the *Arithmetica* had become better known, and progress had been made with the study of Boethius' *Musica*. Adelard of Bath had made several versions of a translation of Euclid's *Elements*. Astronomy had made great strides as Macrobius' *Commentary on the Dream of Scipio* and Martianus Capella's *De Nuptiis Philologiae et Mercurii* were brought together with the study of Calcidius' Commentary on the *Timaeus*, and a search was put in hand for Ptolemy's *Almagest*. Hermann of Carinthia dedicated his translation of Ptolemy's *Almagest* to Thierry in 1143. Nevertheless, the *quadrivium* was still neglected, in comparison with the arts of the *trivium*, and Alan's mastery of these textbooks was unusually thorough. It may indicate – like his familiarity with Boethius' theological tractates – that he spent some time at Chartres; both Thierry of Chartres and Gilbert of Poitiers lectured on the tractates.

For the rest, Alan heard lectures on the Bible and read what he could for himself. The organisation of instruction in the schools was still almost non-existent. A student attached himself to a master as he pleased, made up his own syllabus, beginning with the *artes* and working his way towards the higher study of the Sacred Page if and when he chose, as John of Salisbury did. He spent as long as he was inclined to spend on each subject, changed masters when he wished, and his only qualification for setting up as a master himself was his power to hold the respect of his own students. The result was a certain organisational untidiness, but no lowering of standards. On the contrary, competition for pupils made for enthusiastic teaching. The profession Alan entered was one in which a man got on by hard work and merit.

It was not a career which appealed to John of Salisbury, it

seems. After his ordination to the priesthood, about 1148, he was frequently at the Papal Court, in the hope, perhaps of advancing his ecclesiastical career. He was not disappointed. Alan appears to have remained in the schools, as a master. John of Garland, writing in the mid-thirteenth century, claims that Alan added to the glories of the learning available at Paris,[12] and no doubt he did. An anonymous monk of Affligem confirms the report,[13] and there are testimonies to his presence at Chartres,[14] and at Orleans and Tours.[15]

He did not remain at Paris, certainly, although he seems to have continued to teach there for a long time after John of Salisbury left the schools. Traces of Alan are to be found at Montpellier.[16] Ralph of Longchamps studied there, and it may have been there that he became Alan's pupil. The school at Montpellier was famous for the study of medicine, second only to Salerno. It also had, by virtue of its position, the advantage of receiving early some of the new books which were being discovered by Christian scholars in Spain, works of Arabic science and translations of Aristotle and much besides. Alan would have had every reason to find Montpellier an exciting place to teach.

MASTER AT PARIS

Thirty or forty years elapsed between the writing of the early *Summa Quoniam Homines* and the composition of Alan's last works. These were years of rapid development in the schools. A vast amount of schoolmasterly effort went into the devising of teaching and study-aids, reference-books, dictionaries, collections of extracts. Peter of Poitiers, for example, wrote, in addition to his *Sentences,* a compendium on the genealogy of Christ, an *Allegorical Interpretation of the Tabernacle of Moses,* a *Historia* of the Acts of the Apostles, and sermons.[17] Commentaries were composed on the Creeds, on the liturgy,[18] on Peter Lombard's *Sentences,* a reference-book to the opinions of the Fathers which was to be a standard work for centuries – on textbooks of every sort. Some of these were quite new in the purpose they were intended to serve, and they reflect new requirements in the schools. The most notable in its consequences for the future of scholastic method was the development, out of the *lectio,* or

reading of the glossed text,[19] of the *disputatio*. This was designed
to deal with the questions which arose in the course of the reading.
John of Salisbury commends his master Alberic for finding
questions everywhere. Questions began to be so numerous that it
became necessary to set aside a regular afternoon or evening
session for *disputatio*. Peter the Chanter remarks in his *Verbum
Abbreviatum* that 'if a question arises in the text' it should be
noted 'and deferred until the hour of disputation'.[20] Simon of
Tournai organised his *Disputationes* on a day-by-day basis, referring to 'today's disputation'.[21] Arguments which rested on
reason or authority were assembled, for and against, and a
determination reached, by a process already well on the way to
that which Aquinas polished to perfection in the *Summa
Theologiae*.

Alan was one of the first to write a manual for preachers, a
handbook for priests to use in the confessional, a theological
summa, a dictionary of theological terms; perhaps his most
original attempt at a new *genre* is the *Regulae Theologicae*, by
whose system of theological axioms he hoped to demonstrate the
self-evident truth of all Christian doctrine, and in which he
anticipates by half a millennium the work of the seventeenth
century. Alan wrote liturgical and Scriptural commentaries, in
particular expositions of the Creeds and a commentary on the
Song of Songs, a treatise on angels, and much else besides.
Otto of St Blaise composed a catalogue of Alan's works soon after
his death, in which he credits him with the authorship of 'many
sound and catholic works'. It is clear, then, that Alan of Lille
contributed his share of writings to this industrious beavering.
He was often one of the first in the field, or the author of the
most noteworthy example of the new *genre*. His *Distinctiones
Dictionum Theologicalium* has more entries than any of the other
early dictionaries of Biblical terms, and it covers not only
Scriptural usages of certain terms, but sometimes their meanings
in secular authors, too. Other masters were glad to make use of
his work. Simon of Tournai borrowed from Alan in his *Disputationes* as Peter of Poitiers did in his *Sentences*.[22]

Yet Alan's work proved in many respects inimitable. If he
adopts another man's opinion he makes it his own. Idiosyncratic
and independent, his teaching, like his writing, must have given

the impression that here was a master with a distinctive approach, something more than a pedagogue, the opposite of a Simon de Poissy as John of Salisbury describes him.

Alan never found himself in trouble for unorthodoxy, as far as we know, although some of his teachings were highly eccentric. He is often obscure, and obscurity had helped bring Gilbert of Poitiers to trial at Rheims in 1148. Geoffrey of Auxerre says that Gilbert's gloss was 'more obscure than the text'.[23] But Gilbert was impatient with the slow, and he made enemies. Alan could write when occasion demanded with great plainness and simplicity, and there is every indication that he was a patient and enthusiastic teacher and that he had friends among the other masters. If that is so, his obscurities and eccentricities were likely to win him admiration rather than condemnation, perhaps. He was held to be enormously learned, truly a *doctor universalis*.

It is, to say the least of it, remarkable that no ecclesiastical preferment came the way of so outstanding a scholar, no post in the civil service, nothing by way of worldly reward for his years of teaching in Paris. There can be no 'itinerary' for Alan of Lille like that which can be reconstructed for at least two years of Robert de Courson's life.[24] But Alan may have avoided entering upon a career of the sort John of Salisbury thought so desirable. John was no teacher; only when he was in reduced circumstances did he become a pedagogue. Alan's enjoyment of his chosen profession is amply demonstrated by his continuing to teach into old age.

J. W. Baldwin has brought together what we know of the lives and careers of some of Alan's contemporaries in his time as a master at Paris, in his study of Peter the Chanter.[25] Alan himself makes only a brief appearance there.[26] Baldwin suggests two broad groupings of scholars: those masters upon whom the strongest influence was that of Peter Lombard: Peter of Poitiers, Peter of Capua, Praepositinus, Stephen Langton; and those who may loosely be called *Porretani* because of their debt to Gilbert of Poitiers: Alan of Lille, Simon of Tournai, Master Martin and Peter the Chanter himself. To these we may add the pupils who formed the next generation, such as Robert de Courson.

Of the second group, Simon of Tournai was close enough to

7

Alan in sympathy to borrow from his *Summa*, and familiar enough to do so almost as soon as the *Summa* was ready. He was teaching at Paris from the early 1170s at least, and perhaps from 1165, when he may have taken Odo of Ourscamp's place in the chair of theology at Notre Dame,[27] so that there is every likelihood that he came into contact with Alan personally. He is recorded as a master again in 1181.[28] Matthew Paris says he died in 1202,[29] the same year as Alan.

We should be wary of seeing these groups too distinctly as separate entities. Simon's *Disputationes* and the *Summa* both borrow freely from other masters' works,[30] not only from Alan of Lille, but also from Peter of Poitiers' *Sentences*, for example. In Disputation XIII, Question 1, Simon asks whether it is possible for a man to descend from perfect charity to imperfect charity. Authority has it, he says, that charity either progresses or fails. Here the 'authority' is Peter of Poitiers. Authority also has it that if a man has charity he deserves that it should be increased, and if it is increased charity deserves to be perfected. This 'authority' is Peter Lombard. So it seems that no one can descend from perfect charity to imperfect. On the other hand (*econtra opponitur*), authority has it that when we sin, grace is diminished in us and recedes from us. This time the 'authority' is Alan of Lille. Simon's solution involves a threefold distinction of the ways in which charity may be said to increase (*habitu, diurnitate, intensione*), which is worthy of Aquinas.[31] The community of interest here, the exchange of views, is more important than the classification of a man's opinions as predominantly those of the Lombard or those of Gilbert of Poitiers. Master Martin (Martin of Fougères),[32] author of a *Summa* of the late 1190s, makes use in his turn not only of Simon of Tournai but also of Peter of Poitiers and Odo of Ourscamp.[33] If we look at the range of questions with which Simon was obliged to deal in his *Disputationes* we can see how questions were being raised and discussed on all sides: is the sacrament of the altar greater than the sacrament of baptism (XC.1)? Can the elect be damned (LXVI.1)? Must every prophecy be fulfilled (LXVI.2)? Ought Abraham to have wanted to sacrifice his son (LII.1)? Is perseverance a virtue or a work of virtue (XCIII.2)? It is hardly to be supposed that each master would not make use of all the help he could find, or that his pupils would fail to inform him if he left out a currently fashionable view.

Of the masters of the first group, Peter of Poitiers[34] was a pupil of Peter the Lombard before 1159. By 1167 he was himself a master. In 1169 he took the chair which was left vacant by Peter Comestor. His *Sentences*, in five books, modelled on the *Sentences* of his master but rather differently conceived, were written between 1168 and 1170, at the peak of his academic career. From 1193 to his death in 1205, he was Chancellor of the cathedral of Notre Dame. Administration probably ate up his time increasingly in later years, to judge from the frequency with which he appears in the charters of Paris.[35]

A colleague of his in the running of the cathedral was Peter the Chanter (of whom we shall hear a good deal more as we go on). Peter became precentor of Notre Dame in 1183 and continued there until his death in 1197. J. W. Baldwin finds little evidence that the two Peters shared common academic interests.[36] When Peter of Poitiers died he was succeeded as Chancellor by Praepositinus of Cremona, a Lombard, and another admirer of Peter Lombard, his fellow-countryman. He was a master by 1185, and had been teaching at Paris at least since 1193. He makes use of Peter of Poitiers' work. Peter of Capua is a less conspicuous figure, author of a *Summa* of theological questions,[37] which again owes a great deal to Peter Lombard.

By patient scholarly effort a number of resemblances between passages in the writings of these scholars have been traced in recent years; yet their relationship to one another, as colleagues, or master and pupil, often remains obscure. It is possible to show, in some cases, that direct borrowing has taken place. But it is not easy to say exactly in what sense they can be said to be even loosely grouped together as 'followers' of Peter Lombard or Gilbert of Poitiers. It is likely that rivalry was stronger than community of interest among these masters, as they competed for students.

Perhaps the most important result of these efforts to piece the evidence together is the picture which emerges of the work of the schools of Paris in these decades. Whereas in the first half of the century a master such as Peter Abelard or Gilbert of Poitiers could stand out as a leader of opinion, unchallenged in his supremacy in the schools even if he was not universally approved of, the masters of the second half of the century included no startling figure, unless we propose Alan himself. They were able men, conscientious men, hard-working teachers, but not intellectually ambitious on an Abelardian scale.

There was an air of optimism abroad in the first half of the century, when the possibilities of resolving problems with the aid of grammar and dialectic were still largely untried, and it still seemed possible that human reason might answer all the great problems of theology. It was, in this respect, *mutatis mutandis,* an age of reason comparable with the eighteenth century. We find the scholars of the next generation taking smaller sections of their subject, subordinate questions, giving their energies to the dozens of problems which began to proliferate as grammar and dialectic proved to yield more questions than they resolved. The tendency was for scholarly effort to shift from the writing on major questions of the previous generation, to the organisation into a proper order of a vast number of lesser questions.

Alan is no exception in his preference for making vast compilations of relatively small units, in each of which he deals with a question of a manageable size, or the meanings of a single term, or collects topical material suitable for use in a single sermon. But even amongst the *minutiae* there is a grandness of vision in his work, a sense of the magnitude of the philosophical and theological questions which lie behind. Alan took his habits of thought and work with him to the south. The dictionary which he completed there must have been many years in the making, and he perhaps began it in Paris. But he clearly thought it would be useful to his pupils at Montpellier, and there is no reason to suppose that these features of the theological work of the late twelfth century were peculiar to Paris.

ALAN IN THE SOUTH

Alan did not attain high office in the Church. It may be that he did not seek it, preferring the life of a master. But it is not impossible that it was partly disillusionment over his prospects in the north of France which led him to look elsewhere.[38] Certainly, during his time in Paris developments were taking place in the south which would have been very attractive to him.[39] The cities of southern France played a considerable part in the diffusion of Arabic learning north of the Pyrennees. In 1167, a Provençal, William the Physician, brought back manuscripts of Pseudo-Dionysius from Constantinople to Paris, to the monastery of St Denis, which claimed the Areopagite as its patron. The *Celestial Hierarchy*, the *Ecclesiastical Hierarchy*, *On the Divine Names*, *On Mystical Theology*, were translated from the Greek by John Sarrazin. These translations were literal to the point of crudity, but their merit was precisely that they kept close to the text. In any case, Alan would have had no quarrel with the clumsiness of a method of translation which Burgundio of Pisa describes in his preface to the translation of Chrysostom's St John as *de verbo ad verbum*, 'word for word'.[40] It was words and phrases he wanted for his own use. Like his contemporaries, he had a close eye for a text.

In the south of France, Alan apparently went on teaching, almost certainly at Montpellier itself. His *Dictionary of Theological Terms* is dedicated to Ermengaud, abbot, from 1179–95, of St Gilles, between Nîmes and Montpellier.[41] Alan still calls himself *magister*, and the subject and form of the dictionary itself suggests that he still had the needs of the classroom in mind.

But, more importantly for future developments in his thought, he encountered the Cistercians who were preaching against the heretics in the south of France. He took up the work with enthusiasm. John of Garland commends him for his success in 'taming' heretics. He wrote a treatise, in four books, against heretics and Jews and Moslems, and dedicated it to William VIII of Montpellier (1152–1202). His own experience made him far better informed on the Cathars and Waldensians than about the other two categories of 'unbeliever' to whom the *Contra Hereticos* is addressed, to judge from the amount of space he gives to them. It may have been during these last two decades of the century, when he was actively in contact with the Cistercians and sharing in their missionary work in Languedoc, that he was drawn to the Order, and decided to retire to Cîteaux. His sermons suggest that he preached to Benedictines and Augustinians, too,[42] but the Cistercians were an Order to whose activities he could make a unique contribution. No doubt if he had been born a little later, he would have become one of the Friars Preachers. The Dominican Order in the thirteenth century would have been able to make use of his talents as a scholar and preacher in a way that no single Order or school could do in the twelfth. Alan was obliged to find his own way and to deploy his powers as best he could.

ALAN'S THEOLOGICAL SCHEME

The *doctor universalis*, for all the formidable range of his learning and the impressive list of his publications, was first and foremost a theologian. Even as a poet, he had a theological purpose, just as Bernard Silvestris had had. It is this deep centre of his work with which we shall be principally concerned, for it is upon practical and speculative theology that all his efforts were ultimately concentrated. To take any of his works in isolation is to misrepresent him. We must look at Alan's work as a whole, within the grand – not to say grandiose – framework of his theological purpose, if we are to give him the place he deserves among his contemporaries.

Alan devised a scheme into which all theological studies could be fitted and, *a fortiori,* all the secular studies, the branches of the liberal arts which he, like Hugh of St Victor regarded as hand-maids of theology. The idea that all knowledge might be set out in this way, so as to show how it tended towards the highest knowledge of all, was nothing new. Cassiodorus and Isidore had attempted something of the sort. Hugh of St Victor and the author of the Abelardian *Ysagoge in Theologiam* had produced up-to-date schemes earlier in the twelfth century. Bernard Silvestris explored a similar scheme in the *Aeneid* commentary. Alan was trying something new. He worked out for the first time some of the implications of divisions within theology itself, branches of the subject whose existence was beginning to be widely accepted in the later twelfth century.

Alan found that theology could be divided in various ways. It fell into the speculative and the practical, the theory of the subject and its application to the living of a good Christian life. Again, it could be divided into *theologia rationalis* and *theologia moralis*, matters of faith and doctrine and matters of ethics. Speculative theology may be equated with *theologia rationalis* and taken to refer to the study of the divine and angelic natures. Then we may also call it *superior* or *celestis*. Practical theology may be loosely equated with *theologia moralis* and called *inferior* or *subcelestis*.[43] But Alan himself shows in his writings that there is some overlap. It is possible to consider the theory of moral theology, or to examine the practical aspects of teaching speculative theology, and Alan does both, in his treatise *On the Virtues and Vices*, and in his Scriptural and liturgical commentaries, for example. Nevertheless, the division, taken broadly, is a helpful one when we try to place Alan's own works, because it indicates the lines he was thinking along in writing them.

A second division is one which Alan claims to be common to all sciences. In the commentaries on the Creeds, Alan explains that every science consists in two things, the putting forward of those things which promote or advance it, and the avoidance of those things which impede it. The Creeds are full of *expedimenta* carefully balanced against the *impedimenta*, or objections, with which heretics have tried to create stumbling-blocks to orthodox faith – indeed, one of the reasons why the Creeds were formulated, Alan believes, was to meet the objections of heretics. He sees *impedimentum* theology as the other face of *expedimentum* theology. In his view, no theologian fulfils his task unless he covers both, preaching against the heretics as well as teaching sound doctrine to the faithful.

The *Summa Quoniam Homines*, which can probably be dated between 1155 and 1165, was almost certainly Alan's first substantial work. It shows early promise of that individuality of approach which was to mark everything he wrote. As his editor points out,[44] he took none of the obvious courses. He did not write a commentary on Peter Lombard's newly-published *Sentences*, although he used them as source-material. He did not arrange what he had to say in the form of Scriptural commentary. He did not compose a treatise against the heretics, although he was to do so later, and he was already much aware of the danger and importance of the problem of heresy as he wrote. He attempted instead to give a comprehensive guide to the whole of theology, speculative and practical, superior and inferior, rational and moral, *expedimenta* and *impedimenta* (if Glorieux is right in thinking that the treatise *On Virtues and Vices* was originally part of the lost remainder of the *Summa*). So consistent was he in keeping to this *schema* in his later writings, that the *Summa Quoniam Homines* can be attributed to him beyond a shadow of doubt solely on the internal evidence of its close resemblance to his later works.

A TABLE OF ALAN'S WRITINGS

In the table which follows, Alan's works are set out within his own theological scheme. References are given to M. T. d'Alverny's recent discussions of each text, and to studies published since 1965. Details of editions are given in full. The number of manuscripts of Alan's works is so large that it has seemed best in most cases to refer the reader to De Lage's list, as the most comprehensive so far brought together. Where De Lage has been improved upon, details of more recent work on the manuscripts are included. (This is most noticeably the case for the sermons.) Studies on Alan will be found in section 1 of the Bibliography.

A   THE HANDMAIDS OF THEOLOGY

1   *Ars Poetica*

(a)   *De Planctu Naturae*
Certainly written before 1176, probably between 1160 and 1170 (*Textes*, p. 34).
Textes, pp. 32–7.
MSS, De Lage, pp. 182–4.
PL 210.431–82.
T. Wright (ed.), *Satirical Poets of the Twelfth Century*, vol. ii (London, 1872), pp. 429–522.
N. M. Häring, *Studi Medievali*, xix (1978), pp. 797–879.
J. J. Sheridan (trans.), *Plaint of Nature* (Toronto, 1980).

(b)   *Anticlaudianus*
(Written between 1181–4, possibly 1182–3 (*Textes*, p. 34).)
Textes, pp. 32–7.
MSS, De Lage, pp. 184–6.
PL 210.488–54.
T. Wright (ed.), *Satirical Poets*, vol. ii, pp. 268–426.
R. Bossaut (ed.) (Paris, 1955).

J. J. Sheridan (trans.), *Anticlaudianus, or the Good and Perfect Man.*
(Toronto, 1973).

(c) *Rhythmus de Incarnatione et de Septem Artibus*
Textes, pp. 37–9.
PL 210.577–80.
M. T. d'Alverny (ed.), *Mélanges H. de Lubac* (Paris, 1964), pp. 111–28.

(d) *De Miseria Mundi (Rhythmus de natura hominis fluxa et caduca)*
Textes, pp. 39–40.
PL 210.579–80.
G. M. Dreves and C. Blume (eds.), *Ein Jahrtausend Lateinischen Hymnen-dichtung*, vol. I (1909), p. 288.

(e) Miscellaneous Poems
N. M. Häring (ed.), 'Two Theological Poems Probably Composed by Alan
of Lille', *An. Cist.*, XXXII (1976), 238–46, and 247–50.
'The Poem *Vix Nodosum* by Alan of Lille', ed. N. M. Häring, *Medioevo:
Rivista di storia della filosofia medievale*, III (1978), 165–85.
Poems of doubtful attribution to Alan, see *Textes*, pp. 40–51 (*Hymni
Magistri Alani; Conflictus Iustititiae et Misericordiae et al.*).

II *Commentary*

(a) Commentary on the *Rhetorica ad Herennium*
Textes, pp. 52–5.

III *Quaestiones*

(a) *Quaestiones Alani*
Textes, pp. 55–9.
B. Lawn (ed.), *The Prose Salernitan Questions* (Oxford, 1979), pp. 275–324.
On the authorship of this work and other such collections of 'natural
questions', see B. Lawn, *The Salernitan Questions: an Introduction to the
History of Mediaeval and Renaissance Problem Literature* (Oxford, 1963).

B 'THEOLOGIA SPECULATIVA', SPECULATIVELY CONSIDERED

I *Expedimenta*

(a) The *Summa Quoniam Homines*
Probably belongs to the early period of Alan's teaching at Paris; Glorieux
dates it about 1160. See P. Glorieux, 'L'auteur de la Somme *Quoniam
Homines*', *RTAM*, XVII, 29–45.

Textes, pp. 60–4.

P. Glorieux (ed.), 'La Somme *Quoniam Homines*', *AHDLMA*, xx (1954), 113–64.

(b)   Two Questions on the Faith

Textes, pp. 69–70.

G. Raynaud de Lage (ed.), 'Deux Questions sur la foi inspirées d'Alain de Lille', *AHDLMA*, xiv (1943–5), 323–36. De Lage is cautious, but M. T. d'Alverny believes this to be an authentic work, not merely inspired by Alan.

(c)   *Regulae Theologicae*

Probably belongs to the same period as the *Summa Quoniam Homines*. There are close similarities.

Textes, pp. 66–8.

MSS, De Lage, pp. 175–6.

J. Mingarellius (ed.), *Anecdotorum Fasciculus* (Rome, 1756).

PL 210.621–84.

N. M. Häring (ed.), *AHDLMA*, xlviii (1981), 97–226.

(d)   *Hierarchia Alani*

Probably belongs to the same period as the *Summa Quoniam Homines* and the *Regulae Theologicae*.

Textes, pp. 106–8.

Ed. *Textes*, pp. 219–34.

(e)   Works of doubtful authenticity, or erroneously attributed to Alan

(i)   *Summa de Sacramentis: Totus Homo*; *Textes*, pp. 64–5.

(ii) *Moralium Dogma Philosophorum*; *Textes*, pp. 65–6.

(iii) *De Arte Catholicae Fidei* (*De Articulis;*) *Textes*, pp. 68–9, and see my Appendix 1.

ii   *Impedimenta*

(a)   *De Fide Catholica: Contra Haereticos, Valdenses, Iudaeos et Paganos*

Written *c.* 1185–1200; the section against the Waldensians must have been written after their condemnation at the Council of Verona in 1184; cf. Bernard de Fontcaude, who wrote a *Contra Waldenses* between 1185 and 1193.

Textes, pp. 156–62.

MSS De Lage, pp. 176–7.

PL 210.305–430.

C 'THEOLOGIA MORALIS', THEORETICALLY CONSIDERED

(a) *De Virtutibus, de Vitiis, de Donis Spiritus Sancti*
This work was probably written about the same time as the *Summa Quoniam Homines*, and indeed Glorieux suggests it may be a fragment of the lost ending of the *Summa*, cf. 'La Somme *Quoniam Homines*', p. 115.
Textes, pp. 61–4.
O. Lottin, 'Le traité d'Alain de Lille sur les vertus, les vices et les dons du Saint-Esprit', *Mediaeval Studies*, XII (1950), 20–56; re-edited in *Psychologie et morale aux xii⁰ et xiii⁰ siècles*, vol. VI (Gembloux, 1960), pp. 45–92.

(b) *Liber Parabolarum*
Textes, pp. 51–2, defends the authenticity of this work.
De Lage doubts Alan's authorship; see De Lage pp. 15–16.
PL 210.581–94.

D 'THEOLOGIA SPECULATIVA', PRACTICALLY CONSIDERED

(a) *Distinctiones Dictionum Theologicalium (Summa Quot Modis)*
Textes, pp. 71–3.
MSS De Lage, pp. 177–8.
PL 210.685–1012.

(b) *Elucidatio in Cantica Canticorum*
Textes, pp. 73–5.
PL 210.51–110.

(c) *Glosatura super Cantica*
It is likely that Alan commented upon other books of the Bible. The *Glosatura* may have been put together by pupils from Alan's lectures.
Textes, pp. 75–9.
Prologue ed. *Textes*, pp. 77–9.

(d) *Expositio* of the *Pater Noster*
Written perhaps in the 1190s, at the same time as the *Commentaries* on the Apostles' Creed and the *Quicumque*.
Textes, pp. 79.
N. M. Häring, 'A Commentary on the Our Father by Alan of Lille', *An. Cist.*, XXX (1975), 149–77.

(e) *Expositiones* of the Nicene and Apostolic Creeds
Textes, pp. 79–85.
Ed. *Textes*, pp. 83–4 (Prologue).
Ed. N. M. Häring, 'A Commentary on the Apostles' Creed by Alan of
Lille', *An. Cist.*, xxx (1974), 7–46; 'A Commentary on the Creed of
the Mass by Alan of Lille', *ibid.*, pp. 281–303.

(f) 'A Poem by Alan of Lille on the Pseudo-Athanasian Creed',
ed. N. M. Häring, *Revue d'histoire des textes*, iv (1974), 226–38.

(g) *Expositio Prosae de Angelis*
Textes, pp. 85–106.
Ed. *Textes*, pp. 185–217.

E 'THEOLOGIA MORALIS', PRACTICALLY CONSIDERED

(a) *Quod non est celebrandum bis in die*
Textes, pp. 151–2.
Ed. *Textes*, pp. 290–4.

(b) *Liber Poenitentialis*
Textes, pp. 152–4.
MSS De Lage, pp. 178–9.
PL 210.281–304.
J. Longère (ed.), *Analecta Medievalia, Namurcensia*, xvii–xviii (Louvain,
1965); and 'Alain de Lille *Liber Poenitentialis*: Les traditions moyenne
et courte', *AHDLMA*, xxxii (1965), 169–242.

(c) *De Sex Alis Cherubim*
Textes, pp. 154–5.
PL 210.269–80.

(d) *Ars Praedicandi*
Textes, pp. 109–125.
MSS, De Lage, pp. 179–81.
PL 210.111–95.
G. R. Evans (trans.), in Cistercian Fathers (Michigan, 1981).

(e) *Sermones*
Textes, pp. 109–51.
MSS, De Lage, pp. 181–2.
For a fuller list of known sermons, manuscripts and editions, see *Textes*,

pp. 125–51, and J. B. Schneyer, *Repertorium der Lateinischen Sermones des Mittelalters*, A–D (Münster, 1969), pp. 69–83.

B. Hauréau, *Mémoire sur la vie et quelques oeuvres d'Alain de Lille* Memoires de l'Académie des Inscriptions, xxxii (Paris, 1886), pp. 1–27, includes an edition of a sermon for the first Sunday of Lent and the dedication of the *Liber Poenitentialis*.

B. Hauréau, *Notices et extraits des manuscrits de la Bibliothèque nationale*, vi (Paris, 1890–3), includes an edition of a sermon for Epiphany.

Sermon, '*In die B. Virginis de Assumptione*', ed. P. Glorieux, *Mélanges de science religieuse*, viii (1951), 5–18.

Sermon '*De S. Petro*', ed. L. Hödl, *Zeitschrift für kathol. Theologie*, lxxx (1958).

'*Sermo de sphera intelligibili*', *Textes*, pp. 297–306.

'Un sermon d'Alain de Lille sur la misère de l'homme', ed. M. T. d'Alverny, *The Classical Tradition: Essays presented to H. Caplan* (Ithaca, 1966).

'Variations sur un thème de Virgile dans un sermon d'Alain de Lille', ed. M. T. d'Alverny, *Mélanges d'archéologie et d'histoire offerts à André Piganiol*, ed. R. Chevallier (Paris, 1966), pp. 1517–28.

1 Handmaids of Theology

A DICTIONARY

When Peter, prior of Holy Trinity, Aldgate, London, heard Gilbert Foliot preach, he was so impressed by his facility in recalling to mind the quotations he needed to support his arguments that he thought him 'not a man, but a superman' (*non homo sed superhomo*).[1] He describes how Gilbert varied his talk by exploring various aspects of his theme (*quibusdam distinctionibus variatus*) and how he adorned it 'with little flowers of words and thoughts'.[2] Peter was most impressed, however, by the way in which Gilbert kept to the point: 'he ran backwards and forwards from his starting-point to the same starting-point'. This gave him the idea of compiling a handbook in which texts were collected under themes, in one easily accessible volume, so that those with less capacious memories could imitate Gilbert. He found it a tedious and laborious task, as he complains in his prologue. But the need he perceived proved to be widely-felt and his *Pantheologus* is only one of several collections put together in the last quarter of the twelfth century. The idea was not, even then, entirely novel,[3] but there was something new in the systematic and comprehensive character the compilers strove to give them, and in the hands of the preaching friars of the next century they developed into full concordances to the Bible.[4]

The twelfth-century works, Peter the Chanter's *Summa Abel*, Peter of Poitiers' *Summa super Psalterium* and Alan of Lille's *Distinctiones Dictionum Theologicalium*, have an experimental air. Like the prior of Holy Trinity, their authors had seen a need, and each of them had seen it rather differently. Nevertheless, they agree as to the importance of constructing a practical aid. Prior Peter says that he has provided a series of marginal 'markers' so that the eye can quickly see which book of the Bible is the source of a given quotation. There is often an indication in the margin whether the sense of a term under discussion is literal, allegorical, tropological, anagogical, or of another kind altogether. The most striking novelty is the notion of arranging the entries in alphabetical order. Peter prefaces his first alphabetical list with an *explanatio,* in which he points out this feature of the arrangement with some pride. He has, he explains, set out the words *secundum ordinem alphabeti,* 'so that whoever knows the order of the alphabet can find what he is looking for'. He does not exploit the idea fully; his alphabetical list is merely an index and in the body of the work words are arranged topically. But he has intended to enhance the practical usefulness of the collection by making it easy for the user to find what he needs.

If a preacher wanted to explore a theme, he looked up an appropriate word and found assembled for him the senses in which Scripture uses it, together with contexts for each sense. If he chose 'bed', for example, Peter of Poitiers would provide him with a text in which *lectus* is a 'bed' of Scripture, another in which it is a 'bed' of contemplation, another in which it is a 'bed' of the Church, or a 'bed' of eternal damnation or of eternal blessedness. If he chose 'the way' (*via*), Peter the Chanter would tell him that the *via dei,* the way of God, is sometimes said to be Christ himself, sometimes the keeping of a promise, sometimes the way of the apostles or of the prophets. The choice of a single word for exposition in this way has its limitations. But it enabled the preacher to divide up his subject-matter into several subordinate themes or *distinctiones* in a manner his listeners would find easy to follow – a style already found in Gregory the Great.

Alan of Lille's *Dictionary* has no conspicuous advantages on the practical side, unless we count his inclusion of the extra senses for certain words beyond those to be found in Scripture. But he begins with a Preface which suggests that he saw the purpose of such a dictionary in much more grandiose terms than Prior Peter. Alan had all the consciousness of language of his time, and he is in no doubt about the chief difficulty which faces the contemporary reader of the Bible: the most elementary training in grammar and dialectic made it plain that Biblical usages often conform neither to the rules of ordinary speech (*usus loquendi*), nor to the technically 'exact' usage prescribed by the rules of grammar or logic. The language of the Bible is in a special sense a figurative language, where the word which usually means 'bird' may stand for Christ, Satan, the human mind, pride, or the word for 'mother' be used for Eve, concupiscence, corruption, blessing, the human soul in which Christ is born by grace, the Church militant, triumphant, the synagogue, or the earth itself.

PROPER AND IMPROPER LANGUAGE

1 *Peter the Chanter*

Peter the Chanter looks at the practical implications of the Bible's figurative use of language in his *De Tropis Loquendi*. The particular problem to which he addresses himself is that of the contradictions which appear to be present in Scripture if we do not make allowances for it. Augustine had attempted a reconciliation of the apparent discrepancies and contradictions between the Gospels in the *De Consensu Evangelistarum*, a work Peter imitates in his *Unum et Quattuor*. Cassiodorus had tried to make sense of the *obscuritas* of the Psalms,[5] so as to show that they contain nothing inconsistent with Christian truth. Bede, in the *De Schematibuss et Tropis*, which is commonly found with Peter's *De Tropis Loquendi* in the manuscripts, came closest to Peter's concern. He notes that 'the order of words in the Scriptures is often found to be different from that of the common way of speaking'. Bede concentrates upon a series of figures, *tropi*, such as metaphor, catachresis, metalepsis, anadiplosis, metonymia, and *schemata*, such as prolepsis, zeugma, anaphora, which were familiar to the rhetorically-minded 'grammarians' Bede had in mind in writing. He shows how apparent contrarieties may be made to disappear if one or both the statements involved is taken in a figurative sense.[6] With the difference that he was concerned, not with the area of common ground between grammar and rhetoric, but with that between grammar and logic, Peter the Chanter almost certainly owed the initial idea of writing the *De Tropis* to Bede, and probably some of his terminology, too. But he saw the need for a new work, an up-to-date version, which would meet the contemporary need for a system of reconciling contradictions.

Peter Lombard explains, in a comment on 1 Corinthians 13.12, that *tropica* is a Greek word, and that we use it in preference to *modus,* which is its Latin equivalent, just as we use *schema* more readily than *figura.*[7] The fact that this seems a more acceptable usage is no doubt due to the popularity of Bede's treatise. Bede also provided Peter the Chanter with a definition of *tropica locutio.* Such a usage involves the 'transference' or 'translation' of a word from its 'proper' significance to an 'improper' or 'analogical' significance.[8] Cassiodorus explains the implications of this. Two statements which are in fact not contradictory may appear to stand in opposition to one another if we read both literally; if we look at the 'transferred' sense, they seem to fit perfectly.[9] If, then, those who had attempted to provide a means of getting over the difficulty of the apparent contradictoriness of Scripture before Peter's day had not given him a start in a technical sense by answering the questions which arose in his own day, they had nevertheless given him a set of terms to describe what he was doing, a means of identifying his task in terms familiar to contemporary readers. And they had provided him with one of the fundamental distinctions which give structure to the *De Tropis Loquendi,* that between 'proper' and 'transferred' usages.

But why does the Bible not speak plainly, so that everyone can understand it? Augustine thought it a concession to the weakness of human understanding that God speaks in pictures. Minds from which sin has taken away that clarity of intellectual vision which the angels enjoy can, he held, conceive only of 'bodily images'.[10] When a word is used to signify something in the created world it is used for a 'bodily' thing. Only by means of these 'visual aids' can sin-clouded minds grasp the idea of God. Bede gives two more down-to-earth reasons, for which he is indebted to Boethius on Aristotle. There may be considerations of style, which encourage a writer to speak in a figure. Or the figurative usage may simply be necessary, in the absence of a word which will serve literally. Abelard emphasises the 'necessity' of using language metaphorically because of the shortage of words in our language. In the Bible some such necessity must operate. We cannot believe that anything occurs without good reason.[11] There is no *otiositas* in Scripture, says Cassiodorus. Scripture's figurative language must be 'necessary'.

Peter Lombard's explanation is that these 'transferred' usages in the Bible are helpful to us in understanding something of God, albeit darkly.[12] There is some analogy in these figures or images,[13] which throws light on the nature of God as 'proper' usages cannot, because they, as a rule, refer to created things. Only transferred or figurative usages can begin to speak of God as he is, and even they do so only obscurely. Peter the Chanter takes as his opening text: 'we see now through a glass darkly',[14] the passage on which Peter Lombard was commenting when he set out his views on *tropica locutio*. Peter the Chanter's explanation is straightforward enough, as we should expect. It is, he says, entirely in Augustine's spirit, 'because of the dullness of sense' of sinful man that certain passages in Scripture 'seem to be contrary'[15] although they are not.[16] They are *diversa* but not *adversa*. One day we shall see clearly, but in the meantime we can help our understanding to grow by reading the Scriptures figuratively.

In Peter the Chanter we have a scholar who was comparable with Alan in the level of his technical skill in the *artes* as perhaps Prior Peter was not, but whose more pedestrian approach provides a useful contrast to that of Alan in his speculative flights. J. W. Baldwin has taken Peter as the central figure of his recent study of the *Masters, princes and merchants*, precisely because of the very practicality and common-sense air of his approach to theology. Certainly Peter's writings show a strong predilection for applied moral theology. A number of contemporary masters shared his interest in practical ethics, and Peter can be shown to have exercised a considerable influence upon the development of this branch of theology. It was not, however, Baldwin's purpose to explore Peter's works as a speculative theologian. He mentions the *De Tropis Loquendi* only in a footnote, and therefore fails to show how thoroughly competent Peter was in this area, too.

The discussion of matters of faith and doctrine normally involved the exercise of some technical skill in grammar and dialectic in these decades. It had become a matter of course, but it had not ceased to be a controversial practice, and Peter's use of technical assistance from the *artes* in the resolution of the seeming contradictions of Scripture seems to him to require some justification. Peter knows that some consider it a mortal sin to give time to the study of secular authors, and he himself would go some way towards this view, if such study served no higher purpose. But provided it is borne in mind that the liberal arts are the servants of theology, he sees no objection to it.[17] He himself makes cross-references to Ovid and to *civilibus litteris* in general. He does not hesitate to make comparisons between the laws which apply *in divinis* and those which operate in the natural world and are the study of the natural scientist or physician. He contrasts the change which takes place in the natural world when, for example, wine turns to vinegar, with the change which takes place in the bread and wine of the Eucharist. In the first case there is a change of the substance into another *status* or condition. In the second case, the substance alters, but there is no change in the form of the bread and wine. The latter is rare, he notes, 'and it is found only in theological contexts'.[18] A less developed example contrasts the way the 'physicist' or natural scientist would distinguish between primary and secondary substance, and the way the theologian would do so, if each was asked to define a man. Again, we have the contrast: *sicut in phyisco exemplo*, and *theologicis exemplis*.[19] Used in this way, Peter cannot believe that the study of *ethnice littere*, pagan writings, is to be regarded as *damnabile*. All that is required is to ensure that the handmaid of the Lord[20] does her work. In the light of the help the *artes* can give him, Peter the Chanter tries, in his workmanlike, confident way, to resolve some of the problems raised by the Bible's use of language.

The difficulty which faces theologians in every generation was felt especially acutely, then, by twelfth century scholars: theological language is in certain respects different from ordinary human language; we cannot be sure that the rules we follow when we speak of created things will work when we try to talk about God. For the grammarians and logicians of Peter's and Alan's generation, with their developing skill in handling the laws of the *artes*, the problem of theological language presented the greatest challenge of all. Peter is fully aware of the difficulty. He makes every allowance for the special usages of Scripture. But he is in no doubt that sensible application of familiar rules will make it possible to resolve at least the bulk of difficulties. In this, he takes exactly the opposite stand to Alan of Lille, whose dictionary of theological terms, the *Distinctiones Dictionum Theologicalium*, opens with a Prologue in which he insists that theological language must necessarily transcend all the conventional rules in order to speak of God at all.[21]

There is, then, a substantial tradition behind Peter's treatise and Alan's sharp challenge to those who think the *artes* can be used in the service of theology without undue difficulty. But there is something more behind the challenge than a mere desire to shake the reader out of lazy ways. The twelfth century saw the composition of commentaries on the logical works and Aristotelian commentaries of Boethius, and a great many monographs and reports of lectures, exploring the nature and functioning of language from both a grammatical and a logical point of view. One of the most noticeable areas of growth lay in the treatment of fallacies, which were touched on in the texts of the Old Logic and came into focus with the introduction of texts of the *Sophistici Elenchi* in the middle decades of the century. Alan is asking hard questions about the application of all this to the resolution of the problems of speculative theology. Peter the Chanter is asking the same questions, with the firm intention of showing exactly how the application may be made. Alan chooses commonplaces of grammar and dialectic in order to make his point even to the obtuse among his students. Peter writes for advanced students, making no concessions to the beginner and explaining none of the technical principles he invokes. Alan's response to the presence of apparent obscurities and contradictions in Scripture is to speak of mysteries – mysteries which may be approached, but not resolved with the aid of the reason. Peter's response is to look at the new textbooks on fallacies in a businesslike manner, to see what he can find there which will enable him to explain away the seeming *equivocatio* and *amphibolia* of Scripture, the *fantasia contrarietatis*.[22] But it cannot be over-emphasised that for both the liberal arts provided the starting-point. Nothing can be done without reference to the *artes*, whether their assistance is accepted uncontroversially, or only after they have been suitably modified.

At least three senses of 'propriety' were abroad. In the *differentiae*,[23] Isidore and his Carolingian successors distinguish between near-synonymous terms, explaining which it is proper to use in a given context (*amicus* or *socius*, for example). They drew upon an established tradition among Roman grammarians. This is a grammatical 'propriety', in which the word is employed correctly, in regard to its meaning. Then there is a dialectical 'propriety', which has to do with technically exact usage, as distinguished from the loose usage of ordinary speech. This is a form of 'propriety' much discussed by twelfth-century dialecticians. Finally, there is the theological 'propriety' according to which a word is used primarily of God and only by transference of man and the created world, or, according to the opposing school of thought, 'properly' of man and only by analogy of God.

After his Prologue[24] Peter begins with the heading: PROPRIE. This is – ironically enough, in view of his treatise's over-riding concern with ambiguity – a little ambiguous. He intends the heading to serve for a large class of equivocations arising out of proper usages, that is, cases where, without the introduction of a figurative sense, a word can be seen to have two or more significations. (As when we look a word up in a dictionary we expect to find more than one definition in many cases, none of which is necessarily metaphorical or 'transferred'.) But the first category of such equivocations Peter considers is that which involves confusions over proper names, and so the heading *proprie* may serve for both the large class and its first category. Confusions sometimes arise in Scripture, Peter explains, over two men of the same name. The Herod who died before Jesus returned from Egypt with his parents is not the same as the Herod who was still alive when Jesus was baptised.[25] He moves on to further cases of confusions arising out of 'proper' usages. Scripture does not really contradict itself when it says in one place that it is wrong to swear[26] and elsewhere encourages swearing.[27] Swearing lightly or falsely is one thing; swearing which takes the form of a firm promise or a sacred vow is quite another. It is clear that no figurative sense is involved in either of these instances, but only cases where, because of the poverty of human language, a single word is used for more than one thing in the created world. Such equivocations of words used *proprie*, or literally, are explored for verbs, nouns, adverbs, prepositions, conjunctions, pronouns, and cases where a word is used sometimes as though it is a noun (*nominaliter*) and sometimes *adverbialiter*, and finally for homonyms.

Peter makes it clear in what way he wants 'proper' to be contrasted with 'improper' when he first turns to 'improper' usages. 'It remains for us to deal with multiplicity arising when a word or a saying is used improperly, which the dialecticians call "translation".'[28] He distinguishes, for example, between Matthew's reference to the 'book of the generation of Jesus Christ',[29] and Isaiah's words: 'Who will tell his generation?'[30] In the first example Matthew is speaking of the generation of Jesus Christ according to the flesh, and that is the 'proper' sense of *generatio*. In the second example Isaiah refers to the 'divine' generation which Christ had of the Father without a mother, which no-one can explain in words.[31] We use the word 'generation' for both, *faute de mieux,* but that is 'improperly' said to be a 'generation', for there was no separation of the flesh.[32] Peter explains that in order to speak of such mysteries at all, we must transfer words from their ordinary sense in connection with the natural world, and allow them to have a special sense. When Scripture speaks of fetters, it does not mean the real fetters with which the feet of prisoners are bound, but perhaps the *compes nature*, the fetters of our fallen nature, or the *compes gratie,* the fetters of grace, the bonds which bind us to obedience to the Commandments, or in contemplation, or the bonds of perfection. There are also *compes culpe,* bonds of guilt, from which we must free ourselves. These transferred usages enable Scripture to exploit the possibilities of language far beyond anything which could be achieved by keeping to the 'proper' sense,[33] because they make it possible to speak, even if obliquely, about the Creator. *Translatio* was not a new notion. It is to be found in the ninth-century grammarians, used in much this way. But for its full technical exploitation it awaited Peter Helias and Peter Abelard, and their greater technical expertise in the arts of language.[34]

2 *Alan of Lille*

The comparison between the Prologue to Alan's *Dictionary of Theological Terms* and Peter's *De Tropis Loquendi* is a natural one. The two masters had a number of specialist interests in common. Peter's *Verbum Abbreviatum* shares a good deal of common ground with Alan's *Art of Preaching.*[35] Both begin with reflections on the preacher's task, although Peter is concerned, as Alan is not, to set preaching in the context of the whole exercise of the study of the Bible of which it forms the apex. Both give advice on the best way to adapt preaching to the needs of the audience, especially to listeners of a special type, such as widows or princes or advocates. There are similarities between Chapters 27 and 29 of the *Verbum Abbreviatum* and Alan's *Epistola* against the celebration of the Mass twice in one day.[36] Others thought of them together, too. Otto of St Blaise brackets the two authors with Praepositinus, Chancellor at Paris from 1206–10, in his Chronicle for 1194: *Petrus Cantor Parisiensis et Alanus et Praepositinus magistri claruerunt.*[37] A manuscript from Otto-beuren shows Alan and Peter in conversation in a double portrait.[38]

The duration of their contact with one another can only be guessed at.[39] It is likely that by 1180 Alan had moved to the south of France.[40] Peter was in Paris by 1173 at the latest.[41] He and Alan could have been together in Paris for several years in the 1170s.[42]

Alan's attitude to *proprietas* is not without its ambiguities. In his *Distinctiones* most of the terms are given what he calls their 'proper' sense at the head of the list, and yet that sense is often demonstrably a figurative one. Only thus can 'hail' properly mean the hard, cold heart of the wicked man, and a 'spear' the Son of God.[43] This 'proper' sense is frequently a reference to God, so Alan cannot hold without qualification the view that words are used 'properly' only of created things. Yet one of the axioms of Alan's *Regulae Theologicae* is that 'no name properly belongs to God'.[44] So it seems that words cannot 'properly' be used of God either. This is a position from which he is obliged to withdraw some way, conceding that there may be degrees of propriety in the ways we conventionally speak of God.[45] Within these degrees of propriety no doubt we may accommodate the 'propriety' of speaking of Christ as a 'spear'. Alan seems to want to reserve true propriety for the use of language to describe created things, then, but he is also ready to impute a special 'higher' propriety to cases such as that where *brachium*, for instance, means not 'arm' but 'Christ'. We might sum up his position like this: figurative usages have all sorts of purposes *etiam in naturalibus,* even in speaking of things in the created world, as Alan himself acknowledges. In *sermo theologicus,* however, he holds that ordinary proper usage is impossible, and every word is subject in some measure to a *translatio.*[46] But that, paradoxically, gives it a higher propriety.

In Rule 26 of the *Regulae Theologicae* Alan points out that *translatio* has a further peculiarity *in divinis.* In the natural world the shift, or *translatio,* may be merely nominal[47] or it may involve the thing signified[48] or it may involve both. The principle involved here may derive from a comment of Abelard on Porphyry that since in the definition of a universal or species or genus only the words are involved,[49] it is necessary to 'transfer' the word to the thing when we wish to speak of a particular thing, the *res speciei* or the *res generis.*[50] This rule is not altogether illuminating in this connection, however, and Abelard himself goes on to say that the use of *translatio* is difficult to understand.

It is clear that the point Alan wishes to make is that in speaking of God we must assume that the transference applies only to the word and not to the thing, for no shift or change can take place in God. Peter the Chanter has perhaps something of the same distinction in mind in a comment on Luke 14.26 which helps make Alan's intention plain. We are told there that no one can be a disciple of Christ unless he hates his mother and father and wife and sons and brothers and sisters. Elsewhere we are told to love them. There is an *equivocatio* involving a shift in *res,* the object of love or hate, not in the word 'love' says Peter.

Augustine and Boethius, writing on the Trinity, had both insisted upon the existence of only two categories or predicates which apply to God. We may speak of the divine substance or essence, and we may speak of the relationships which exist between the Persons of the Trinity. We cannot speak of quantity or quality, for all the divine attributes of goodness, mercy, omnipotence, are substantial, not accidental. They cannot be taken away from the divine essence, because they are themselves that essence. Nor can God be said to be 'here' or 'there', or 'now' or 'then'. Alan of Lille mentions this principle several times in his writings. In the *Regulae Theologicae,* for example, Rule 32 states that every name which is said of God has to do with his essence or with the Persons.[51] Rule 22 puts it succinctly: 'Every theological predicate shows what God is, or in-relation-to-what he is.'[52]

This peculiarity of theological predicates raises difficulties over the propriety of the use of the verb 'to be' of God. Alan would go so far as to say that God is 'improperly said to be',[53] for every noun used of God is used improperly. The impropriety lies, not in the 'being', for God exists more truly than any of his creatures, but in *saying* that he 'is'.[54] The rule, as Alan states it, is that 'every simple thing properly exists and is improperly said to exist'.[55] Accordingly, all affirmative statements made about God, the only truly simple Being, are 'improper', for if we cannot even say that he exists, what can be said of him? In speaking of God, says Alan, in Pseudo-Dionysian tradition, only negative statements are both true and proper.[56]

Alan shows himself one of the Porretani here. Gilbert of Poitiers regarded the statemen*t Deus est* as meaningless, and proposed as a solution the use of the ablative case rather than the nominative in speaking of God. Thus the theologian discusses that 'by which' God is, how he is great by virtue of his greatness, powerful by virtue of his power, and so on.[57] That is one way in which language may be 'transferred' or 'translated' to make it apply to God. Everard, author of a dialogue strongly influenced by Gilbert of Poitiers, describes the process by which names are transferred from their 'natural' reference to created things, to give them a theological reference.[58]

Peter the Chanter is not so pessimistic as Alan about the possibility of speaking about God's existence with at least some degree of propriety. Nowhere is Peter's sturdy common-sense so strongly contrasted with Gilbert's extreme position, and Alan of Lille's adaptation of it for his own purposes. Some transferred usages are improper, says Peter, some, which involve analogy, are 'more proper',[59] but there is one word entirely proper to God, and that is 'to be'. 'Note that every word said of God affirmatively is used improperly, except this word "to be", which is said properly only of God and of God alone, of any other in a transferred manner', he goes on.[60] Since, as Peter argues at length, we cannot properly say that anything but God exists, we are in some difficulty over the use of the verb 'to be' for other things. Peter has a sensible solution to offer. The verb 'to be' can be adapted: *Potest enim aliter assignari,* since 'The verb "to be" is properly assigned to God.'[61] 'Of those things which are, some subsist, some exist in things, some exist in the presence of things, some forward things and some stand in the way of things.'[62] 'Being' (*ypostasis*) is peculiar to God, but things made up of matter and form subsist; *insunt qualitates et quantitates,* qualities and quantities exist in things; *assunt relationes,* relations exist in juxtaposition to things; the virtues *prosunt* and the vices *obsunt.*[63] Thus we can speak of things in the created world using special forms of the verb 'to be' which are proper to them.

BREAKING THE RULES

It is beginning to be clear in what terms Alan would want to argue for the primacy of the 'theological' sense. He describes in the Prologue to the *Summa Quoniam Homines* how 'when words are transferred from natural to theological' uses 'they wonder at their new meanings and seem to seek their old ones'.[64] Taken together with a number of other passages where the *translatio* takes place in the same direction, from created things to the divine, this would seem to suggest that Alan sees the *nova significatio* as the 'theological' one and the *antiqua significatio* as the 'natural' one.

We must make a distinction here between the actual order of events and the primacy of a higher sense over a lower one. Alan accepts that in fact words are normally first used for created things, at least in human experience, and that from a human point of view, they seem to be 'transferred' from the natural to the divine when we use them to speak of God. He sees a word as something rather like a human soul, a limited, created thing, which begins its life upon earth, but is intended by God to reach a higher level and to be, in the end, quite at home in heaven. Only when it reaches heaven is the human soul in its proper place. Only when it is applied to God is a term used 'properly', in the 'theological' sense of the word.

This is a principle on which Alan builds a very great deal, here and elsewhere in his writings. If it is theological language which is normal and correct, then it sets the standard of normal usage even when it appears to break the rules of grammar and dialectic.

That is not to say that the rules of these and the other arts have no force. Theological language breaks the rules by transcending them, by setting an altogether higher standard of 'propriety', and in this way it turns them into new, higher rules.

In adopting this view Alan was running counter to a strong current of contemporary opinion about the 'propriety' which attaches to technically correct usage, which can be seen as early as the end of the eleventh century in the work of St Anselm. When Anselm says that a term is used *proprie*, he means that it is employed with technical exactitude; 'When the Lord said that he who does the truth comes to the light' 'he wanted "to do" to be understood, not for what is properly called "doing" only, but for every verb.'[65] So 'he who does the truth' may be someone who suffers persecution for righteousness' sake, although he is not really 'doing' anything, but rather having something done to him. This is a common enough usage of *facere,* and it is by no means incorrect, but it cannot be said to be quite 'proper', technically speaking.[66] When Alan claims that 'arm' (*brachium*) 'properly' means 'the Son of God',[67] he is saying that Scripture's usage is 'proper' although it is not literally correct. He thus turns much contemporary opinion on its head.[68] Alan works out this principle in detail for all the liberal arts, so as to show how the Bible's language breaks each of their rules by transcending it.

He begins with some general remarks on the dangers of not knowing the force of the words used in the Bible: 'It is dangerous not to know the powers of the theological nouns in the Sacred Page', he warns.[69] Sometimes, for example, there are simply no words for the things we want to discuss, and so the Bible has had to give a new meaning to an existing word. This consciousness of the inadequacy of the vocabulary available, in Latin in particular, was more general even than it had been in Bede's day, since Boethius' theological tractates had come to be more widely studied. In *Contra Eutychen* III Boethius complains of the shortage of words in Latin (*inopia verborum*). Thierry of Chartres explains that this makes it impossible to teach the arts adequately in Latin, and Gilbert of Poitiers looks at its theological implications, for the formulation of the doctrine of the Trinity in Latin. 'We Latins, because of shortage of words, have properly kept a borrowed term' (*persona*), where 'the Greeks correctly (*recte*) say *hypostasis*'.[70]

Alan sees a further difficulty. Even where we have the words we need, they may not be adequate. That is, they may not speak of the thing they signify as it really is.[71] This problem, he feels, is bound to arise where human language, a created thing, is used to speak of the Creator. Words have a tendency to wander from their 'proper' senses and to take on strange and novel meanings[72] under such pressure. If God has come down to meet human understanding in framing the text of Holy Scripture, however, we must take it that he himself has adapted them for their special purpose. We must, therefore, treat their strange meanings with respect and revise our notion of what is 'proper'. Scripture's figurative sayings are not mere images. They are God's own usages, and that is why they are truly 'proper'.

Alan makes his point by presenting his readers with a series of paradoxes, designed to sharpen their appreciation of the way in which the divine Author of Scripture breaks the rules of the arts. He does not elaborate – he is writing for readers who may be expected to appreciate the point at once. Keeping to technical commonplaces, he lists the ways in which Scripture deviates from the technical rules of the arts. All the arts are included, specifically or by implication, not only grammar and dialectic, which would seem the most likely to be affected.

The first of the respects in which Scripture transcends the rules is in making its nouns behave like pronouns on occasion. Grammatical theory allows for the possibility that a pronoun may stand in place of a noun.[73] Peter Helias – a pupil of Thierry of Chartres and a master of some note in the teaching of grammar and rhetoric from the 1130s, in Poitiers and Paris – is the author of a commentary on Priscian which became so much the standard work on the subject that Alan is able to make use of it and expect his readers to be as familiar with it as he is himself. The principle in question is commonplace enough, but it is likely that Peter Helias is Alan's direct source; he certainly knew Helias on rhetoric, and it is entirely probable that he relies upon him for grammar, too.[74] Peter Helias explains how a pronoun may stand in place of a noun, in his discussion of Priscian *Ars Minor*.[75] A pronoun normally signifies a substance without a quality.[76]

It can, however, be used in such a way that the qualities denoted by the noun for which it stands are to be understood, too. When we read *hic* instead of 'Virgil' we understand readily enough that 'this' in this particular case refers to the poet and *hic* signifies all the attributes of Virgil with his subsistence.[77] There would be nothing worthy of remark, then, if Scripture simply made pronouns behave like nouns. But Alan claims that the Bible sometimes makes nouns behave like pronouns, emptying them of their content and making them purely designative and not descriptive. Thus the noun ceases to denote both quality and substance and comes to denote substance only. Scripture reverses the principles of grammar when it behaves in this way: we have, not the common sight of pronouns behaving like nouns, but the curious sight of nouns behaving like pronouns.

Scripture also shows us adjectives behaving like substantives,[78] Alan claims. Here we are in a noted area of disagreement between grammarians and dialecticians. Grammarians included adjectives in the class of nouns, among the parts of speech, and they held that all nouns signify substance and quality. The dialecticians took the view that adjectives signify quality only, that to call a horse 'white' is to attribute a quality to him but not to refer to his substance.[79] Only a dialectician, then, would feel that a rule had been broken when an adjective denoted substance. Again, there are discussions in Peter Helias which bear on this point, and similar considerations arise for William of Conches, another noted grammarian, in his exposition of Priscian.[80] A passage in Rupert of Deutz's *De Victoria Verbi Dei,* written much earlier in the twelfth century, makes practical use of the same principle in the interpretation of Scripture. He discusses the difference between the description of Satan as the *antiquus serpens,* and God as the *antiquus dierum.* Satan is called 'the old Serpent' adjectivally. His 'oldness' is merely a quality. God is called *antiquus* as if to refer to his very substance, for he is 'oldness' itself.[81]

Alan's next technical point is again perhaps a direct quotation from Peter Helias, with the addition of a *non* which turns it on its head: 'ubi verbum non est nota eius quod de altero dicitur'. The origin of the principle is to be found in Boethius' first *Commentary* on Aristotle's *De Interpretatione.*[82] A word is normally 'a sign of something which is being said of something else'.[83]

In theological language that is not always the case (for the Word of God signifies himself directly). Here and in the next example, we are on dialecticians' ground.[84] Alan next says that in Scripture there is sometimes predication without inherence. Contemporary dialecticians were divided between those who held that in an affirmative proposition the copula states that a 'universal nature' such as 'whiteness' inheres in a particular individual who is designated by the subject-term (the inherence theory). Those who preferred the 'identity theory' held that the subject-term and the predicate-term of a proposition refer to the same thing.[85] Alan is saying, then, that theological language breaks the rules of the inherence theory.

Alan's next example is perhaps a reference to the doctrine that, at the consecration of the bread and wine of the Eucharist, the accidents remain, but the substance of the bread and wine is changed. The accidents therefore persist even when the *materia* in which they normally inhere is removed. In his treatise against the heretics, Alan remarks that it is not surprising that the God who is able to make all things from nothing is able to cause accidents to exist without material substance.[86] The expression he uses in the preface to his dictionary is: 'ubi sine materia subiectio'. In Scripture, as in the consecration, properties may be detached from those things in which they usually inhere and treated as though they were able to exist independently.

His next principle, which we have already met in the discussion of the *proprietas* of saying that God exists, states that in Scripture affirmative statements are not 'proper', but on the other hand, negative statements are true.[87] A similar claim is made in Rule 18 of the *Regulae Theologicae*.[88] Alan's explanation of the meaning of this paradox in the *Regulae* throws some light on his intention in the preface to the *Dictionary*. An affirmation is said to be *composita* or *compacta* when it signifies composition; for example, 'Peter is righteous',[89] means that righteousness is being attributed or in some way 'added' to Peter.[90] When no 'composition' is signified, the affirmation is not 'composite', as when we say that God is righteous. God is not merely righteous; he is righteousness itself.[91] We attribute nothing to him when we call him righteous, because we are speaking of his substance, not of a mere property. In the preface to the *Dictionary* Alan calls such affirmations 'improper' perhaps because they are not properly speaking affirmations, in the usual technical sense. Alan goes on to explain, in the *Regulae*, that 'negations said of God are both true and proper, insofar as what does not belong to God by inherence is removed from him'.[92] Alan is asserting in the *Distinctiones*, then, that affirmative statements are not, in cases where they are made of God, technically proper, but negative statements are both true and proper. It would be true and proper to say of God that he is in-finite, for example.

Alan brings what he has to say in the Preface to an end with some comments of a more general kind about each of the *artes* in turn, designed to show that the language of the Bible transcends the rules of all the arts. In the Bible, the construction of sentences is not subject to the laws of Donatus.[93] Alan's choice of Donatus rather than Priscian for his 'grammarian' here is no doubt an echo of Gregory the Great's dictum. In a famous passage, Gregory says that he thinks it entirely improper to attempt to confine the words of the 'heavenly Oracle under the rules of Donatus'.[94] The saying became a commonplace. In the twelfth century Abbot Ernald, a scholar of Bonneval near Chartres, commenting on Psalm 132, wrote that it was no great matter to sin against Priscian, if by such a sin one was able to strengthen the faith of the Christian reader. Even if the Latin sounds oddly[95] the appropriate sense edifies.[96]

Peter Helias' commentary covers the subject of 'construction' thoroughly, and it is to Peter Helias on Priscian, not to Donatus, that we must probably look for Alan's notion of *constructio*. *Constructio est congrua dictionum ordinatio*, he explains, and the 'congruous' ordering of words is to be understood to refer both to the words and to the sense.[97] A sentence may make enough sense for the meaning to be understood, but be grammatically inaccurate; or it may be grammatically accurate nonsense. The 'sense' is what the listener can reasonably understand. A *locutio* is like a picture, for just as a picture depicts something, so a saying 'depicts' a meaning or 'understanding' (*intellectum*). That is its sole purpose.[98] Alan is saying that in the case of the statement of the Bible words may, when they are arranged in a *congrua dictionum ordinatio*, mean something which is independent of the rules of grammar.[99]

Next, Alan tells us that in Scripture the *translatio* is often foreign to the laws of Cicero.[100] This seems to be a reference to Cicero's *Topics*, which has an echo in Peter the Chanter's *De Tropis Loquendi*; there we meet the notion that in the Bible differences of meaning occur sometimes *proprie* and sometimes *transsumptive et aliene*. The terms *transsumptio* and *translatio* were in process of finding their place as technical terms in the commentaries on Boethius of Gilbert of Poitiers and the school of Thierry of Chartres. Thierry prefers *translatio* but Gilbert makes use of both terms. In Peter Abelard *transsumptio* is explicitly linked with Cicero's *Topics,* in the *De Divisionibus Themistii et Tullii. Transsumptio* takes place, he says, when a question has been posed and not yet settled, and another question is raised and settled in order that the proof which has been arrived at may be applied to the resolution of the first question.[101] It seems likely, then, that the particular *regulae Tullii* Alan has in mind are the rules of the *Topics,* and that he expects his readers to understand readily that he is referring to this work of Cicero, not, for example, to the *De Inventione*. The *Topics* had a place, not so much in rhetoric as in dialectic. As for logic, we are told next that in the Bible *enuntiatio* wanders from the *documenta* of Aristotle. *Enuntiatio* would place us in the context of the *De Interpretatione* of Aristotle. Alan sums up with the general remark that in Scripture 'faith is remote from the argument of reason'.[102]

This long series of commonplaces of the contemporary study of the *trivium,* all turned on their heads by the higher rules which the language of Scripture obeys, looks laborious enough to the modern eye, because we are not steeped by long habit in these matters, as Alan's students had been during the years of their training in the *artes*. Alan intended his reversals of the rules to make their point immediately, perhaps even to amuse the reader, although their purpose is serious enough.

The principle he wants to make clear is that Scripture does not break the rules clumsily or by chance. There is all the difference in the world between the rule-breaking which goes on here, and that of fallen nature, as it is described in the *De Planctu Naturae,* which Alan calls a *vitium* and not a *translatio*, an error and not a transference of meaning:

Non tamen ista tropus poterit translatio dici; In vitium melius ista figura cadit.	That artificiality cannot be called metaphor; rather, it sinks into error.

Translatio is a term of approbation. The *vitium* of fallen nature involves a degeneration. The man who denies his manhood is a barbarism:

Se negat esse virum, naturae fac-
    tus in arte
Barbarus.   Ars illi non placet,
    imo, tropus.
	He denies that he is a man,
	barbarously, although he is made
	by Nature's skill; Art does not
	please him as much as artifice.

This is a kind of logic which causes the laws of nature to perish:

Hoc modo est logicus, per quem conversio simplex Artis, naturae jura perire facit.	He is too fond of logic, through whom a simple conversion causes the rights of Nature to perish.

Nature's 'writing' does not scan:

Sic pede dactilio Veneris male
    iambitur usus
In quo non patitur syllaba longa
    brevem.[103]
	Thus the iambic measure does not
	keep pace with the dactylic foot
	of Venus, in which the long
	syllable impedes the short.

The imagery of rule-breaking in the arts is extended to cover every aspect of the failings of the natural world Alan can contrive to make it fit. Here, he intends the breach of rules to be seen clearly as a shameful thing, a sign of the effect of sin.

There is, by contrast, a spanking confidence about the Bible's use of language. Its divergences from the rules are not *vitia*, *barbarismi* or *solecismi*. They are not errors. The Holy Spirit knows everything, and when he inspired the writers of Scripture, he knew the rules of grammar better than they. The divergences from the rules to be found in the Bible cannot, then, be the result of error or ignorance. They must be deliberate. That is why Alan wants his readers to treat the Bible's special usages with respect, to make an effort to distinguish between the meanings of 'theological terms' in a way which will be worthy of the Bible's language (*dignum*), and in that way to bring into the light what appears at first sight to be obscure.

The dictionary itself is a practical attempt to help in this task. Alan explains that he has set out the different senses of his *theologicae dictiones* in order. In that way, he has opened up the way (*introitus*) into the Sacred Page.[104]

THE THRESHOLD OF THEOLOGY

1 *Powers of Mind*

Alan sees the soul as a four-wheeled chariot, running along on the two front wheels of *ratio* and *intellectualitas*. Sense-perception and the mind's power of forming images of things perceived by the senses,[105] roll their way like two more wheels, over the dark lower things of this world. Reason and intellectual understanding move upwards towards heavenly things.[106] If the rear two wheels turn in the wrong direction, the soul becomes a beast. If reason or intellectual understanding go astray, the consequences are even worse; for these are spiritual powers, and a spiritual being who goes wrong becomes – as Satan did – a devil.[107] This is an image we shall meet again, and which Alan may have drawn from Bernard Silvestris.

These 'powers of mind' are a favourite theme of Alan's. In a sermon for Epiphany he explains that the three Kings who offered their gifts to the infant Christ are to be identified with the three *anime potentiales, ratio, intellectus, intelligentia,* but not, it should be noted, with the two lower powers of the four-wheeled chariot.[108] In the *Contra Haereticos* he interrupts his discussion of the question of the relation between body and soul, to explain that 'to the incorporeal spirit belong...five powers, that is, sense, imagination, reason, *intellectus* and *intelligentia*'.[109] Of these, *intellectus*[110] and *ratio*[111] are defined in Alan's *Dictionary of Theological Terms* as *potentie anime*.

But this gives us only half a picture of a man. Human beings have bodies as well as souls. The soul must govern the body. The head rules the heart and the heart keeps in order the improper desires of the lower part of the body. In this, Alan thinks, man is a microcosm of divine government. In the universe, God rules, the angels carry out his orders and man obeys. In man, there ought to be a similar most orderly arrangement.[112] The head has its wit,[113] its reason,[114] its memory. The heart has its magnanimity, which acts under the direction of prudence. The *renes* are like the suburbs of a city, for their desires spread out in all directions shapelessly, and they do not willingly obey the direction of the heart,[115] but it is their duty to be obedient to the powers set in authority over them.

There is a parallel, too, with the division we have been considering, between those things in the natural world which may be discussed according to the laws of the liberal arts, and those higher truths of which the *artes* cannot speak unless we modify their rules. The proper order of learning requires us to keep the 'bodily' rules of the secular *artes*, so that we do not talk nonsense about created things. But it also requires us to see those rules in the light of the superior laws of theology. If we confine ourselves to the secular arts on the grounds that we cannot by an act of reason go beyond them, we are like a chariot with only three wheels, the wheels of sense, imagination and reason. A man ought to exercise his *intellectualitas* (*intellectus, intelligentia*) and be a theologian, or he is not using the powers of his mind as God intended.

The first practical necessity – and Alan is always practical, even when his speculations are most daring – is to determine the nature of the boundary between the world of secular studies and the realm of theology, and to show where it lies. Where, in other words, do the ordinary rules break down?

2   *The Breakdown of Every Rule*

In the *Dictionary of Theological Terms* Alan of Lille subordinates speculation to practical considerations. He warns his readers that they are to expect something out of the ordinary in their reading of the Bible; he draws their attention sharply to its rule-breaking propensities in a series of witty reversals of technical principles so familiar that any student of the *artes* would be inclined to take them for granted. But he does not explore the implications of this startling claim because he wants first and foremost to provide them with a practical aid to Bible study. Elsewhere he allows himself to range speculatively rather further afield. The question to which he returns again and again is this: what is the relationship between the understanding of God and the created world which may be attained by the exercise of the reason, that is, as he sees it, according to the rules of the arts and sciences, and the knowledge man may have of God in ways beyond reason? Have the higher powers of the mind a capacity to penetrate so far?

Alan is interested above all in the boundary he perceives between the two, the 'reason' which may be given for a 'mystery' when the mystery is all but within reach of reason, but not quite. In his sermon for Epiphany he says that there is a 'reason for the mystery' that a star appeared above the house where the child was, 'for the divine favour illuminates the human mind in which Christ is born by grace'; in the sermon for Pentecost we learn the 'reason for the mystery' that the feast continues for seven days. The seven days signify the seven gifts of the spirit. In the same sermon, there is a 'reason' given for the 'mystery' that the apostles were 'sitting' when the Holy Spirit came upon them: there are some who lie prostrate, who are bent only on earthly things, some who sit, with their minds half upon earth and half upon heaven, and some who stand, with their eyes fixed exclusively upon heaven. In the sermon on the Cross of the Lord, we learn the 'reason for the mystery' that pilgrims to Jerusalem wear the sign of the cross on their shoulders on the outward journey, and on their breasts on their return. In all these instances, Alan uses the expression: 'nec vacat a mysterii ratione'.[116] His instinct is to apply reason to matters of faith, so as to see how far it will take him towards understanding.

He does not expect reason to be able to take him all the way. He is acutely aware that human reason fails in the face of divine mysteries. He often speaks of the stupefaction felt by even the trained mind, how even the scholar, the academic theologian, learns about God chiefly from his own bafflement. The function of the reason, and of the liberal arts which furnish the reason with technical procedures and instruments, is to map out the approach to the mystery with as much exactitude as possible.

In the Prologue to his *De Trinitate* Boethius describes the height of the divine mystery[117] and warns his readers against trying to press beyond the proper limits set to reason. He points out that some limit is set[118] in all the arts, beyond which reason may not reach, and theology is no exception. Indeed, it is the most difficult subject of all for the reason to work upon.

Boethius' picture of a boundary which marks the limit of what reason can do attracted Alan of Lille. As he sees it, theology begins where the secular arts and the sciences of human reason leave off. The idea is worked out in several of his writings, and in some detail. It constitutes a distinctive contribution to the resolution of a classic problem for the educated Christian, and a particularly pressing one in Alan's day, when enterprising scholars were ready to experiment with the possibilities of finding out more about God by any means that technical and scientific advance opened up.

Among the logical treatises which survive from the second half of the twelfth century is an elementary handbook on fallacies, the *Fallacie Magistri Willelmi,* which was written, according to a note at the end, for the use of 'ignorant theologians'.[119] Master William sets out the Aristotelian fallacies, and gives examples to illustrate each of them, chosen for their 'theological' complexion. In the case of a fallacy *secundum equivocationem,* for example, where the 'deception' comes from a difference of signification between two terms, we have:

Omnis caritas est qualitas mentis.	All love is a quality of mind.
Deus caritas est.	God is love.
Ergo Deus est qualitas mentis.	Therefore God is a quality of mind.

Caritas, the magister explains, has two meanings here: first, it is the name of a created virtue, and secondly the name of something uncreated, a noun signifying the very divine essence.[120] There is therefore in reality no common middle term, and the conclusion does not follow from the premisses. The implication of the whole treatise is that theologians will have little trouble with the apparent paradoxes which modern dialectic puts before them, if they understand the rules of argument correctly.

It is fairly clear that one of the most significant divisions among those contemporary scholars who chose to make full use of their knowledge of the liberal arts in the study of the Bible and in speculative theology, lay between those who thought that the ordinary rules of the *artes* applied to theological problems directly, and those who held that they did not. Like Peter the Chanter, Simon of Tournai, a scholar of the most moderate order in his use of the techniques of the *artes,* consistently looks for solutions in terms of the ordinary rules of grammar and dialectic. He reminds us that when we ask 'whether God always wills what he once wills' we must remember that 'according to the rule of the grammarians',[121] verbs of willing and desiring are construed with present, past or future infinitives, according to their different *affectus*.[122] Before the creation of the world, God willed the world to be created in the future; while it was being created, he willed it to be created in the present; when it had been created, he willed it to have been created in the past. We must therefore listen for, or understand, the appropriate tense of the verb[123] when we speak of God's willing something at any time.[124] The will is eternal; its direction, or *affectus*, appears, from our temporal standpoint, to alter with the passage of time. It might be argued that Simon has bent the rules of grammar a little here, in order to accommodate a special theological case. But he has tried to give an explanation in terms of the normal rules of the grammarians.

Not every writer of the mid-twelfth century would be so optimistic as Simon about the possibility of reconciling theological usages with the ordinary usages of grammar and dialectic merely by stretching the rules a little. The author of the *Sententie Parisienses* of the School of Peter Abelard declares plainly that 'philosophers cannot learn anything properly of God by the rule of the human arts'.[125] Peter of Poitiers points out in his *Sentences* that statements about God are often made ungrammatically.[126] He himself attempts solutions which make use of the rules of the arts, in deciding, for instance, whether a singular or a plural verb should be used for the Persons of the Trinity.[127] But he is always alert to the problems which theological language ultimately raises for the student of the *artes*.

To judge from the frequency with which he returns to the problem – it is his starting-point in both the *Regulae Theologicae* and the *Summa Quoniam Homines* as well as in the *Distinctiones* – no scholar of the second half of the twelfth century gave more systematic thought to the matter than Alan of Lille. Certainly no-one was more conscious of the role of 'rules' (*regulae*) of both the *artes* and theology itself. He cites Boethius as his authority for the view that when words are used theologically they undergo a complete change.[128] There are, he insists, special rules for theological language. The implications of this view are followed through at considerable length in the *Summa Quoniam Homines*, where Alan examines the rules which govern the use of the words *persona* and *trinitas*, terms which are said to be 'especially theological',[129] and other *nomina theologica*. Of theological *nomina* in general, some are *essentialia*, like *caritas*, which we have already met in this connection in Master William's treatise, and *Deus, deitas, essentia, natura, usia, substantia, iustus, pius, fortis*. They signify the essence of God without *distinctio*. Others are *coessentialia*; they signify the relationships which the *divina usia* bears to other things; if we call God *dominus, principium, origo, causa*, we are saying something about God in his relation to his creatures. Some *theologica nomina* (*persona* and *trinitas*) refer principally to the Divine Essence, but they also refer to the distinction of Persons; they are therefore *partim personalia, partim essentialia*. Still others are *personalia*, and predicate what is proper to the Persons (*Pater, Filius, Spiritus Sanctus*), and others are *compersonalia*, signifying that one Person is not the same as another (*distinctus, differens, alius*). Out of all this it is possible to draw a rule[130] by which it may be determined that every noun which means the same in its dictionary definition as it does in its specific reference in context[131] is said of the three Persons individually and the three *in summa*, in the singular not in the plural.[132] Alan goes on to explore and consider the apparent exceptions to this rule.[133]

In the Prologue to his *Regulae Theologicae* Alan explains the general principle which he believes lies behind this talk of rules.[134] He points out that every science has its rules. He found a list of the rules proper to each of the *artes* in Gilbert of Poitiers' commentary on Boethius' *De Hebdomadibus*: the art of dialectic, for example, has its *maximae*, music its *axiomata*, rhetoric its common topics, or *loci communes*, geometry its theorems, or *theoremata*.[135] The 'heavenly science' of theology has its rules, too, rules of a higher and finer kind, with an absolute binding force which the rules of the other sciences cannot claim, for they are obedient to the course of nature.[136]

Can we, then, use the rules of the *artes* to answer theological questions? It would seem, on the face of it, that Alan thinks not, because theology is clearly not subject to the rules of the *artes*.

Yet his theological writings, like those of many of his contemporaries, are full of technical terms of the *artes* – indeed, they are notably rich in such technicalities. But, as we are beginning to see, Alan has an answer to the problem which permits him to make full use of the skills he possesses, even though he believes that theology cannot be subject to these lower *regulae*.

In a sermon addressed to clerks who neglect their theological studies, Alan says that 'after they have led us to the threshold of theology',[137] 'to the door of the heavenly queen',[138] 'the liberal arts are to be left in peace'.[139] He envisages the existence of a firm line of demarcation, a 'threshold' to which the arts can take us, but beyond which they can help us to progress further only by showing us exactly what lies beyond their normal scope, where the accent lies on 'normal'. In so doing they perform at least one very considerable service; they make the position clear.

In the sermon from which our quotation comes, Alan castigates the clerks of his day who waste their time with 'vain and transitory sciences'[140] and despise the *celestis scientia*. Yet he certainly does not regard the liberal arts as intrinsically bad or unworthy. God does not condemn them, for they are instituted by him.[141] He has ordained them for one purpose only: to be handmaids of theology.[142] This picture of the arts as handmaids of heavenly wisdom was a popular one in the twelfth century, especially among monastic scholars. Hugh of St Victor has it, and in Rupert of Deutz's *De Trinitate et Operibus Eius* there is a lively description of the arts as wayward girls who run about and chatter until they are taught to serve their divine Master. He, too, contrasts the *philosophia inanis et fallax* with the *philosophia sana et vera*; he, too, insists that God does not condemn the schools of the grammarians and dialecticians, but blames them when they fail to seek that higher wisdom which he intended the arts to serve.[143] Once Rupert's *artes* have come to their senses, they are able, he says, to declare faithfully what it is fitting for them to tell of the Creator:[144] then they are serviceable and worth studying, and neither Rupert of Deutz nor Alan of Lille would want to discourage anyone from making use of them.

There is an important difference between Rupert's view that the *artes* are able to speak of God – even if only in a limited way – and Alan's contention that (in their ordinary guise) they can take him only to the threshold of theology. Rupert would not, perhaps, want to claim that the arts of language can apply to the more than human language of God himself, to the Word; it is as Creator that they speak of God, because human language is a created thing and it can only refer directly to the created world. Alan, however, goes further than Rupert in making the difference quite explicit. He holds that the *artes* can take a man only as far as his powers as a human being allow him to go. He cannot have the full knowledge which God himself has (*theosophia*); he cannot even see God as the angels do.[145]

It is in the *Summa Quoniam Homines* that Alan first examines the powers or faculties of the mind (*potentie anime*): first there is *thesis* or *ratio*, the reasoning power which is exercised upon human and earthly things. Natural science or *naturalis philosophia* is its field. Secondly, there is *extasis*, the higher faculty, which enables a man to see some way into those mysteries which go beyond the reach of natural philosophy. This, in its turn, Alan separates into two: *intellectus*, by which a man understands *spiritualia*, spiritual beings, angels and souls, and the *intelligentia* by which he has some perception of the Trinity.[146] In order to understand anything at all of the nature of God himself a man must in some way 'become God'; he cannot do it by his own powers or his own efforts.[147] Thus man's natural powers are extended by God himself, so that man may know something of God, 'where divine excellence descends, so that human understanding may ascend',[148] as Alan describes it in the Prologue to his *Dictionary of Theological Terms,* the *Distinctiones Dictionum Theologicalium.* In this way only may we speak of a *humana scientia,* a human science by which God is understood by man.[149] Such a 'science' is quite different from the ordinary 'human sciences', the liberal arts. There is a clear dividing line between the two, which a man can cross only with divine assistance.

In Book v of Alan's *Anticlaudianus,* Phronesis meets the Heavenly Queen (*regina poli*), who appears to stand for the queen of sciences, *Theologia.* Phronesis represents the highest wisdom to which man can attain; she has a stature and a nobleness of mind which Reason lacks. Yet she is humble and respectful in her salutation of Theology, because she recognises how far short she falls of the full knowledge possessed by the Heavenly

Queen of the sciences. When, at the beginning of Book VI, they arrive at a point in their journey from which Phronesis can at last look upon God's realm, she is stunned at the sight; she cannot comprehend what she sees; she faints and has to be helped to stand.[150] The brightness dazzles her eyes; the novelty of the things she sees stupefies her mind; she cannot look upon them and her innermost mind is dazed by the glare. Here Alan gives an allegorical dress to his description, but the presence of the threshold is clear enough. Phronesis cannot cope by her own efforts with the subject-matter of Theologia.

What is this science, then, which Alan tells us begins where other sciences end? He sees it stretching upwards in stages or degrees of remoteness from the reach of human sciences, rather as he envisages the Jacob's ladder[151] the Christian is to climb, from confession, to prayer, to thanksgiving, to thorough reading of the Bible, to asking someone more experienced about his difficulties, to the exposition of Scripture, and finally, to preaching.[152]

In the *Expositio Prosae de Angelis,* in which he is much concerned with the notion of hierarchy, and in the *Summa Quoniam Homines,* Alan distinguishes between apothetical and hypothetical theology. Hypothetical theology deals with things heavenly, with angels and the heavenly city.[153] Apothetical theology deals with Unity and Trinity, with what is above the heavens (*supercelestia*).[154] He emphasises the height to which the seeker after theological knowledge must aspire,[155] in the sermon on the *Intelligible Sphere.* If human power is like the positive degree, and natural power like the comparative degree, divine power is like the superlative degree.[156]

Alan gives a general picture of the hierarchical structure of knowledge, then, and the most important point he can show us is the threshold which divides the liberal arts from theology. Beyond that threshold, the further we look, the deeper the mystery becomes. The rules of theology (*theologiae maximae*) are also known as enigmas (*aenigmata*) because of their obscurity; *emblemata,* because of the inward splendour of their *intelligentia*; *enthymemata,* because they lie deep within the mind.[157] We may speak of the hidden places, the *arcana Dei,* the depths of the divine mind, *divinae mentis abyssum.*[158] It is of the essence of theology, for Alan, that it should be secret and hidden from the unworthy. He follows Boethius in the *De Hebdomadibus* in this.

Yet theology has visible fruits. In the sermon which Alan addressed to the clerks who did not study theology as they should, he describes how theology grows green in the mind, sprouts leaves in speech, flowers in the manifold fragrances of the meanings it draws out of the text, and bears fruits in the practical living of the Christian life. It is like a great tree.[159] We can, too, say of theology as of other sciences[160] that it has a defensive and a positive function: the theologian must defend the faith against heretics, and expound it positively for the faithful, and to do that he must teach and think about it.[161] Like other sciences, theology has rules, *regulae*. In practical terms he treats it as though it were accessible to study, finding more than a hundred such rules in the *Regulae Theologicae*.[162]

Alan's solution, then, is not to turn from reasoning to contemplation. He looks to the *artes* for help. Yet it is not at first easy to see how this may be if, when human wisdom looks upon the realm of theology, she is stupefied; Alan's contention is that the rules of theology may be understood best if we know the rules of grammar and logic, and the other liberal arts, thoroughly. Then we shall be able to understand exactly where they break down, and accordingly, to make inferences about the nature of those matters they cannot touch unless we modify them for theological purposes. The exact position of the threshold is of crucial importance here. The *stupor* of Phronesis' mind is not a mindless confusion, but a sense of helplessness, when she sees that all her laws of thought have failed her simultaneously at the moment when she looks into the heavenly realm.

In the poem on *The Incarnation of Christ and the Seven Liberal Arts* Alan examines the point of breakdown of the rules for each of the arts. The Incarnation is envisaged in terms of a proposition, as he does in his *Dictionary of Theological Terms*. Here, Christ as the Word itself (*Verbum*) acts as a *copula*. Grammar, applying the laws which govern activity and passivity in verbs, finds that here alone 'action conceives passion'; rhetoric discovers a new 'colour of rhetoric' in the conjoining; arithmetic finds unity becoming something other than itself (*alteratur unitas*) and discovers diversity in sameness (*in idem identitas*); music's harmony has no rules for such *proportio*; geometry has the curve of its circle converted into a straight line; logic blushes at its own fallacies; astronomy sees the Sun rise in Virgo (the Virgin). Each of the arts in turn discovers that

In hac Verbi copula   'in the copula of this Verb every
Stupet omnis regula.   rule is confounded'[163]

The rules of the arts, then, are confounded in ways which can be clearly stated; we can see exactly where theology begins because we can see exactly where the *artes* end.

The moral Alan wishes to draw is that the rules of the *artes* must never be over-extended in their application without being adapted for theology. 'When terms are transferred from the natural world to the theological', he explains in the Prologue to the *Summa Quoniam Homines,* 'they are amazed at their new meanings, and they seem to want to return to their old meanings'.[164] As a result, those who have not mastered the liberal arts so that they are correctly led by their knowledge of their limitations, fall into various errors when they try to deal with the *ineffabilia* of theology.[165] When they press on across the bridge which the liberal arts provide at the threshold of the realm of theology, they fall into the waters of heresy beneath.[166] The liberal arts, then, teach the theologian above all where to stop.

In the *Regulae Theologicae* and the *Summa Quoniam Homines,* as we have seen, Alan makes a serious effort to work out the implications of the principle. In the *Anticlaudianus* he treats it rhetorically. At the sight of the Virgin Mother, 'nature is silent; the force of logic is banished; rhetoric's judgment is destroyed; reason wavers'. In God we have 'a beginning without beginning; an end without end; what is immense without measure, strong without strength, powerful without vigour, directing all things without motion; without place, filling all places; enduring without time, and so on. When ordinary language tries to speak of these divine things[167] she loses her powers of speaking, and desires to return to the old meanings with which she is familiar. Her sounds die into silence and she is scarcely able to stammer.[168]

3   *New Men, New Rules: the Theologian's Qualifications*

Alan was not one of those twelfth-century scholars who thought 'new' a synonym for 'dangerous'. We have seen how his own adventurousness led him to try out novel literary *genres*. His was the first manual on the *Art of Preaching* to anticipate the methods of the university-style sermon of the thirteenth century. His *Liber Poenitentialis* and the *Dictionary of Theological Terms* were among the first of their kind. His *Regulae Theologicae* was a novelty.[169] There was more to this than the attempt to meet new needs in the schoolroom. Alan approved strongly of what was new; he employs the terms *novitas* and *novus* with the utmost respect. They are, he believes, the distinguishing mark of theological language. In theology words have a *novus sensus*. As he explains in the fifth book of the *Anticlaudianus*, the very face of Theologia herself is alight with *novitas*. As the travellers reach the threshold of heaven at the beginning of Book VI, everything seems 'new'. In the *Summa Quoniam Homines*, too, Alan speaks of the novelty of the meanings words have in theological contexts, their *novas significationes*.[170]

Gilbert of Poitiers admits the existence of these novel meanings, but he would like to reduce them to order, to bring them under the conventional rules of the *artes*. In his first Prologue to the commentary on Boethius' *De Trinitate*, he says that he sees it as the commentator's task to suppress novelties and oddities of usage, so as to demonstrate that theology is subject to intelligible rules: 'We, undertaking the duty of interpreters,...restore transposed words to order[171] and subject novelties to rule.'[172]

There is no evidence in Gilbert of Poitiers' surviving writings that he possessed the responsiveness to the mysterious which Alan of Lille had in such large measure. Gilbert is all hard reason. Alan is emotionally and spiritually, as well as intellectually, stirred by the picture Boethius paints of the 'heights of divinity'.[173] He has a good deal to say in several of his works about the way in which man may ascend to God by means other than plain reasoning. In a sermon on the spiritual unity of abbot and monks, he describes the kiss 'which comes about through the spiritual conjunction of the soul and God'.[174]

When we say that Alan preferred to celebrate these novel

meanings, to throw them into relief; that by emphasising the stupefaction of human reason and the arts of language he tried to reflect glory upon the mysteries of theology which are beyond reason, we are saying something important about his philosophical position. It is not that Gilbert is unaware of the existence of what Boethius calls the *secreta theologie altioris*. It is rather that he believes that with the aid of the liberal arts human reason can penetrate the mysteries.

4 *The Deification of Man*

If Alan insists that human reason stops short at the threshold of theology – and reason is agreed by common consent to be the faculty which distinguishes men and angels from mere beasts and makes them able to lift their understanding towards God – how is man ever to advance beyond the threshold to receive this 'kiss'? How is man to understand even in part what only God knows of himself? To understand Alan's thinking here, we must look at a work which influenced him profoundly: the *Asclepius*, attributed to Hermes Trismegistus (the Egyptian god Thoth), author and patron of knowledge. The *Asclepius* was one of a number of 'Hermetic' writings of the second and third centuries AD, in which Platonism, Stoicism and oriental elements were brought together in a mysticism concerned with the 'deification' of man through knowledge. Bernard Silvestris made use of the *Asclepius,* too, especially in his *Cosmographia,* but it was a work by no means universally known even in Alan's day.

The author of the *Asclepius* examines the nature of God and the nature of man. He suggests that in some respects man is capable of approaching so close to the nature of God that it is as if he were himself a god – or perhaps even God himself; the Latin is not clear:

> Hoc enim in naturam dei transit, quasi ipse
> sit deus.[175]

The treatise explores at some length the question of the precise nature of the 'divinity' which man may be said to attain; the ambivalence of *ipse sit deus* is not left unresolved. Alan drew from the treatise a number of ideas of which he was able to make use in constructing his own theory of the way in which it is possible for man to rise above the threshold, to go beyond the point to which reason takes him in his search for God.

Certain passages in the treatise rightly struck Augustine as requiring careful analysis if the nugget of truth they contained[176] was to be made accessible to the Christian reader. In Augustine's day, the paganism of the *Asclepius* represented a living tradition. When he discussed the pagan gods in *The City of God*, he was writing for angry exiles from fallen Rome, who protested that the collapse of the Christian Roman Empire had come about because the gods were angry. Augustine was defending the Christian faith. His mediaeval successors faced rather different problems in their attempts to understand the teaching of the treatise and to adapt it for Christian use.

Augustine discusses a small part of the *Asclepius,* the part which explores the possibility that gods have bodies and souls: the spirit of the god is its 'soul'; the statue in which it resides is its 'body', says the *Asclepius*. The chief interest of this for the mediaeval reader lay in the distinction this leads to, between the gods which men make (in their own image) and the gods which the Supreme God creates.[177] The gods men make are idols. But what are the gods which God himself makes? Gods of this sort are mentioned in Scripture, in Psalms 49 and 81, for example, and Augustine discusses what we are to make of them in his *Enarrationes in Psalmos*.[178] He did not draw together the teaching of the *Asclepius* and the teaching of Scripture explicitly, and he left mediaeval scholars with a task of some importance to complete.

The only other piece of the *Asclepius* which was widely known in the Middle Ages is cited in the Pseudo-Augustinian *Adversus Quinque Haereses*.[179] The passage in question says that 'the Lord and Creator of all the Gods made a second Lord';[180] to Peter Abelard this seemed an excellent example of the way in which a pagan writer, under divine guidance, could be seen to be groping towards an understanding of the doctrine of the Trinity. Several times in the *Theologia Christiana* and the *Theologia 'Scholarium'*, Abelard examines the principles involved, in an attempt to see how close 'Mercurius' has come to the truth.[181] Alan of Lille discusses the passage in Book III of his four books *Contra*

Haereticos; he, too, is anxious to make out a case for the ortho-
doxy of the *Asclepius*. When Mercurius says that 'the eternal
God makes eternal gods', he asks, what is to be understood by
'God', but the Father, and what by 'eternal gods', but the Son
and the Holy Spirit, 'who are said to be gods, that is divine
Persons, and truly eternal'?[182]

In order to see more clearly what was new in the borrowing of
twelfth-century scholars from the *Asclepius*,[183] however, we need
to look rather more closely at the notions of *deificatio*, both
hermetic and non-hermetic. These were relatively commonplace
in the twelfth century because they were to be found in the
Fathers. The first question to be answered is what kind of *deus*
the *Asclepius* describes. There is a clear-cut division in the
Asclepius between the Supreme God and other gods. God the
Creator is *gubernator omnium*, ruler of all things. He made the
world to be a *receptaculum* of every kind of species.[184] To this
God man can raise himself, or be raised, only in his understanding
(*intelligentia*).[185] The lesser gods to which humanity may be said
to conform itself[186] are, as we have seen, themselves made up of
a twofold nature: *ex divina* and *ex ea quae intra homines est,
id est materia*. These gods are physically of the same stuff as
human bodies, and it is not difficult to see how men may resemble
them; indeed, men made them in their own likeness, while the
'eternal gods', made by God himself, resemble the supreme
God;[187] we have seen how readily these *deis aeterni* lent themselves to identification with the Son and the Holy Spirit. But the
divinity of which all the gods partake, and man himself at his
highest, is the divinity of the supreme God; there is only one
divinitas just as there is only one *humanitas,* uniting all gods and
all men respectively. There is, then, a blurring of the clear-cut
division at its most crucial point. In some sense, both the supreme
God and the lesser gods are divine in the same way; a common
divinity is what makes them gods.

The *Asclepius* says that man is divine in spirit and reason,[188]
and that this is the part of him which is other-worldly; it is not
the *pars mundana,* that 'other part', which makes man mortal.[189]
This is dangerously close to the Manichean heresy that the
human soul is a spark of the divine, a fragment of God himself.
When a Christian writer speaks of *deificatio*, we are in a system

of thought where *deus* can be none other than the supreme God, and to 'become God' has another and more mysterious meaning altogether. Gregory the Great discusses the argument that the man Christ Jesus was created *purus homo,* but made God by grace.[190] He uses *deificatio* to describe the making of man into the supreme God. Augustine speaks of *deificari in otio,*[191] the holy quiet in which a man may approach God. Here he does not refer to a literal making of man into God, but he certainly intends the reader to understand that the God in question is the Supreme Being, and not some lesser god. When the Christian seeks to pass beyond the threshold of theology, then, he seeks not merely to understand things which are not of this world, to 'become a god' in the hermetic sense, but also to approach the supreme God. He seeks to explore not only the 'hypothetical theology' which is concerned with the angels and created spirits, but also the 'apothetical' theology which is concerned with God himself.

Scripture presents the reader with some difficulties here, because it speaks of 'the God of gods', and thus appears to be countenancing the distinction which the author of the *Asclepius* makes between God himself and the lesser gods the pagans worship. In his *Enarratio* on Psalm 49, Augustine goes at some length into the question of the meaning of: 'The Lord God of Gods has spoken.'[192] Here we have the Psalmist, inspired by the Holy Spirit, apparently stating that there are other Gods beside God himself. 'These gods of whom God is the true God, who are they, or where are they?', asks Augustine. He notes another passage, in Psalm 81, where God is said to stand in the meeting of the gods, in their 'congregation'. But the same Psalm provides us with a clue. 'I have said', the Psalmist writes, 'that you are all gods, and sons of the most High.' It is clear, then, Augustine argues, that since the Psalmist refers to men as 'gods', he means us to understand that men may be gods, but he emphasises that men are 'deified' by divine grace; they are not gods in themselves *de substantia sua,* but *ex gratia deificatos,* not sparks of the divine light as the Manichees say, but made gods by grace.

Augustine expands the point. Those whom God justifies, he 'deifies', for by justifying them he makes them sons of God, and 'if we are made Sons of God, we are also made gods'. Only the Son of God himself is God in his very nature; men can be made gods only by adoption. It is not necessary, then, for us to postulate the existence of intermediate gods, such as the pagans worship. The 'gods' of the Psalmist are simply the elect among men.

We can dispense with the notion that the 'gods' of the pagans may be fallen angels, even though, in Psalm 95, the Psalmist speaks of 'the gods of the gentiles', or *daemonia*. Here, says Augustine, it is necessary to make a distinction between the devils and the men who have become sons of God. He cites the passage in Mark 5.7, where the *daemones* acknowledge Jesus to be the Son of God. 'We know who you are; you are the Son of God', they say. It seems that they are like the faithful among men in that they confess God. But there is a difference. God indeed makes into gods those who confess him in love: *deos illos fecit.* Those who do not love him show clearly that they are not gods.

5   *Man: god or beast?*

A man is made up of body and soul, spiritual and material parts. That makes him unique in creation, and in one especial way it makes him godlike. That is what we should expect to find; Alan points out that the very hierarchy of the universe is *deiformis*; it is godlike both in the heavenly hierarchy, which was 'created in the image and likeness of God', and in the earthly hierarchy, 'which is conformed to God through likeness'. The angels are even more 'like God' than men because they are purely spiritual beings.[193] The emphasis is everywhere upon 'likeness'[194] and 'conformity'.[195]

Man is alone in creation in demonstrating how a spiritual part, the soul, can be united to a material part, the body. He is a living analogy, showing how it was possible for an uncreated spirit to be united with a creature, a thing which would equally defy the laws of the universe if it had not been shown to the world in the Incarnation.[196] The Incarnation was something incomparably greater and more marvellous. Nevertheless, the composition of man gives some idea of what was involved. In the Incarnation there was a unity or union of human and divine far closer than the vague *cognatio* or *consortio* of the *Asclepius*.[197] It was an act of 'becoming' God without parallel when the human nature of

Christ was united with his divine nature. But because the Son of God demonstrated that it could be done, man need not despair of becoming, in a humbler way, himself a god.

There is a darker side to this doubleness of man. His spiritual part may be raised, but equally, his animal and material part may degenerate, taking the whole man with it. Indeed, man can descend so far below the level of godlikeness which he was created for, that he can lose the capacity for 'divinity' which the *Asclepius* attributes to him,[198] and which, with appropriate Christian modifications Alan sees as the theologian's essential qualification.

Bernard Silvestris describes in his commentary on the *Aeneid*, the four ways in which it is possible for a man to go down into hell. There is the way of nature, the way of power, the way of vice, the way of the magician. When a man is born, his soul enters this fallen world in the course of nature (*naturaliter*), and so it is already on its way to hell. Some professors of theology have said that the descent of the soul into the human body is clearly a come-down in the universe. The human body is a poor specimen even among bodies. It lacks the majestic size of the elephant, the strength of the bull, the speed of the tiger. The soul which enters it is moving in a direction which will take it away from its own divinity,[199] and towards bestiality. As the author of the *Asclepius* emphasises, not all men are capable of achieving that union with the gods in which they enjoy the status of gods,[200] but only those who possess *intelligentia,* and direct their efforts upwards. Others turn the opposite way, and their nature changes – as Alan describes it in his image of the four-wheeled chariot of the powers of mind[201] – from that of the best of animals into that of a wild beast.[202] A man's middle position, his natural *thesis* as Alan of Lille calls it, places him between god and beast.

He makes this Neoplatonic commonplace his. The theme reappears in the *De Planctu Naturae*, where Alan distinguishes between the sensual urges[203] and the rational promptings[204] of the human mind, which lead him, respectively, into vice or virtue.[205] The former turns a man into a beast by making him degenerate; the latter transfigures him into something which is almost a god.[206] The first drives out light and plunges the mind into darkness. The second illuminates the night of the mind with light. The first makes man wallow with the brute beasts. The second makes him able to conduct a rational conversation with angels.[207]

There are, Alan suggests, three walls between the saints and God: the wall of *cognitio*, the wall of *operatio*, the wall of *charitas*. The saints must climb these walls as though they were a heavenly ladder, and then, although they are in the flesh, yet they will arrive at the contemplation of the divine.[208] He stresses that spiritual striving is a necessary part of intellectual effort – in very much the way that Augustine does. He brings out this twofold intellectual and contemplative *theologia* in a number of passages where he makes use again of Bernard Silvestris' picture of man rising above his natural state or sinking below it. In the *Sermon on the Intelligible Sphere*, he describes how by sense and *imaginatio* the soul becomes man; by reason the soul becomes spirit; through understanding[209] the soul becomes a god.[210] In a sermon for Ash Wednesday he describes how man was made in the image and likeness of God, intended to go to heaven, but has turned to earth instead, and, worse still, is on his way to hell. Alan exhorts him to look upward, so that it may be said of him: *deificatus es, et ascendes ad Deum*. In the chapter of *The Art of Preaching*, which is directed *contra luxuriam*, Alan points out that it is through *luxuria* that a man turns into a beast, his imagination sluggish, his senses slow, his understanding darkened; indeed, he descends below the level of a beast, for a beast feels desire only at the proper time, but man is lustful all the time.[211] In Alan's view, then, the natural state of man (*thesis*) is something from which he can move upwards only by developing the part of him which has a capacity for *divinitas*, and downwards only by allowing rein to the part of him which is like a beast.

He moves in either direction by intellectual endeavour, and spiritual and moral striving. *Theologia*, in its wider sense can, then, be explored in two ways, by the exercise of the mind, and by prayer and contemplation. *Theologia* in the *Anticlaudianus* does not look downwards; there is nothing earthly in her face;[212] the 'exhortation to prayer' in the *Ars Praedicandi* compares prayer with her who 'comes up out of the wilderness' in the third chapter of the Song of Songs, to smoke rising up from fire, to a pillar pointing straight upwards;[213] the two must always go together.

Alan makes a distinction between *thesis* and *exstasis*, between

intellectus and *intelligentia*. The raising of the understanding to
God which Alan calls *intelligentia* is discussed in much the same
terms in *Asclepius* 6. 'Of all animals, only the human is raised by
God to an understanding of himself.'[214] Alan calls this upward
movement *apotheosis*, and describes it as a kind of deification[215]
when man is rapt in contemplation of the divine, in contrast to
the *hypothesis* into which he falls when he becomes a beast.[216]
That *apotheosis* raises man above himself[217] and enables him to
see what he could not otherwise perceive. Much of this is in
Thierry of Chartres. He makes *Asclepius'* point, that not all men
are equal in their capacity for understanding, in his commentary
on the opening of the second chapter of Boethius' *De Trinitate*.
He goes on to explain that man has four modes of perception:
sense, imagination, reason and *intelligentia*. When the soul employs only sense and imagination, it is held back at the level of a
beast; when it employs reason, it is able to take up the position of
a man. When it aspires to the supreme simplicity of God himself,
the soul is raised to its highest power of understanding, and
becomes a god.[218] Thierry is a little unhappy about the expression:
fit deus. He qualifies it by saying 'according to Mercury'. But he
adopts the general scheme of the *Asclepius* in his search for an
explanation of the way in which man may cross the threshold of
theology, just as Alan does.

Alan links this human capacity to move up or down with its
divine counterpart. He says that God himself has an *apotheosis*,
which is his natural and proper state, just as man's natural state
is that of *thesis*, but, descending from it, God emptied himself,
taking the form of a servant, and humbled himself as far as the
thesis of our nature:[219] he even came down *usque in hypothesim
nostrae miseriae*, to the 'hypothesis' of our wretchedness, not in
blameworthiness, but in the punishment he accepted.[220] The
parallel with the Incarnation was not new. Anselm comments on
the difference between God being made man, and man being
made God in the Incarnation. He wants to emphasise that this act
of humility is to be understood to have been no sign of a change
in God; the nature of man was exalted, not the nature of God
brought low.[221] Thierry of Chartres puts it like this; in the
Incarnation alone: *deificata est humanitas*,[222] humanity is truly
deified.

There is no attempt to extend what happened in the Incarnation to common human experience. When an ordinary man ascends towards God by contemplation, there is no second Incarnation. In his account of the way in which man may pass beyond the threshold, Alan of Lille has in mind something closer to Bonaventure's *Itinerarium Mentis in Deum*. The mind journeys upwards, first by making use of all the evidences about himself which God has placed in created things – the subject-matter, in other words, of the seven liberal arts and the human sciences in general. At last, it arrives at an *excessus mentalis et mysticus*; it passes beyond itself wholly (*totaliter*); it passes into God (*in Deum*).²²³ Then, at last, a man is truly a theologian.

6 *The Deification of the Arts*

Just as we saw that words are limited and prevented from attaining their 'proper' meanings in theology, by the limitations of the human beings who use them, so the liberal arts are held back by the failings of sinful human masters. They are, as we have them, the sciences of human reason. In the *Anticlaudianus* Reason cannot go beyond the stars into high heaven, and when Theologia tries to take Prudence or Phronesis (human wisdom) further, she faints at the brightness of the heavenly realm. She cannot endure it. Nevertheless, the sequences of our reasoning are directed towards the discovery of divine mysteries. The human mind longs with sighs of yearning to discover and to understand. As long as reason tries to find the way alone, she will go astray, but she cannot resist the temptation to try. As Alan puts it in the *De Planctu Naturae*: 'Now how far the line of our reasoning goes astray, which dares to raise itself to treat the ineffable mystery of deity; [yet] the sighs of our mind long to understand it.'²²⁴ In the *Anticlaudianus*, it is faith which comes to the rescue. In the *De Planctu Naturae* nature compares her own powers with those of Theologia. Nature tests faith against reason; Theology tests reason against faith. Nature knows so that she may believe; Theology believes, so that she may know. Nature assents to what she knows and Theology feels that to which she gives assent. Nature scarcely sees what is visible; Theology comprehends the incomprehensible in a glass. Nature measures with scarcely any understanding and Theology measures with almost boundless reason. Nature creeps about like a beast on the ground, and Theology strides about the secret places of high heaven.[225] Again, faith makes the difference. The approach of Theology is quite different from that of Nature because she reasons with faith.

But there is another difference, too. The arts, in Theology's hands, are capable of a kind of *deificatio*, when they are raised to a level where they can very nearly deal with divine truths. The limitation proves to lie not in themselves, but in natural man who uses them. There is, for example a special rule which allows us to use Aristotle's *Categories* in theology. Alan explains it in the treatise on virtues and vices.[226] All words which would, if they were used of created things, refer to qualities and quantities, 'predicate the divine essence' if they are transferred *ad divina*. Thus a man might be called just or holy or good, great or single or huge, but any of these properties might be subtracted from him because they are merely attributes. We are not describing his very being in calling him just, for he might at any moment commit an unjust act. If we describe God as just or holy or good, we are speaking of his very being, the divine substance. We have two special categories for God, not ten, as for created things: *predicamentum in quid, predicamentum ad aliquid*, which refer respectively to that which God is in himself and that which God is in relation to others. All words which refer to the divine essence (*divina usia*) describe the 'substance' of God, and into that category fall nine out of the ten Aristotelian categories. Words which speak of the relations which obtain within the Godhead (Fatherhood, Sonship) fall into the second 'theological category' of relation. These are not of course new thoughts. Augustine and Boethius had trodden the ground thoroughly, but Alan was making a new use of the idea, in suggesting that when the liberal arts are thus raised into a higher dimension, they become transformed into 'theological arts'.

Things go wrong not because the arts thus dressed for theology are totally inadequate for theological purposes, but because men try to use them without adaptation. Men who have allowed their rational faculties to decay[227] are really no longer men at all, but they continue to masquerade as men.[228] They have, in other words, transferred the name of 'man' from its true sense, the sense God intended it to have to a debased one. From this false position they cannot make a proper use of the arts even in connection with the created world, and they live in a world of fantasy[229] where they see no objection to trying to raise the liberal arts to purposes higher even than those of the *celestis scientia*. Thus they diminish the dignity of theology itself.[230] They turn the world of learning upside down. While they are confounded by the *miraculosae significationes* of *divina verba* they make up monstrous meanings of their own. Inevitably they fall into error, and when they push their way over the bridge by which the liberal arts give admission to the imperial realm of theology, they fall over the precipice into various heresies and are drowned.[231]

Now this is clearly not the fault of the *artes*, which are themselves being abused. An adherence to proper procedure and an orderliness of mind are essential. Then the arts will take man safely to the threshold of theology, where, undergoing a transformation, they themselves can serve 'theological science'. Alan did not leave all this in the realm of theory. He tried to work out in detail exactly what rules theology can use, in his most adventurous work, the *Regulae Theologicae*, to which we must now turn.

2 Theologia Rationalis

Among the works of Alan of Lille which are printed by Migne is a treatise of unusual interest, whose authorship has long been a matter of dispute. The *De Arte Catholicae Fidei* is a complete systematic theology in five books. The truth of a series of points of doctrine is demonstrated as though they were Euclidean theorems, with the aid of definitions, postulates and axioms. A superficial similarity of 'axiomatic method' between Alan's *Regulae Theologicae* and the *De Arte Catholicae Fidei* encouraged the attribution of both works to Alan of Lille, not only by modern scholars, but also by the copyists of several of the manuscripts of the work.[1] M. T. d'Alverny gives the work to Alan's contemporary, Nicholas of Amiens, on the basis of a comment of his own in the preface to his Chronicle, that he has discussed a certain point more fully in the *Liber de Arte Catholicae Fidei*. The preface is so close in subject-matter to the *De Arte* that there can be no doubt that this attribution is correct.[2] Even if we take this work away from Alan, the *Regulae Theologicae,* which antedates it by a decade, remains a pioneering work comparable with Proclus' *Elements of Theology* in its theological audacity.

The exercise attempted by Alan of Lille and Nicholas of Amiens appears to have attracted few imitators – unless we count the extra book someone added to Nicholas' treatise. No-one seems to have attempted anything on such a scale until Sebastianus Foxius Morzillus in the middle of the sixteenth century,[3] and Johannes Baptistus Morinus in the seventeenth,[4] composed axiomatic systems which are remarkably similar to that of the *De Arte Catholicae Fidei* in their adaptation of Euclidean *method*. The *De Arte* was still being read, and it is not impossible that it exerted a direct influence here.[5]

If we are to understand what Alan was trying to do – and Nicholas after him – we must look at a group of treatises of the second half of the twelfth century which make a distinctive use of *regulae* or axioms. The first of these is the *Liber de Causis*,[6] which appears to have been translated by Gerard of Cremona between 1167 and 1187, from an Arabic compilation of laws concerning various aspects of causation. It was only slowly taken up by Western scholars, and Alan may have been one of the first to encounter it. *The Liber de Causis* was, in its turn, drawn from the *Elements of Theology* of Proclus, a work which was not translated into Latin until 1268.[7] Both the *De Arte* and the *Regulae* deal with causes, the *De Arte* at the beginning, the *Regulae* at the end. They treat the subject in quite different ways, but the common ground with the subject-matter of the *Liber de Causis* may be of some significance.

The second of these 'axiomatic' works is the *Book of the Twenty-Four Philosophers*.[8] This contains a series of sayings, which purport to have been proposed by twenty-four philosophers, who had met together to discuss the question. 'What is God?' Each was to put forward his own proposition, in the form of a definition (*sub definitione*) in the hope that they would find that a common agreement would emerge (*ut ex propriis definitionibus excerptum aliquid de deo communi consensu statuerunt*). Perhaps the mediaeval author conceived the plan in imitation of the way in which Rufinus describes the Apostles meeting together to contribute their respective clauses to the *Symbolum Apostolorum*. In the *Liber XXIV Philosophorum*[9] each proposition is followed by a self-contained demonstration of its truth. The propositions are not related to one another except incidentally, and the demonstrations do not make use of material from other parts of the *Liber*. No attempt is made to draw out the promised *communis consensus*.

Nevertheless, despite the lack of system and the undeveloped nature of the 'axiomatic method' as it is employed here, the piece has some claim to be set beside the *Regulae Theologicae* and the *De Arte Fidei Catholicae*. Several of the demonstrations end, like those of Nicholas of Amiens, with *Et sic patet propositum*. Two, at least, of Alan's *Regulae* are also to be found in the *Liber*. Alan's third Rule, that the Monad begets the Monad and reflects its ardour in it (*in se suum reflectit ardorem*) is the first proposition or definition of the *Liber*. His seventh Rule, the famous 'God is the intelligible sphere whose centre is everywhere and his circumference nowhere'[10] appears as a definition of God as the *sphera infinita* in the *Liber*.

All these pieces contain a series of *regulae* or axioms, with short passages of exposition or demonstration for each. Although several different kinds of axiom are involved, copyists seem to have thought that they were sufficiently similar to treat them in much the same way. Typically, the axioms are written in the manuscripts in a larger script or in capitals or in red, or else they are underlined, and the exposition, demonstration or discussion of the axiom is set out beneath in a smaller script, so that at first glance the page looks much the same for all these works.

The text of Euclid normally contains diagrams, but otherwise it, too, has the same general appearance. In one manuscript from the thirteenth century, an English collection, now Bodleian Library Oxford MS. Auct. F. 5.28, the juxtaposition of texts is striking. First comes the text of Adelard of Bath's Euclid (*Versio* II), ff. ii–15^r. This has been bound with a group of treatises which includes the *De Causis* (ff.153^r–8^r) and, following on immediately in the same hand, the *De Arte Catholicae Fidei*, here with its alternative title *Liber de Articulis Fidei* (ff.158–60). Later in the manuscript are to be found other pieces which are associated with our group of 'axiomatic' works. The *opuscula sacra* and the *Consolatio Philosophiae* of Boethius are freely used by Alan of Lille in the *Regulae*. He also attributes to Boethius a passage from the *De Unitate et Uno* of Gundisalvus, which shows that the book was already widely current under Boethius' name.[11] Regula LXVIII is taken directly from the *De Hebdomadibus*,[12] and Rule after Rule at the beginning of the treatise is supported by a passage from the *Consolatio*, from the *De Trinitate*, from the *Contra Eutychen*, from the *De Hebdomadibus*.[13] Boethius' *De Trinitate* is to be found in our manuscript ff.170^v–2^r, Gundisalvus' *De Unitate et Uno* ff.172^r–3^r and his *De Ortu Scientiarum* ff.173^r–86^v.

SELF-EVIDENT THEOLOGY

Where lay the attraction of these often obscure and always
difficult works for the select few of Alan's contemporaries who
took an interest in them? It may have lain partly in the very
challenge they posed. John of Salisbury writes in Book iv.6 of the
Metalogicon[14] that the *Posterior Analytics* of Aristotle is neglected
because it deals with this same art of demonstration 'which is', he
says, 'the most demanding of all forms of reasoning'. As a result,
he claims, it has almost totally fallen into disuse in his own day.
Only mathematicians use it, for it is 'most subtle' and very few
can make sense of it.

This was not likely to be a discommendation to Alan, who was
always attracted to what was difficult, and for whom the remoteness and refinement of the method would be a strong indication
of its suitability for the purposes of the theologian. In Boethius'
De Trinitate ii we find a description of theology as that subject
which it is proper to treat *intellectualiter* and without resort to
images.[15] The axiomatic method[16] is supremely the method of the
theorist. It makes no use of argument from analogy with the
created world, but rests its case on those things which are self-
evident to the mind when it looks inside itself. In addition, the
method had the strong recommendation that it was comprehensive. When Alan wrote a book he liked to cover the whole field.
For this reason, too, he was appropriately called *doctor
universalis*. The axiomatic method at its most highly developed
supposed it possible to proceed from principles self-evident to
everyone, to principles which were derived from these, and so to
build up a complete system.

There were at least two distinct modes of doing this for Alan
to choose from, worked out in detail in two of the textbooks
available to his contemporaries: the *Elements* of Euclid and the
De Hebdomadibus of Boethius. In the *De Hebdomadibus*
Boethius makes use of a method which he identifies as that of the
mathematical sciences, but not specifically as the method of
geometry;[17] he applies it to the solution of a single problem: how
can substances be good by virtue of their existence – for all that
exists is good – without being absolute goods? The method he
employs is a strictly limited one. Only 'bounds' and 'rules'

(*termini* and *regulae*) are allowed; Boethius eliminates definitions and postulates, hypotheses, corollaries, lemmata, all the terminology and apparatus of the full Euclidean method. He deliberately refrains from explaining how the axioms are to be applied to the argument; the reader is instructed to make the connection for himself.[18]

Euclid's textbook is concerned exclusively with geometry. There is no preliminary discussion of the appropriateness of the method of demonstration he has chosen, and nothing to encourage attempts to extend or adapt the method for use with other subject-matter. Proclus' commentary on the first book of Euclid's *Elements* goes some way towards bridging the gap. It may indeed have provided Boethius with a number of starting-points for his own thinking. There are certainly some common ideas: the notion, for example, that the mathematical mode of understanding stands in an intermediate position between the highest mode of understanding possible to man, which Alan of Lille identifies with theological knowledge, and the lowest, sense-perception, is to be found in Proclus and in Boethius' *De Trinitate* II.[19] Proclus says that it is peculiar to mathematical sciences – and in particular to geometry – that propositions are proved from first principles; he insists that the first principles of such a science must be presented separately from its conclusions, and that no arguments must be given for the principles, but only for the theorems which are derived from them.[20] These are rules which Boethius himself adopts in the *De Hebdomadibus*.

But if he was indeed drawing upon Proclus in framing the theological method of the *De Hebdomadibus*, it is notable that Boethius appears to take no account of the lengthy discussion which follows in Proclus of the differences between hypotheses, postulates and axioms. Proclus reviews the contemporary differences of opinion with which he is familiar. The Stoics wanted to call all statements, even hypotheses, 'axioms'. Some called all propositions 'theorems', where Proclus would prefer to distinguish between 'problems', which involve such concrete operations as the construction of figures, and 'theorems' proper, which involve the demonstration of the inherent properties in each figure, that is, the theoretical aspects of the figure. Aristotle, too, discusses the need to make distinctions, in the *Posterior Analytics*. He defines the axiom as something which is necessarily true, the hypothesis as a proposition which the teacher assumes and the pupil is prepared to concede to be true, a postulate as a proposition which the teacher assumes and with which the pupil has no quarrel, and a definition as something which makes no assertion about the thing defined to which assent may be given or from which assent may be withheld. A definition need only be understood.[21] There is nothing like this in the *De Hebdomadibus*. Boethius dis-tinguishes only two kinds of *communis animi conceptio*, those notions whose truth is obvious at once to everyone everywhere, and those which are evident only to the learned.

There can be no doubt that Boethius deliberately refrains from employing the full technical vocabulary of the Euclidean method which he had at his disposal. When he refers to the geometers in the *Consolation of Philosophy*, he mentions *demonstratio* of a peculiarly geometrical kind, involving not only *propositiones*, but *porismata* and *corollaria*.[22] Yet it would be misleading to place too much emphasis upon the choice of technical terms. *Hypothesis,* for example is a technical term of both logic and geometry. In the twelfth century, Thierry of Chartres readily identifies Boethius' use of a hypothesis.[23] Clarembald of Arras, too, refers to *ypotesis* in his remarks on the *De Hebdomadibus*,[24] yet neither has a geometrical usage in mind. *Demonstratio,* too, is a term of logic as well as of geometry, as Gilbert shows in his reference to the 'deducing of a demonstration from propositions'.[25] Boethius himself was largely responsible for the transmission of these terms in their logical sense. There is little more to be learned from the rendering of Euclid's Greek terms in the Boethian *Geometria*.[26] The *De Hebdomadibus* is tantalisingly silent on the subject. The important point is not perhaps that the terms *hypothesis, definitio* and so on are missing from the *De Hebdomadibus* (for their inclusion would not necessarily indicate that Boethius had made use of Euclid's *Elements* or the *Posterior Analytics* or Proclus directly) but that Boethius chooses to describe his *communis animi conceptiones* as *reguli* or *termini*.

These were the terms which attracted the attention of com-mentators from Carolingian times.[27] In the twelfth-century com-mentaries *termini* are envisaged as 'boundaries', which cut off the 'area of thought' of each *regula*: *cogitandi spacium* as Thierry of

Chartres puts it.[28] Gilbert of Poitiers describes the *regula* as something like a place, or container of many things.[29] Alan of Lille inherited the same idea (*quasi quibusdam terminis certis clauduntur*).[30] In the thirteenth century, with a knowledge of Aristotle's *Posterior Analytics,* Aquinas was able to arrive at a rather more sophisticated conception of *terminus.* He says that the *regulae* are called *termini* because 'upon first principles of this kind rests the resolution of all demonstrations'.[31] Here the terminus is an 'end' in the sense of 'resolution', but it still performs the function of cutting off one area of the self-evident, or *per se notum,* from another. Aquinas thinks that the *regulae* are so called because they rule and direct the thinking of the man who uses them.[32] All these commentators are agreed in regarding the method Boethius has chosen as being 'axiomatic' in some special sense which depends upon the meaning he is to be supposed to have given to these terms, and in particular upon the notion of *regula.*

When Alan asks himself what is the nature of the *regulae* he himself proposes to use in the *Regulae Theologicae* he begins, like Gilbert of Poitiers, by considering what kinds of 'rules' are used in the specific sciences with which he is familiar.[33] Both scholars undoubtedly take their cue from Boethius' comment at the beginning of the *De Hebdomadibus* that he intends to use rules such as mathematicians employ. Every science, Alan explains, rests upon its rules, as if upon its own proper foundations.[34] The important point here is that the rules are specific to the sciences (*suae regulae; propria fundamenta*). This is again a subject on which Aristotle has a good deal to say in the *Posterior Analytics.*[35] Aristotle contends that there can be no science from whose principles the principles of all other sciences can be demonstrated; such a science would hold a supreme position over all others, and although Plato would contend that this is the case with dialectic, Aristotle prefers to regard the rules of each science as peculiarly its own, and incapable of demonstration.[36]

Gilbert of Poitiers[37] and Alan of Lille and Clarembald of Arras[38] were all prompted by their study of the seven liberal arts to attempt to identify the *regulae* or *communes animi conceptiones* of each of the arts. Alan of Lille's list opens the *Regulae Theologicae*; he has removed the discussion from the context of commentary on the *De Hebdomadibus*.[39] Both Clarembald and Alan clearly depend upon Gilbert in their framing of the list of rules of the arts, and both follow Gilbert in making an important distinction between the rules of grammar and the rules of the other arts. Grammatical *regulae* are *positivae,* that is, as Alan explains, they are 'imposed' by men, according to their own wishes. They are not as Boethius of Dacia and later *modistae* would have it, universally self-evident. For not all men speak Latin as all men understand that two and two make four. True *regulae,* the rules on which a science is built, must be absolute and axiomatic.

Aristotle says in the *Posterior Analytics* that the first principles of any science are those facts which cannot be proved, but which we must take as given.[40] He emphasises that we should not expect to be able to find general laws of the sciences, and that where it happens that a principle is common to more than one science, that is merely a matter of chance; certain rules happen to have a specific application within more than one science. That does not make them general laws. He cites the very example which Boethius gives in the *De Hebdomadibus,* and which is also Euclidean: 'If equals are taken from equals the remainders are equal.' These, then, are the *regulae* of the axiomatic method Boethius employs in the *De Hebdomadibus,* as they appeared to the eyes of twelfth-century scholars.

Boethius himself cannot be said to have followed the rules of any specific science. He says merely that he has done as is done in mathematics and other such disciplines, and laid down the rules by which he will proceed. The rules themselves are not the laws of a known science, but merely those he will require for the purposes of the specific argument in hand. In practice, this is Alan of Lille's procedure, too; he lays down in his *regulae* the laws he finds he needs as he goes along; but he makes a claim for his *regulae* which goes beyond anything in Boethius or in Gilbert of Poitiers. He calls them *regulae theologicae,* theological laws, the laws of a science which has hitherto not been treated, as a whole, by the mathematical method of arguing from first principles which are themselves beyond demonstration.

Alan of Lille is confident that theological *regulae* are of a higher order than the laws of other sciences. There are two ways in which they may be said to be 'higher'. Either they are

principles of the kind whose existence Aristotle wants to deny –
that is, general first principles from which the first principles of
specific disciplines may be demonstrated. Gilbert of Poitiers seems
to have something of the kind in mind in his commentary on the
Contra Eutychen. There he says that the statement: 'In Christ
was made a union of God and man' is a *regula generalis* which is
self-evidently and necessarily true for every science and in every
context,[41] but in the *Regulae Theologicae* Alan prefers to see
theological laws as 'higher' in another sense, closer to that which
Boethius himself hints at in his remarks on the importance of
keeping high secrets from the unworthy by a deliberate obscurity
of expression.[42] In the *Regulae Theologicae,* then, Alan prefers to
see theological laws as 'higher' in the sense of being superior in
kind to the laws of other sciences. Their elevated nature is a
matter of *dignitas* and *excellentia.*[43]

They have two distinctive features – an obscurity and a subtlety
which keeps them from being fully understood by any but the
learned, and an absoluteness which is beyond anything to be
found in the laws of other sciences. They are known in the deepest
recesses of the mind;[44] they have an inner brilliance.[45] The rules
of other sciences are self-evident certainly, but they have only a
contingent necessity,[46] which depends upon the ordinary course
of things in the natural world.[47] The necessity of the rules of
theology is not contingent, but *absoluta* and *irrefragibilis.* There
are two kinds of statement here about the nature of theological
laws. Alan emphasises their absoluteness, but he is interested
chiefly in their difficulty of access to human understanding, their
mystery and profundity.

We have seen how theological *regulae* are called *aenigmata*
because of their obscurity, *emblemata* because of their inward
splendour, which makes them understandable only to the most
refined perceptions of the mind,[48] *enthymemata* because they lie
hidden within the mind; they are known as *hebdomades,* too,
because of their dignity and honour. They are also called *para-
doxae,* again for two reasons: because of their absoluteness[49] and
because of their glorious subtlety.[50] They therefore have the two
essential ingredients of a paradox in its more usual modern
technical sense. Their component parts cannot be discarded or
proved false; and they have the effect of dazzling the mind with

their apparent incomprehensibility. Gilbert of Poitiers places his emphasis on the capacity of the paradox for exciting the wonder and admiration of philosophers, but Alan takes us a little further. He presents us with paradoxes among his *regulae*:

Only the Monad is Alpha and Omega without Alpha and Omega (Rule 5). God is the intelligible sphere, whose centre is everywhere and his circumference nowhere (Rule 7).

Rules 15, 16, 18, 20 and a number of others have an air of paradox about them, too. Alan discusses them with a view to showing how, despite their appearance of self-contradictoriness, in the special case of God they are plain statements of the truth. He defines the terms of the paradoxical *regulae* in keeping with their divine sense. To say that the Monad is Alpha and Omega is to say that he is the beginning and end of all things, but because he is *simplex,* and there is nothing composite in him, he himself has neither beginning nor end. So God is Alpha and Omega without Alpha and Omega, beginning and end (of other things) without himself having beginning or end. In the second example (Rule 7) God is called a sphere because, like a sphere, he has no beginning and end. He is not a bodily or corporeal sphere; he is an 'intelligible' sphere. We should not allow the image of an ordinary sphere to rise before us when we think about God in this way. In a corporeal sphere the centre is a geometrical point, which occupies no space at all, and can scarcely be said to be 'anywhere', and the circumference is in many places. In the intelligible sphere the centre is the created world, which is 'everywhere' in the sense that all 'places' are themselves created things. The circumference is the immensity of God himself, and because he is not circumscribed by place, the circumference is said to be 'nowhere'. And so God is the intelligible sphere whose centre is everywhere and whose circumference is nowhere.[51] Alan handles these paradoxes by trying to redefine the terms in which they are expressed so as to show the difference between their usual meaning and their special meaning when they are applied to God. In this way he shows that there is no contradiction embodied in them. We are invited to wonder at the God who reconciles contradictions in himself.

Alan's *Regulae* are not only full of mystery, and absolute, they are also *indemonstrabiles*,[52] not susceptible of demonstration. It might be argued that he does attempt to demonstrate them, or at least to show how one rule is derived from another. In the early passages of the *Regulae Theologicae* Alan consistently explains that a given rule follows from its predecessor, or from a rule given a little earlier. Boethius gives him some authority for this, in his distinction of the two kinds of *communis animi conceptio,* those which are obvious to everyone, and those which only the learned can understand. The second kind are dependent for their force upon the first.

Boethius does not attempt to make a systematic application of his axioms in the *De Hebdomadibus.* He suggests that the intelligent reader will be able to supply the arguments which are appropriate at each point in the discussion.[53] The twelfth-century commentators are not satisfied with this. Clarembald of Arras, Thierry of Chartres' pupil, systematically identifies the axioms employed (explicitly and implicitly) by Boethius throughout the *De Hebdomadibus.* 'He applies (*aptat*) in this proof two laws which are self-evident to the learned', he says of the beginning of Boethius' demonstration. One comes from Book III.10 of the *Consolation of Philosophy* (everything which exists tends to the good): the other is the ninth of the *regulae* of the *De Hebdomadibus.* Clarembald shows how, with the aid of these two, Boethius is able to prove his first point, that all things which exist are good.[54] As he goes on, Clarembald notes that one point depends upon the sixth and eighth Rule, another is shown to be true *iuxta septimam regulam.*[55] He sums up by saying that he has, as far as possible,[56] applied the *communes animi conceptiones* to their proper places.[57]

Thierry of Chartres exclaims over the difficulty of the task Boethius has set his readers. 'He would have to be careful who wanted to apply the proper arguments to the problem in the right places!'[58] He warns again that we must proceed cautiously, so as to see how they may be properly applied in the right places.[59] Gilbert of Poitiers is not so ready to acknowledge the difficulty. His comments are brisk and to the point. 'It should be noted that the necessity of this argument depends upon the first and ninth Rule'; 'It should be noted that this depends upon the third and fourth and sixth Rules'; 'according to the seventh Rule already stated', and so on.[60] But like Clarembald, both Thierry and

Gilbert carefully apply the nine Rules with which the *De Hebdomadibus* begins, as Boethius instructs the intelligent reader to do. They adduce one, two or more *regulae*, as they are needed, and Gilbert, in particular, is careful to leave out none of the axioms – for it is scarcely conceivable that Boethius would have included a superfluous rule in so tight-knit a treatise. There was evidently some variation in interpretation in the schools; Clarembald does not give the same *regulae* as Gilbert for Boethius' first point, for example; but the notion that proper study of the *De Hebdomadibus* required the student to apply the *regulae* to Boethius' argument seems to have been general.

In his adaptation of the method of the *De Hebdomadibus* in the *Regulae Theologicae* Alan does not attempt to apply his own rules. He gives no argument to which they might be applied. Instead – in a manner quite different from Boethius' practice in the *De Hebdomadibus* – he expounds each *regula,* indicates what it may be said to demonstrate, and explains how each is related to the rule with which it is most closely linked. He begins with the oneness of God. The first *regula*: *monas est, qua quaelibet res est una* (the monad is that by which anything is one) is the starting-point for several chains of *regulae*. It becomes, like the *unum argumentum* of St Anselm's *Proslogion,* a principle which can be used to prove everything which we believe about God.[61] From it other rules proceed.[62] Occasionally a rule is said to 'prove' another.[63] In this sense, Alan might be said to have substituted 'demonstration' for the 'application of the rules' with which his contemporaries were busy.

From the first Rule: 'The monad is that by which anything is one',[64] Alan is able to draw the second, third and fourth immediately. The monad is not merely 'one'; it is unity itself, in which there is no plurality. Multiplied by itself, it remains one; it gives rise to its own equal. This is good Pythagorean number theory, and when Alan applies it to the Deity, he is able to show that God, too, has no origin but himself, that he begets another of himself who is like him – that is, the Son – and that he gives rise to his own equal, that is, the Holy Spirit.

The second Rule is drawn from this, by an extension of the same analogy with Pythagorean number theory. One is not a number, but the origin of number. According to some commentators, two is not a number, because it is the beginning of difference, or 'otherness'. Three is the first number, and therefore the first thing which can be called truly plural. Alan's second Rule, stated in the Pseudo-Dionysian vocabulary of his own *Hierarchia*, puts it that: 'above the heavens there is unity, in the heavens there is otherness (*alteritas*), beneath the heavens plurality'. This Alan explains by saying that what is above the heavens is God himself, who is unity. In the heavens are the angels, who were created first by God, and who were therefore the first things other than God to come into existence. The rest of creation, which is under the heavens, is truly plural.[65] It is positively profuse in its multiplicity and variety.[66] By an arithmetical analogy, which Alan regards as a plain statement about the nature of God, we have now placed creation in its proper relation to the divine unity.[67]

The third Rule is the first definition of the *Liber XXIV Philosophorum*.[68] It states that the monad begets the monad, and reflects its own *ardor* upon itself.[69] Alan's exposition is his own, however. He refers back to his description at the end of the exposition of Rule One: (God begets another of himself, and so on). The *ardor* proceeds from the monad, that is from the Father, in such a way that it does not leave him, for it is of the same essence with him; he turns it back upon his 'other self' (*in se alterum*), that is the Son. The *ardor* is the Holy Spirit. Its author is the Son, together with the Father.

The fourth Rule follows from this: 'In the Father there is unity, in the Son equality, in the Holy Spirit the union of unity and equality.' The rule itself is taken from Augustine's *De Doctrina Christiana*,[70] but Alan thinks it can be drawn from what has been said so far.[71] Here ends the first group of rules. Alan's procedure is to examine the meaning of the *regula*; as he opens out its compressed message he provides himself with statements which he considers to be implied in each rule, and those statements lead him on to further rules. The method is akin to that of argument by equipollent propositions, but the extent to which each *regula* is the equivalent of some implication within the one before has to be shown by careful exposition of each rule. The relationship between the rules is indeed self-evident only to the learned and those who have been taught how to perceive it.

Now we return to *Regula* I, from which the fifth Rule proceeds directly.[72] 'Only the monad is alpha and omega without alpha and omega', that is beginning and end of other things without itself having a beginning and end. The seventh Rule, the famous 'God is the intelligible sphere whose centre is everywhere and whose circumference is nowhere', performs a new function in the system of the *regulae*. It proves or tests[73] Rule 5. Rule 6, which is derived from Rule 5, states that every finite alpha and omega[74] is either good by virtue of its beginning[75] or good by virtue of its beginning and its end. That is, all created things are good in their beginning because God made them. Rational beings, whose intended end is blessedness, are good by virtue of their ends, too.[76] Here ends a second self-contained section.

With Rule 8 we go back again to the first *Regula*. From 'the monad is that by which anything is one', we draw the Rule 'God is that by whom whatever is has all its being.'[77] We now enter upon a structurally complex section of exposition, in which Rules 9 and 10 follow directly after 12, and Rule 11 depends on Rule 8. Alan wants to show that, since whatever we say of God we say as *unum et idem,* it is the same thing to say of God that he is a substance, that he is merciful, and so on. Rule 11 says that whatever is simple (and God is simplicity itself) has as one its existence and whatever it is. This is Boethius' seventh Rule in the *De Hebdomadibus*.[78] When we arrive at Rule 12 we are in a position to say that in any statement about God[79] we speak not of what, in a created thing, would be 'in' the subject, but of the very essence of the subject himself. This is the burden of Boethius' discussion of the theological application of the Aristotelian *Categories* in the *De Trinitate*, and Alan goes on in later *regulae* to discuss the problems of theological predication at some length.

Now, with Rule 13, we turn to a discussion of form and matter, which runs up to Rule 17, and which echoes the discussion of Boethius in *De Trinitate* II. With Rule 18 we begin in earnest on a lengthy and detailed consideration of the way in which human language may properly be used of God, with the Pseudo-Dionysian distinction between affirmative and negative statements which is to be found in Thierry of Chartres' commentaries on the *opuscula sacra*.[80] It is Rule 19 which Alan wants to link directly with Rule 17. From 19 we go on to look at *theologica praedicatio* (Rule 22) and the fact that normal grammatical rules for nouns and adjectives, pronouns, verbs, must be adapted for use in the special case of God, so that *sermo theologicus* (Rule 34) becomes a special language. Alan is carrying out the promise of his preface and showing us, by detailed comparison, how much more profound are the laws of theology than those of the liberal arts.

St Anselm has a good deal to say about the ways in which will, power and necessity work together, in the *Cur Deus Homo*. The topic had become a familiar one in the course of the twelfth century, and Alan gives up a series of *regulae* to it (beginning at Rule 54), as an introduction to that part of the treatise which deals with foreknowledge, predestination, grace and free will. Rules 100–6 cover the Incarnation, Rules 107–15 the sacraments. There is a rich fund of contemporary learning here, most fully developed in the earlier *regulae* where those questions of divine unity, the nature of God and problems of theological language which are the subject-matter of the *opuscula sacra* are discussed. It is in these earlier *regulae,* too, that we find him most careful to explain exactly where one Rule proceeds from another. Insofar as the *regulae* constitute a methodically unified system, they do so in the first part of the treatise, where the subject-matter is closest to that of Boethius, and where it lends itself most readily to the treatment outlined at the beginning of the *De Hebdomadibus.* The later part of the work, especially the section on sacraments, begins to resemble a more conventional *summa* of the day.

The methodological procedure becomes strikingly Boethian again only when we reach the section which begins after Rule 115 in some manuscripts. In the second chapter of the *De Trinitate* Boethius distinguishes three *speculativae partes*: *naturalis, mathematica, theologica.* With the possible exception of the *regulae* which deal with form and matter, the bulk of the *regulae* which draw upon sciences other than theology are not concerned with *naturalis,* but with *mathematica* and with the problems of predication which arise in connection with the arts of the *trivium,* grammar, logic and rhetoric. But now Alan promises that he will deal with the *regulae* which *ad naturalem pertinent facultatem,* and especially in their relation to theology.[81] Boethius does not use the word *facultas* for the branches of speculative science, but it is to be found in Gilbert of Poitiers' remarks on this part of the *De Trinitate* and on the *De Hebdomadibus*.[82] He even suggests a parallel for the exercise Alan is about to attempt. Human language,[83] he says, is forced to transfer words from their application to the ordinary world, so that we speak of God as *magnus* even though he has no quantity, and the meaning is quite different from that which we should attach to *magnus* in *corpus est magnum*. He describes this as a transference *a naturalibus ad alias facultates*.[84] Alan's pattern throughout is to consider whether each *maxima* or *regula* is common to both *facultates*, or belongs especially to nature. Rules 116 and 119 for instance, are said to be common to both, while Rule 117 belongs to the *naturalis facultas*. Then the precise attribution of each rule to the natural and to the divine is set out, so as to make the contrast clear. In this last section of the *Regulae Theologicae* Alan has moved a long way from Boethius in the *De Hebdomadibus* in his subject-matter, but nowhere among the technical principles or ideas from the mathematical sciences which he imports into the treatise is there any trace of Euclid's influence.

We have come full circle, back to Alan's preoccupation with the threshold of theology, the point at which we must modify the rules of the *artes* so that they will be applicable to divine truths; or transfer our thinking from categories appropriate to the natural world to categories which fit theology. It is not perhaps without significance that Alan uses the word *translatio* at the beginning of the *Arithmetica* and elsewhere, to refer to translation from one language to another, from Greek to Latin. There is a sense in which he regards the language we use to discuss the natural world and theological language as two distinct languages. Man's native language must be translated, and its grammatical rules modified accordingly, and a new vocabulary mastered, if he is to speak theological language correctly.

In the *Regulae Theologicae* Alan has attempted to provide a revised set of rules, a theological grammar, to show in detail how the laws of the *artes* must be modified if they are to be used in theology. He did not succeed entirely in sustaining the philosophical level or the conceptual elegance of the first *regulae* in the series, for the very good reason that he presses the method beyond the point where Christian doctrine lends itself to philosophical methods. This was probably one of his less helpful manuals to the would-be theologian. It may be, to judge from the variation in the number of *regulae* which are found in the manuscripts, that Alan himself was unable to bring the work to a satisfactory conclusion.

Nevertheless, it is not surprising that he should make the attempt. It is a working out in practice of a theory of exceptional audacity about the existence of 'theological arts', special theological rules for the *artes* which would make them helpful beyond the threshold, in the realm of theology itself.

3 Theologia Moralis

Like 'rational theology' moral theology has two categories. Into
one fall the virtues and into the other fall the vices.[1] Alan's
treatise on the *Virtues and Vices and the Gifts of the Holy Spirit*
has a strong claim to be a section of the lost conclusion of the
Summa Quoniam Homines. Certainly, Alan treats the subject of
moral theology in this work as though it were itself part of speculative or rational theology, in exactly the way he had dealt earlier
with topics such as the unity and nature of God. The virtues are
the *expedimenta*, the vices the *impedimenta*, of this branch of
theology. We must pause briefly over this theoretical examination
before we come to Alan's practical theology since Alan himself
would place it with the *speculative*.

In this treatise then, Alan attempts a definition of virtue which
owes everything to philosophy and nothing to common observa-
tion of good men's lives. In man, he begins, a virtue is a quality,
not a substance.[2] To call God righteous is to speak of an attribute
of his very substance. To call a man righteous is to speak of a
quality he may lose at any moment. God is justice; man is just.
More precisely, we may describe virtue as the 'habit of a well-
ordered mind'.[3] We must also take into account the further
meaning of *virtus* which makes it a 'power'. These are our three
starting-points.

When Alan frames a definition, he likes to present it ready-
made for consideration and analysis, rather than to show step by
step how he has arrived at it. He knew the formal procedure for
arriving at a definition well enough. But whereas Anselm in the
De Veritate and elsewhere allows all the discussion and analysis
to precede the definition, Alan makes the definition precede the
discussion.

His analysis has an air of Aquinas about it, even at this early date, in its Aristotelian talk of 'power' and 'act'. What is this 'habit of a well-ordered mind'? We must first distinguish between those powers which are bestowed upon a rational creature at its creation,[4] and the true virtues. There are powers which are potential in a man from birth, such as 'walking' or 'reasoning'. From the first he is potentially able to walk,[5] potentially able to resist the vices,[6] but we should not properly speak of a merely potential power as a 'virtue'. We call a grown man 'brave', 'just', 'temperate', because he exercises his inborn power, not because he has the potential to do so. Such *denominationes* derive rather from the exercise of a power than from the possession of a power.[7] A man is not called *intelligens, ratiocinans, memorans* because God gave understanding, reason and memory, but because he is actively engaged in understanding, reasoning or remembering.

Merely to have *dispositiones*, tendencies towards virtues, does not, then, make a man virtuous. Everything depends on *usus,* exercise. To be chaste is not a virtue, if chastity is preserved solely to win the world's approval, Alan thinks. *Usus,* the exercise of virtue, properly comprises two things: *officium* and *finis*.[8] To act well is the *officium* of virtue, its task or duty, but the good act must also have its proper purpose (*finis*) if it is to be a virtuous act. *Officium* or duty is the *congruus actus* of each person, according to the customs and ways of the country. The *officium* of the Christian religion is the *congruus actus* of each person according to the customs and ways of the Church; that means, 'directed towards God and done in charity'. The *usus virtutis*, the one who exercises virtue will be 'well-ordered' and he will have, not a disposition towards virtue only, but a habit of virtue, a will to persevere such that in no way can he be turned from it.[9]

Now that we know what virtue is, we can place it in the category of moral theology as the supreme *genus*.[10] Next below it come the four cardinal virtues. From them proceed the others, as from their source. Prudence, for example is divided (by philosophers) into: *intellectus, ratio, prudentia, circumspectio, docibilitas, cautio.*

So much for virtue; what of vice? In one sense of the term it is the opposite of a *naturalis potentia*. Man is born with the power of seeing; if he is blind that power is flawed. Man is by nature able to hear; if he is deaf that power is flawed. Health, too, may be regarded as a *naturalis potentia* to which sickness is the opposing *vitium*. We saw in the case of the *virtus* which is merely a power, that there is no 'virtue', in the proper sense, in possessing it. Similarly, there is no vice, in the proper sense, involved in being blind. 'It belongs to logic to discuss this kind of vice and its *oppositio* in its many kinds, and so we must leave it out', Alan says firmly.[11] He thus distinguishes sharply between the theological use of the word and the use of the word in relation to the natural world.

Apud theologum vice is differently defined, as the *actus interior vel exterior*, the inward or outward act, which does not come to its proper end. Evil will is the interior act; evil-doing the exterior act. This is called *vitium* because it is out of order[12] in being without its due and proper end. In case it should not be clear to his readers in what the 'privation' consists, Alan gives two examples. It is a vice 'not to believe in God' (*interior actus*) or 'not to go to church' (*exterior actus*). Here we can see clearly from the 'not' that a negation is involved.[13] Within the *genus generalissimum* of vice fall the subsidiary *genera* of vainglory, anger, envy, sloth, greed, gluttony, lust. These are called *capitalia,* because from them spring all the vices.[14]

One might be inclined to say that Alan anticipated Aquinas,[15] in the assumptions on which this is based, and indeed Alan, like Aquinas, is able to use the principles he has set out to settle a number of further questions. Are virtue and vice *immediate opposita,* in the sense that if anyone lacks a particular virtue he has its opposing vice? If so, we can show that the virtues are interconnected, so that a good man has all virtues if he has any at all. Thus, if he had one virtue and not another, he would have the vice which was opposed to the other virtue, and then the same man would be both virtuous and vicious, which is impossible, because he would be a living contradiction.[16] Are virtues conferred in baptism? (Yes, in *habitus,* but not in *usus.*) Did Adam have virtues before the Fall? (Only natural *potentiae*.)[17]

Alan's final thoughts in this treatise are on the gifts of the Holy Spirit. He is anxious to distinguish between *data* and *dona*, so as to show that the *dona* of the Spirit are something more than the *naturalia data,* the natural gifts bestowed on all created things.[18]

There is, for example, the spirit of knowledge, by which man conducts himself in the world, the spirit of understanding, by which he grasps the truth of things he cannot see, and the spirit of wisdom, by which he tastes heavenly delights.[19] Such gifts are not in themselves virtues, but they make it possible for a man to behave virtuously: the *virtus*, then, is an *effectus*, a result of the gifts of the Holy Spirit.[20]

This is dry matter, and Alan works his way a little wearily through his definitions. Moral theology lends itself to an academic treatment readily enough, but its natural sphere is that of practical theology. When Alan speaks of the virtues and vices in his *Ars Praedicandi* he is able to give earthy, practical advice, and he writes with the light of battle in his eye. 'If the preacher wants to invite his listeners to avoid gluttony, he can use these authorities'; 'The body is to be chastised so that it may serve us'; 'The more a servant is indulged the more he slips into laziness'; 'The better a beast of burden is fed, the more inclined he is to kick his master'; 'How zealously then should we avoid gluttony, which reduces the habitation of the body, the receptacle of spirit and soul, to a dung-heap...which inclines the soul, the true school of the virtues, the rule of reason, the temple of the Deity, the foundation of immortality, to the pomp of the vices, the filth of crime, the mire of sin, the theatre of uncleanness.'[21] Against envy he writes, again giving a list of authorities first, 'You have heard, dearest brothers, how Holy Scripture deals with the plague of envy...Therefore the plague of envy is especially to be avoided, which first vexes itself and infests its possessor, and hurts itself before anyone else, and turns its wounds back upon itself. This it is which grieves at another's prosperity, is sorrowful when someone else is happy, rejoices in the adversity of another. O vice more to be despised than any vice, more lowering than any plague!'[22] Spiritual joy, by contrast, is 'the house of Solomon, filled with different fragrant oils, for the gifts of charity smell sweet in purity of heart. This is the throne of God, the palace of Christ, the couch of the heavenly Bridegroom. There the soul, who is the bride, rests with Christ her husband...There Jacob rejoices in the sweet embraces of Rachel; there Mary Magdalen offers most precious ointment to Christ.'[23]

In the chapters of the *Art of Preaching* Alan considers gluttony, luxury, avarice, sloth, envy, anger, pride, and then turns to the despising of the world and the hope of heaven, spiritual grief and spiritual joy, before turning to patience, obedience, perseverance, mercy, justice, love of God and love of neighbour, peace, prudence, fortitude and temperance. He looks at the need to govern the tongue, at lying and detraction. He considers prayer, contrition, confession of sins, penitence, almsgiving, fasting, vigil, learning, hospitality. Here is a complete moral theology made, not speculative but practical, and it is to this department of Alan's thought that we must turn next.

4 Expedimenta

ALAN THE PREACHER

'Few have said much about what preaching ought to be, whose task it is, to whom it should be addressed, what subjects it ought to cover, how and when and where.'[1] In his *Art of Preaching* Alan proposes to repair this deficiency in two ways: firstly he tries to answer some of these questions with general advice, and, secondly, he provides the would-be preacher with a substantial body of material so that he can put the advice to practical use.

Was he right in thinking that such a handbook was needed? In general he seems to have had an eye for a gap in the literature of any subject which he himself was competent to fill, and this seems to have been no exception. In Paris in the late twelfth century the preaching of sermons became something of a fashion among academics. As it had been in the days of Jerome and Augustine, the sermon was seen as a form of exposition of Scripture. At the beginning of his *Verbum Abbreviatum* Peter the Chanter describes the laying of foundations by *lectio*; the building of the walls by *disputatio* and the construction of the roof by *predicatio*. An additional spur was the need for missionary preaching against the heretics in the south of France and elsewhere, which was felt with increasing pressure as the twelfth century wore on.

How were these new preachers to learn their business? One way was certainly by imitation. The homilies of the Fathers had for centuries provided all that was needed for reading to members of monastic communities. Indeed, it seems to have been so rare for anyone to supplement them with an original sermon in the late eleventh or early twelfth century, that St Anselm's preaching and his 'table-talk' aroused enthusiasm in the monasteries he visited almost as much for their novelty as for their excellence.[2]

In the twelfth century, heads of monastic houses often took advantage of the licence the Rule gave them to speak for the edification of their monks, indeed such talks were normally the centre of spiritual direction in a well-run abbey. Hugh and Richard of St Victor, Peter de Celle, Peter the Venerable and, surely the most copious preacher of the century, Bernard of Clairvaux, all made a name for themselves as preachers, to their own communities and those they visited.

These were men who could set and maintain high standards, but there was a danger that lesser men might lead others astray if they took to preaching. Guibert, abbot of Nogent, a younger contemporary of Anselm who remembered with gratitude the spiritual direction he had received from him as a young man, composed a *Book on Making Sermons*,[3] with this thought in mind. He examines the motives which should lead a man to preach, the principles by which he should be guided, the state of mind in which he should begin. He emphasises, as Augustine had done, that prayer should come before preaching,[4] that is, that the preacher should prepare himself spiritually so that he would be receptive to the guidance of the Holy Spirit as he spoke. He envisages the preacher's task in terms of the needs of the monastic community, and he is cautious. He writes in the hope of curbing the excesses of the over-enthusiastic and instilling sound habits in him.

In his *Art of Preaching* Alan has not altogether turned his back upon these considerations, but it has a very different air. Alan is concerned with practical mastery of the methods of preaching. His instruction is detailed and methodical. Guibert may give the same advice – for example that the preacher should adapt his sermon to the capacity of the audience – but he does so in more general terms. 'While he speaks to the unlearned plainly and simply', he advises, let the preacher 'introduce those greater profundities which befit the more learned, when he speaks to them'.[5] Alan explains exactly how to do so, and provides collections of suitable texts and examples for use with different kinds of audience.

Alan wrote within a scholarly milieu very different from that of the monasteries in which Anselm and Guibert lived and worked. He certainly preached to monks, but he addressed himself to fellow-scholars, too, to the heretics, to mixed popular audiences, and, if we are to take as it stands the evidence of some of the later chapters of the *Art of Preaching*, to groups of widows or soldiers or princes or lawyers. The sheer variety of his experience had taught him a great deal about the practical needs of the preacher. The picture we have of the range of his preaching is likely to be one-sided, because his surviving sermons are all in Latin, and most of them clearly have an educated audience in view. There may have been simpler sermons, given to ordinary people, which neither Alan nor those who made notes or copies of his sermons thought important enough to record for publication, but if we compare like with like, the change which had taken place between the time when Guibert wrote a book on preaching and the period when Alan composed his manual, is obvious enough.

Alan's method is closer to Cicero's technique of composing speeches; an opening and closing passage are given special attention and perhaps learned by heart, and he relies upon mnemonic devices for the rest; Alan is a pulpit orator. Like the authors of some of the books on letter-writing – another mediaeval branch of the ancient rhetorical art – Alan provides a set of samples at the end of his treatise. Instead of pattern-letters he gives pattern-sermons – a collection now known as the *Liber Sermonum* – and covering the principal feasts of the liturgical year.

We must pause here and look at a work which brought practical theology to its fullest twelfth-century development, and which has, on the face of it, a strong claim to be set beside Alan's *Art of Preaching* as the first manual of preaching in the university tradition. Peter the Chanter's *Verbum Abbreviatum* begins with a lengthy discussion of the virtues of brevity – a virtue Peter sees as especially appropriate in the practical man. It covers more than the preacher's needs, but Peter places preaching at the top of his list of the theologian's tasks, and it might be argued that everything he has to say is intended to serve the preacher's purposes directly or indirectly.

The three stages in the study of the Bible are considered one at a time. We are shown first why it is best for the lecturer to keep his gloss or commentary short. For the practical needs of the private reader comment must be self-explanatory.⁶ For the use of students in the school difficult points may be raised.⁷ In either case too much detail is burdensome.⁸ Scripture was not given us so that we should waste our time asking frivolous questions about it, or trying to establish details of time and place, genealogies and the precise architectural points of buildings. From *lectio* Peter moves on to *disputatio*. Here, too, we must be on our guard against wasting time on frivolous questions; we must confine ourselves to serious matters, such as have to do with righteousness and holiness and modesty – with virtuous living.

Finally Peter comes to the advantages of brevity in preaching, which, like a roof, completes the building of which *lectio* is the foundation and *disputatio* the walls. Again, this is a brevity of tightness, appropriateness; it reflects a sensible and practical approach to achieving the proper end of preaching. The preacher should be himself a good man, burning with zeal, so that he can arouse his listeners to good intentions. Peter tells a story of St Bernard, who preached to an audience of German-speaking laymen with such fervour that they were reduced to tears, even though they did not understand what he was saying. When a monk who was an excellent and accurate translator repeated what Bernard had said in German they did not respond at all, because he spoke with dull precision and did not fire their hearts.⁹ This is the practical way of driving the point of a sermon home, not the use of rhetorical devices and elaborate stylistic contrivances which merely titillate the ear. The general tone of this advice is entirely in keeping with Alan's discussion at the beginning of the *Art of Preaching*, but Peter has placed what he has to say in a larger context – that of the whole *exercitium* of the study of Scripture.

In a similar way, Peter includes not only the discussion of virtues and vices and other appropriate topics for the preacher who wants to help his congregation live a more holy life, but a great many chapters on abuses in the Church. Alan mentions some of these abuses in his *Art of Preaching* and elsewhere, but he does not seem to have been so moved to protest by what he saw on every side as was Peter, who, as precentor of the Cathedral of Notre Dame, was daily perhaps having to deal with abuses among the clergy with whom he came into contact. On one occasion, indeed, he broke up a dispute which was coming to blows in the nave of the Cathedral.[10]

We might compare the arguments the two scholars advance against the celebration of the Mass more than once a day. For Alan the key to the offence lies in the greed it displays (*cupiditas*), that is, in the sin of the individual. For Peter – although he mentions *cupiditas* too – the horror lies in the monstrosity of the act. Two-headed Janus, the seven-headed hydra, Briareus of the hundred heads, a monster with two or three bodies, none of these is to be compared with the monstrosity of a two-headed, twice-celebrated Mass, or worse, a thrice-celebrated Mass. Peter sees the horror of the act as an offence against the Church. No doubt Peter's objections were in part motivated by his abhorrence of priests who found the multiplication of masses a source of lucrative fees. Elsewhere in the *Verbum Abbreviatum* he censures the corruption of justice by bribery, simony in every form, and all the ways in which, through his performance of sacred functions, a priest can add to his income or can enhance his worldly standing by bribing influential voices to speak for him in high places, and so come to enjoy exaggerated respect flattering to his ego. Peter is sensitive to the confusion of the spiritual with the temporal.

The proportionately less thorough treatment of these matters in Alan's writings should not perhaps be over-emphasised. Alan certainly cared deeply about those abuses on which he does have something to say. But the inclusion of so many chapters on such topics in the *Verbum Abbreviatum* serves to distinguish its purpose from that of the *Art of Preaching*.[11] Not only is it larger in conception, dealing with every level of the study of Scripture, but it is larger in scope, dealing at far greater length with abuses in the Church as well as with the vices and virtues treated in both works.

Peter everywhere gives the impression of having his feet planted more squarely in the practical realities of the contemporary world than Alan. He tells stories of his contemporaries and masters of an earlier generation, holding them up as moral examples. These have been collected together by Baldwin in a chapter of his study of Peter's moral theology,[12] but we might add two episodes from the *De Tropis Loquendi* by way of additional illustration. There is a brief reference there to Ivo of Chartres' teaching on the rights and wrongs of selling the preacher's skill by accepting offerings in payment, and a story about an occasion when Bernard of Clairvaux refused to apply medicine to his eye when he was suffering from an eye disease. He explained that Scripture must be taken seriously when it says that if the eye offends us it is to be cast out.[13]

One result of Peter's more comprehensive approach and his firm view of contemporary events, is that his *Verbum Abbreviatum* cannot be said to be strictly or solely a manual of popular ethics; it undoubtedly seeks to meet the needs of the preacher, but it lacks the pointed application to the requirements of the master who wants to learn an art of preaching which is recognisably that of the university-style sermon in embryo. In making exactly this provision, Alan's manual, together perhaps with that of Maurice de Sully (d. 1196), another Paris master of Stephen Langton's time, is a forerunner of something new. In the thirteenth century, especially after 1230, a number of preaching-manuals were put together, in which the theory of preaching was given a full academic development.[14]

It seems that Alan really did see a new need, and tried to meet it by exploring the ways a preacher could best reach his audience, in the light of the developing skills of his contemporaries in the arts of argument. There is a characteristic blend of the theoretical and the practical in his approach to preaching.[15] In his sermons themselves he puts into practice his own advice to adapt preaching to the capacity of the audience. To a group of clerics he preaches a sermon in which he apologises in case he is insulting their intelligence by making his message too simple. Stephen Langton gives the same advice. 'A preacher should not always use polished, subtle preaching', he explains, 'but sometimes...rude rustic exhortation...Whereas the laity are easily converted by rude, unpolished preaching, such a sermon to clerks will draw scarcely one of them from his error.'[16]

Alan's surviving sermons vary a good deal in the demands they make on the listener, but there is little 'rude, rustic exhortation' in them. He makes only sparing use of stories from the lives of saints or from the Bible itself, and although he recommends the preacher to give *exempla*, such as moral fables and tales, stories of everyday life, tales from the secular classics – all the apparatus with which the preacher to a popular audience tried to capture the interest of simple men in the later Middle Ages[17] – Alan does not address himself to those who would prefer to hear a story, something close to their own experience or aspiration, rather than a literary anecdote or a speculative exploration of an idea. Such stories as he tells are analogies, a little dry and schematic; though rich enough in texture, even at their most colourful they are stereotyped. In the eighteenth sermon of *The Book of Sermons,* a sermon for Palm Sunday, he describes how certain members of the angelic army, rebelling against their King, and becoming disloyal to their Prince, wished to steal the lordship of his castle for themselves. Thus he tells in allegory the story of the fall of the angels. His imagery of castle and moat, wall and tower and rampart makes use of familiar 'props' of the feudal scene. In the same sermon Christ is compared with a warrior going into battle, as he goes to be crucified.[18]

Scholar though he is in his approach, Alan does not go so far as the thirteenth-century preachers were to do in subjecting his sermon to methodical treatment. First, a theme is proposed, usually, if not always, a text from the Bible. Alan himself describes the textual theme as the proper beginning of a sermon. Then in the thirteenth century the academic preacher set about winning his audience's attention and interest with the protheme, perhaps by inviting them to pray with him. This part of the sermon corresponds to the *captatio benevolentiae* of the art of letter-writing. Alan explains that 'the preacher ought to capture the goodwill of his listeners'.[19] The theme is then expounded, either by argument or by narration, the story-telling method clearly being more suitable for a popular audience. Once it is clear to everyone what the sermon is to be about, the theme is divided into three parts. If possible, these should be labelled with words which terminate in syllables with the same sound, so that they will lodge the better in the reader's memory. In a sermon for Advent Alan speaks of the threefold coming of the heavenly kingdom, first *in caritate,* when Christ visits us by grace, secondly, *in carne,* when he visited us in mercy, and thirdly *in claritate,* when he shall judge the world in glory. Alan employs the rhetorical devices of later manuals: *digressio, correspondentia, circulatio, unitio, convolutio,* and so on, and it is probable that he could have given some of them their technical names. But these correspondences are also points of contrast, for Alan gives each technical device only enough weight to make its application clear. He is not interested in developing their technicalities for their own sake. Preaching is an art in his hands, but above all a practical art.

THE BOOK OF EXPERIENCE

Alan's peculiar blend of the conventional and the natural, the contrived and the spontaneous, gives him great flexibility as a preacher. He is able to cajole and threaten and soothe to such effect that it is easy to believe that he is speaking from experience when he warns the preacher to watch his audience carefully for signs of emotion. When they are in tears, it is well for the preacher to pause and allow them to become calmer, he advises, 'for nothing dries up faster than a tear', according to Lucretius, and it is better for a lasting change to be worked upon their minds than a passing change upon their emotions only.[20]

The ability to respond to the needs of the moment depends upon the preacher's presence of mind, and upon something else: his possession of a stock of arguments and illustrations which he can draw upon at a moment's notice. The classical orator was taught the art of memory[21] and encouraged to equip himself with 'topics' in this way. The collections of *exempla* made for the use of preachers in the later Middle Ages served exactly the same purpose – and indeed preaching was recognised as a rhetorical art which was unique among the mediaeval 'rhetorical arts', of poetry, preaching and letter-writing, in its need for such material. There is no exact equivalent for the art of letter-writing or the art of poetry. Alan had therefore hit upon a practical requirement when he began to assemble the collections of quotations and citations which make up the chapters of the *Art of Preaching*.

Underlying his own lively and apparently free adaptations of certain *topoi* there is certainly the conscious use of a convention. The study of 'topics' was very much alive in twelfth-century schools, but in the context of dialectical studies, where it meant general types of argument capable of being applied in many ways, rather than in a rhetorical connection, where it was used for stock examples, illustrations and other commonplaces. Peter

Abelard devotes a considerable part of his *Dialectica* to topics, leaning heavily upon Boethius.[22] When Boethius wrote his own works on topics, he was aware of a pressing need of his day for a distinction of rhetorical and dialectical uses of *topoi*. He commented upon Cicero's *Topics*[23] and in the *De Differentiis Topicis* he attempted a resolution of the disparities between the logicians' use of topics as set out by the fourth-century scholar Themistius in his paraphrase of Aristotle, and the rhetoricians' topics of Cicero.[24] It was the *De Differentiis Topicis* which served as a basis for Abelard's *De Divisionibus Themistii et Tullii*.[25] The emphasis of these studies is upon the *topos* as an aid to logical argument,[26] rather than upon its usefulness in providing the orator with ready-made material for his speeches, both illustrative and argumentative. The same emphasis upon applications in logic is detectable in commentaries upon the *De Inventione* and the *Ad Herennium* of the twelfth century.[27] There can have been only a limited appreciation of the orator's difficulties where a written not a spoken rhetoric was being studied. Quintilian's *Institutio Oratoria* might have helped contemporary scholars understand something of the richness of classical rhetoric, but it was little-known, and only a small part of the whole was available.[28]

Alan was therefore adventurous in making use of the *topos* as the classical rhetoricians did, and he did so in the context of one of the new mediaeval rhetorical arts.[29] There can be no doubt that he intended to revive the rhetorical *topos* for its sheer practical usefulness.

The 'topical' character of the chapters of the *Art of Preaching* is clear enough. These are not, perhaps, as has been suggested, simply 'model sermons', sermons in miniature.[30] Alan's sermons are normally on a single text. Each of the chapters of the *Art of Preaching* gives a selection of several suitable texts, Scriptural, patristic and secular.[31] These are, as Cicero defines them (in Aristotelian terms) 'seats of argument', not arguments fully developed into sequences of argumentation.[32] They are simply collections of source material, and the preacher is intended to draw upon them selectively, taking what he needs for a particular sermon, rather than expanding them as they stand into full-length sermons.[33]

Alan includes a few analogies in his collection – some of his own favourites, which he employs himself in more than one sermon. He speaks, for example, of the Book of Experience, and compares it with the Books of Knowledge and of Conscience. In one chapter of the *Art of Preaching,* Alan sets out a schematic pattern for the *topos.* The Book of Knowledge is a volume where a man may read of his final end; in the Book of Experience he can read about himself; in the Book of Conscience he can discover himself. The Book of Knowledge is written on pages which are bound into an actual volume; the Book of Experience is written in the body and the Book of Conscience on the heart. In the Book of Knowledge we read 'Know Thyself'; in the Book of Experience we read 'The flesh wars against the Spirit'; in the Book of Conscience we read, in the words of Statius, 'The dreadful day of the mind circles on ever-present wings.'[34] An alternative scheme for extending the metaphor is to be found in Chapter 14, where the same quotation from Statius[35] recalls the topic to Alan's mind, this time in connection with the theme of 'spiritual joy'. Since Chapter 3 is devoted to 'despising oneself' it is clear that such topics may be employed irrespective of the context, wherever they happen to have something pertinent to add. Where 'The dreadful day of the mind circles on ever-present wings' there is the hand-written Book of the Devil, inscribed in letters of the deepest black; there the page is the bad conscience, the pen freedom of choice and the ink the enormity of sin.[36] Alan goes on to exhort the reader to wipe out what he has written in the book, by confession, repentance and penance, so that the conscience may find no reason to condemn, the Devil no grounds for accusation, and God no reason to judge. 'And thus', Alan promises, 'you will return to spiritual joy of the mind.'

The image was not new. It was something of a patristic commonplace,[37] but the fact that it was well-worn could only recommend it the more strongly to the compiler of a collection of useful *topoi.* Familiarity with an image is thought to aid the listener's understanding, and to make it easier for him to remember what has been said to him.

Alan makes use of this *topos* several times in his sermons. In a sermon on despising the world we are told that Job read of his condition of wretchedness in the Book of Experience.[38] Here the

Book of Experience is the body. Alan does not develop the image, but he evidently expects his readers to call to mind the baggage of associations which belong to it. By contrast, in another sermon, St Nicholas reads of mercy in the Book of Experience.[39] Elsewhere the two descriptions of the image in the *Art of Preaching* are brought together, and we are shown how the Book of Knowledge is written in a volume, the Book of Experience in the body, the Book of Conscience in the heart; how the Book of Knowledge is written in letters of gold, the Book of Experience in letters of lead, and the Book of Conscience in hideous letters.[40] The Book of Experience is said to be the human body and the Book of Conscience the mind, and we are told that in the Book of Knowledge we may read 'Know Thyself'.[41] Later in the same sermon the quotation from Statius is once more associated with the 'book' image and again ink is the enormity of sin, the pen freedom of choice and the page a bad conscience. The listener is exhorted to wipe out his sins through confession, repentance and penance, in exactly the same way as before, so that his conscience, the Devil, and God himself, can bring no charge against him.[42]

A further example of the use of topical material from the *Ars Praedicandi* occurs in a sermon on the spiritual unity of abbot and monks. There, Alan has a passage on mirrors which is also to be found in the third chapter of the *Ars*. In the *Ars*, Alan speaks of a threefold mirror, that of Scripture, that of nature, and that of creation. He goes on to describe the different kinds of mirror, that in which the left appears on the right and the right on the left, that in which the right appears on the right and the left on the left, and that in which the image is inverted. These stand, respectively, for the mirror of the senses, the mirror of reason, and the mirror of the flesh.[43] In the sermon, the same three mirrors stand for good and bad prelates.[44] Alan's source of information on mirrors may have been Lucretius or Seneca,[45] but he makes his own varied use of the *topos*. As before, certain phrases stick in Alan's mind. The *Ars* has:

> quaedam est species speculi, in qua sinistra videtur
> esse sinistra, et dextera videtur esse dextera...
> Aliud vero est speculum, in quo dexterae partes videntur
> esse sinistrae et sinistrae videntur esse dexterae...
> Aliud est speculum in quo facies videtur inversa.

The sermon has:

Est speculum in quo sinistrae partes sinistrae et dextrae videntur dextrae...Est aliud speculum, in quo sinistrae partes dextrae et dextrae sinistrae videntur...Tertium speculum est, in quo superiores partes hominis videntur inferiores et inferiores superiores.[46]

Topical material is being re-used, in a quite different context, but in very much the same words, which indicates that the *topos* travels as a ready-made unit.

Alan loved new and unusual words, especially those with a Greek element, and some of those he discovered or devised became favourites. In the fourth chapter of the *Art of Preaching*, he describes the worship of Bacchus rather than of God, as 'Bacchus-worship': *bacchilatria*. 'This is one of the daughters of idolatry, whose stomach is her God, and who worships Bacchus. For this reason, to invent a word for it, we speak of "Bacchus-worship".'[47] Whether or not Alan invented the term, he was certainly sufficiently pleased with it to make use of it again. In a sermon for the Annunciation when it falls on Palm Sunday, we find:

ut autem fictis vocabulis liceat nos loqui, prima potest dici bacchilatria; secunda nummilatria; tertia carnilatria.[48]

Again, he claims to be inventing words, this time for three daughters of idolatry, the love of the stomach, the love of money and the love of the flesh.[49]

Something rather similar has happened in the case of a curious phrase which occurs in the third chapter of the *Ars*. 'O man, remember that you were a seed in fluid, how you are a vessel of dung, how you will be food for the worms.'[50] *Sperma fluidum* seems to have puzzled the scribe of at least one of the manuscripts,[51] but the passage appears in exactly the same form in the *Sermo in Die Cinerum*.[52] Alan perhaps took a liking to this trio of clauses, and used them again.

Elsewhere, the same thing has happened to the antithesis of *Ars* Chapter 31, between *judex soli* and *judex poli*, the heavenly and the earthly judge.[53] In a sermon for the Feast of St Augustine, Alan speaks of a crown of earth and a crown of heaven[54] and in a sermon for Epiphany of a law of heaven and a law of earth.[55] The 'heaven and earth' *topos* was not invented by Alan in this form – it occurs in St Bernard, too – but, again, he evidently found it sufficiently pleasing to be worth employing again and again with variations. Whether he invents words of his own, or borrows unusual terms from his reading, Alan's use of topical themes extends to the smallest *minutiae* of individual words and phrases. His varied use of the same or similar terms in different contexts emphasises the flexibility of application which is a feature of the classical rhetorical *topos*.

The topic is not by any means always so brief. Alan repeats much longer passages in his pastoral writings. The sermon composed for the Annunciation when it falls on Palm Sunday[56] coincides in a number of passages with another sermon for Palm Sunday.[57] Perhaps the author was simply saving himself trouble by reshaping a ready-written sermon, but it is perfectly in keeping with the notion of the *topos* that he should include quite substantial pieces of one composition within another. In Chapter 36 of the *Ars Praedicandi* Alan uses the stock image of the despoiling of the Egyptians by the children of Israel;[58] thus he allows a place for the study of the secular arts in the Christian scholar's programme of learning. A *Sermo ad Scholares* expands the notion, but gives it a twist in the opposite direction: Egypt becomes the world itself, Pharaoh, Satan; and those who trust themselves to secular studies embark in paper boats made of the papyrus reeds of the Nile.[59] Such large borrowings, then, demonstrate as clearly as the smaller borrowings of words and phrases, Alan's flexibility and his masterly use of the topical art.

It would be absurd to suggest that Alan was consciously following the teaching of the classical rhetorical textbooks in a way which distinguishes him from his contemporaries, but he was a notably conscious artist in an age of conscious artists. It so happens that in Alan's *Art of Preaching* we have an almost unique example of a collection of topical material designed to be used in speaking aloud to an audience, and in his *Book of Sermons* we have a companion volume containing a number of examples of the way in which it was actually used. Thus Alan's work brings us closer than any other to the original purpose of the *topos*: in order to speak fluently and convincingly in public it is necessary to prepare one's material. A stock of ready-made illustrations and images must be the stock-in-trade of any public speaker. Alan himself, in the first chapter of the *Ars* links preaching with *concionatio*, public-speaking, which is designed for the public good,[60] and thus relates it to the purpose of ancient oratory.

There is a grave disadvantage for an editor in the use of such a collection by an author. It is difficult to suggest a date of composition for most of Alan's pastoral writings, or to be sure that other hands have not made insertions or polished a version 'pirated' on an occasion when a sermon was delivered. Anyone could use topical material. Even if this is the case – and it would be impossible to establish that it was not – the whole procedure would still be perfectly in keeping with the spirit of the classical rhetorician's use of the *topos*. There was no 'copyright' on the material, and every orator built up his private collection by borrowing from others. Patterns of argument and turns of phrase which could be used again in various connections formed part of the rhetoricians' stock and might easily become the property of his admirers and imitators.[61]

Thirty-five years ago, J. P. Bonnes attempted to unravel one of the numerous problems which surround the identification of the authors of the Pseudo-Augustinian works.[62] In considering the sermons *Ad Fratres in Eremo*, which are printed by Migne after the Maurist edition,[63] he discusses the identity of the 'Geoffrey' who appears to be their author and the probable date of composition of the sermons. Although he mentions borrowings from Peter Comestor and Geoffrey Babion,[64] he nowhere remarks on the striking similarities between passages from these sermons and passages from Alan of Lille's *Ars Praedicandi*.[65] If the author of the *Ad Fratres in Eremo* did in fact write the sermons during the thirteenth century, as J. P. Bonnes asserts, there can be no doubt that the direction of the borrowing was from Alan and that Alan did not himself, on the contrary, include pieces or material which he believed to be Augustinian. If this is the case, we have an example of the *Art of Preaching* being actually used for the purpose for which it was designed: to furnish topical material to intending preachers.

We began by suggesting that Alan was nothing if not practical in his advice to preachers. How practically effective were these sometimes rather worn *topoi* in awakening his audiences from their spiritual torpor or their moral turpitude? Perhaps more so than might now seem likely. The classical rhetoricians who refined the method were not practising an art for its own sake, but as a means of persuasion in the political arena or in the law-court. Alan, too, intended his *Ars Praedicandi* to be, not a fine art, but a useful art.

5 Impedimenta

In 1116 Henry, a renegade monk, entered Le Mans preceded by
two disciples bearing a cross. He had formed the view that the
clergy should live like the seventy apostles Jesus sent out two by
two into the towns and villages to preach (Matthew 10.7–13),
poor wanderers, without the backing of the great institutional
structure of the Church. His thinking seems gradually to have
hardened into a vigorous anticlericalism. He taught the laity to
confess to one another, saying that priests had no power to forgive
men their sins. He rejected the doctrine of the Eucharist, and
indeed all the priestly functions of administering the sacraments.[1]

He represented a type of holy rebel not uncommon in the late
eleventh and early twelfth century, often a monk who had grown
dissatisfied with the monastic life of even the best of Benedictine
houses (and there were many which left much to be desired); the
ideal of the Apostolic Life, envisaged as a missionary, or pastoral
or spiritual ideal, possessed a powerful attraction for such individuals. Out of these attempts to rediscover true Christian life as
it was lived among the first followers of Christ, came some of the
greatest and most respected movements of the twelfth century.
Robert of Molesme led a group of friends to a new poverty of
monastic life, and a young convert called Bernard was drawn to
the house he founded at Cîteaux with a group of his friends and
family. Norbert of Xanten founded an Order of preaching
canons; his Premonstratensians followed the Augustinian Rule in
much the same spirit as the Cistercians followed that of Benedict,
and relations between the two great movements were always close
and cordial.[2]

But such original spirits with a vision of a higher religious life
did not always succeed in remaining respectable in the eyes of the
Church. As Robert of Arbrissel and Bernard of Tiron found, a

fine line divided an acceptable zeal for a primitive purity of life from a dangerous attractiveness to men ready to sneer at authority and to separate themselves from the established Church.[3]

Peter the Venerable, abbot of Cluny from 1122–56, heard of the existence of a popular preacher of whose sect he believed Henry to be a member. His name was Peter of Bruys, and he was more extreme in his views than Henry with, it appears, some notions he had got, not from following through the logical implications of his own vision, but by talking to others, perhaps the Bogomils; they held views which Augustine would have recognised as Manichean, and which were to be characteristic of the Cathar heretics of the second half of the twelfth century.[4] Peter rejected the Old Testament as the dualists did, in the belief that it told the story of the creation of a material world by a power who was a principle of evil, and who was opposed to the principle of good, the God of the New Testament. In the dualist belief that all matter is evil, the outward and visible things which Christians used as symbols of their faith, the Cross, Church buildings, even Church music,[5] seemed to Peter misleading, things to be repudiated by true believers.

Peter the Venerable addressed himself to Peter of Bruys and his followers in a treatise *Contra Petrobrusianos*; he cannot have hoped to break the hold of this popular preacher by publishing an academic monograph; yet there was little to be done in his day beyond making an attempt to change the heretics' heart by argument, and, as an extreme measure, bringing about public condemnation at Synod or Council.

These were the methods used in the first decades of the spread of popular heresy, and their general ineffectiveness may be judged by the way in which Peter's views spread into south-west France, into Narbonne, Toulouse, Arles, Gascony, before his death about 1140; while Henry the monk preached in Languedoc,[6] which became the centre of activity in the late twelfth century when Alan was at Montpellier.

The pattern began to change as numbers grew and the diffusion of heretical ideas came to depend less on the rise of individual preachers with a talent for demagogy.[7] Heresy which had no obvious leader was harder to deal with and, if anything, more alarming. Bernard of Clairvaux remarked with concern on this new anonymity.[8] The only way to deal with it appeared to be to preach against it, to meet preaching with preaching, and in extreme circumstances, to march against it on Crusade. That was to be the method of Alan of Lille's own day, which saw extensive preaching by Cistercians in the south of France, in which Alan joined (perhaps already himself a Cistercian monk); and the Albigensian Crusade was to follow, in the early thirteenth century.[9]

Two sects appeared most dangerous in the last thirty years of the twelfth century: the Cathars, and, from the early 1180s, the Waldensians.[10] The Cathars were dualists; and Alan was able to identify them with Augustine's Manichees at many points, and thus to write against them on the basis of patristic authority. The Waldensians emerged rather as some sects of the earlier twelfth century had come into being, as a movement led by a single individual with a vision of an Apostolic life revived. Valdès, the founder, had been a rich townsman of Lyon. He heard a wandering singer or *jongleur* recounting the life of St Alexius. Alexius, too, had been a wealthy man, but he gave up his bride and his inheritance to live a life of poverty. Valdès sent his daughters to Fontevrault as nuns and provided for his wife; and set off to follow Alexius' example. His offence consisted, not so much in unorthodoxy, as in his independence of the Church and what it provided for the faithful through the sacraments. The authorities mistrusted him, moreover, because he was a preacher without a licence. More: he encouraged the laity to educate themselves and read the Bible in their own language, and make up their own minds about the Church's teaching. He was condemned at Verona in 1184, but the movement did not come to an end. Archbishop Bernard-Gaucelin found it necessary to make an enquiry into Waldensian beliefs and to issue condemnation in 1185 and 1187. Count William VIII took action in Montpellier. In 1192 the bishop of Toul was ordering the rounding-up of 'Wadoys', and in Aragon, Alfonso II in 1194 and Pedro II in 1198 were still issuing edicts against the sect.[11] The movement was well-organised by now, its preachers getting by heart a vast array of biblical texts in schools run by the movement, so that they could call men to repentance with authority.[12] Certainly those who wrote books against heretics in the latter years of the twelfth century commonly refer with exasperation to this heretic habit of quoting Scripture as though it were theirs by right to do so.

Alan had a strong sense of the importance of taking action against heresy: by preaching, and by writing. He was clearly justified in thinking that there was a need to keep the faithful informed about the danger in which they lay. At Metz at the end of the century it seems that when laymen were found in un-authorised meetings reading the Bible together, no-one realised that they were Waldensians.[13]

A MULTIPLICITY OF OBJECTIONS

One of the most worrying features of popular heresy to the churchmen of Alan's generation was the way in which it chal-lenged the Church's authority, questioning the need for priest and sacrament alike. The Church claimed sole power to administer a mystery without which no-one could be saved. As the author of the Abelardian *Sententie de Sacramentis* puts it, 'He who despises the sacrament will not obtain everlasting life.'[14]

In response to this challenge, there was a renewed effort on the part of the Church's apologists to determine what is the *essence* of a sacrament. Two definitions were current. A sacrament could be seen as the 'visible form of invisible grace'[15] or the 'sign of a holy thing'.[16] Both imply that in the sacrament there is more than one element. Stephen Langton, with many of his contemporaries, held that each sacrament is composed of several elements, the sacrament itself[17] – the water of baptism, for example – the ablution of baptism which is also a spiritual cleansing[18] and the infusion of grace,[19] which is the mystery, the significance of the sacrament. Langton takes the view that the essence of a sacrament is determined by its principal *res*. This emphasis on its inner reality directly confronts the contention of the heretics that the sprinkling of water can have no effect, beneficial or otherwise, on the state of men's souls, but it was impossible to leave it there. The schools themselves bred controversy. It was the habit of scholars to worry away at definitions.

Alan wrote a good deal about the sacraments, and particularly about the Eucharist. One short treatise which we have already met deals with the reasons why the Mass should not be celebrated more than once a day. Alan regards two abuses as equally simoniacal in character: the celebration of two or more masses by the same priest on the same day, and the combining of two or three offices in the same Mass.[20] Alan is also the author of a sermon *Ad Sacerdotes in Synodo* addressed to priests who 'sell' the body of Christ in various ways, and especially by 'celebrating the Mass simoniacally'.[21]

Alan knew a great deal about the Eucharistic debate of the previous century and its recent developments. Six of the first seventy-six chapters of his book against the Cathars are devoted to the subject. He explains in an early version of this book that his concern had been aroused by the sheer multiplicity of the objections he knew to have been raised to the orthodox view.[22] Because he held the Eucharist to be of the first importance for every Christian, he saw no alternative to dealing with them all systematically. Not all of them by any means are distinctively Cathar or Waldensian positions, but it is convenient for Alan to treat them all at once so that his book will be a comprehensive manual and arranged so that each topic will be readily accessible.

Before we look at the grand sweep of Alan's polemical writing, it may help to convey something of its flavour if we examine his handling of this single question in detail. It aroused his intellectual curiosity more than most of the topics he took up against the heretics and it was a matter over which he himself felt especially strongly. Moreover, the Eucharistic controversy had a particularly long and a rather unusual history among contemporary disputes with 'unbelievers'. There had never been a single sect of eucharistic heretics, to correspond with the Cathars or Waldensians. To question the real presence of Christ in the consecrated bread and wine had tended to be a heresy of the schoolroom taken out into the world rather than a 'popular' heresy. Alan was most at home with classroom difficulties; he knew where he stood with an academic problem, and so we see him here in his element, marshalling arguments for and against, listing every objection, however minute, that he thinks may be pertinent to the discussion.

Two recent studies have traced the emergence and development of the eucharistic controversy of the eleventh century, and attempted to set it in its doctrinal and historical context.[23] Their authors have confined themselves largely to the period of perhaps seventy years, from the late 1040s, when the views of Berengar of Tours were beginning to attract widespread criticism, to the first decades of the twelfth century, when Alger of Liège wrote his monograph on the Eucharist. After that, scholars seem to have felt the matter of transubstantiation less pressing, if not closed.[24] The excitement went out of the controversy, and Alan's revival of these old issues is of considerable interest in its own right for what it shows of the development in thinking on detailed points which had been going on in the middle of the century in the schools.

Peter Lombard merely refers to the heresies of those who say that the body of Christ on the altar is only a sign (*signum*), and he supports the orthodox case, not with reasons, but with authorities. He deliberately avoids making any attempt to reproduce the arguments of the dialecticians. 'If it is asked what kind of change this is, whether it is "formal" or "substantial"; or of another kind, I cannot define it, but I know that it is not formal, for the species of the things which were there before remain, and the flavour and the weight.' If the reader asks how that may be, Peter answers *breviter,* that the mystery of the faith may be believed 'savingly' (*salubriter*) but not investigated.[25]

The list of headings in a *De Sacramentis* which may be the work of Peter Comestor owes a good deal to Peter Lombard, but it also reflects the increasingly wide range of aspects of the Eucharist which interested later twelfth-century writers. Written in the 1160s, the treatise includes sections on the name of the Eucharist, its institution, the reason for its institution, its form, what the word 'sacrament' means, and the word 'thing' in this context, the spiritual and physical ways of eating, why the body of Christ is given under the form of bread and not as it really is, why there is bread and wine, and not only one of the two, by whom the consecration should be carried out, when and where and with what instrument, the power and effect of the Eucharist. Finally we come to a selection of the questions Alan considers. In what are the accidents of the bread and wine after the substance has been changed into that of the body and blood of Christ? What is it that is broken or divided? What becomes of the body of Christ once it is eaten? What enters the mouth of a mouse who finds consecrated bread set aside, and eats it?[26]

Alan's account is far more detailed than either of these, within a much narrower frame of reference. His concern is with what happens when the bread is consecrated; what, in other words, is meant by the doctrine of transubstantiation? This is the heretics' question, for as they shrewdly point out, no mention is made of the matter in the Creeds, and the Creeds, as Alan would be the first to concede, contain every article of faith (*Contra Haereticos* 1.59). Alan cannot believe that the significance of Eucharist is a matter which may be left to individual opinion. It is clearly far too important for that, if it is true that without it no-one can be saved. He proposes one or two lines of explanation. Perhaps it was so obvious to everyone in the primitive Church that the bread and wine were changed, that no-one doubted the literal truth of what Christ had said in the Gospel: 'This is my body.' Perhaps there was no heretical opinion to be refuted; that would explain why there was no need to make mention of the matter in the Creeds. Topics upon which there were heretical opinions (the doctrine of the Trinity, the subject of the Holy Spirit, Incarnation, Resurrection) are mentioned in the Creeds. Alternatively, we may say the phrase *sanctorum communio,* 'the communion of saints', makes brief implicit reference to the Eucharist.

These remarks are of interest for two reasons. Firstly, they show how conscious later twelfth-century heretics were becoming of the ancient parentage of certain contemporary heresies. Indeed, Alan himself had made the point in the Prologue to the *Contra Haereticos* that in many details the modern problem can be met by reference to patristic teaching against earlier heretics, but that there remains a task for the modern theologian, who faces new versions of old errors.[27] In this respect, as Alan notes, the Eucharist stands apart. The heresy with which he has been concerned in these chapters is not as ancient as many others, but it is none the less pressing for that, and the modern apologist has little, beyond some passages of Ambrose and Augustine, to turn to among the Fathers.[28] The task of fitting a discussion of the Eucharist into the whole scheme of polemical theology was, then, consciously recognised by Alan to be an especially difficult one.

All this has a bearing on Alan's distinction between *expedi-*

menta and *impedimenta* in theology. He reflects upon the special difficulty which is presented by a topic not fully dealt with in the Creeds, but which is, manifestly, the subject of heresy. Here we may certainly learn what *not* to believe from the heretics, but we must learn what we ought to believe by other means than by studying the Creeds, for although Alan himself adheres to the view that the Eucharist is mentioned in the phrase *sanctorum communionem*, the Creeds cannot be said to be informative on the subject of transubstantiation.

The greatest advances of the twelfth century in discussion of transubstantiation were, ironically enough, in the very area where Berengar had been so proud of his powers: that of dialectic. It cannot be said that much more was done with the central issue: does the bread and wine of the Eucharist become literally the body and blood of Christ after consecration? Instead, a large number of peripheral questions were raised, and Alan gives an account of the solution he finds most satisfactory to several of these. The Eucharist, with the problems it raised about the change in the substance of the bread and wine and the reasons why the qualities it had before persist if their substance has changed, was by no means the first matter of doctrine to receive thoroughgoing dialectical analysis. The doctrine of the Trinity had presented itself as a suitable candidate to Augustine, and even more forcibly to Boethius, because the technical terminology of *substantia* and *relatio* irresistibly suggested recourse to the *Categories*; but the doctrine of transubstantiation was perhaps the first mediaeval doctrine to be formulated with the aid of the principles of dialectic. It certainly stood out in the eleventh century for its susceptibility to handling in this way, and even in Alan's day, when dialectic had a role in the discussion of almost every doctrinal problem, it retained a certain prominence in this respect.

Guitmund of Aversa, the author of one of the clearest expositions of the eleventh-century controversy, gave an account of an increasingly complex problem about 1073–5 in his *De Corpore et Sanguine Domini*. He describes how the problem came into existence. Berengar was arrogant, it seems, even as a boy at school. He despised his fellow-pupils, and the textbooks of the liberal arts (for at that time, Guitmund comments, the liberal arts

were little studied in France). Berengar set himself up as a leading
exponent of the art of dialectic, putting forward 'new interpreta-
tions of words'. Lanfranc confounded him readily enough, for
Lanfranc was very learned in the liberal arts, but Berengar
'impudently' turned his attention to the mysteries of Holy
Scripture, and showed that he preferred to be famous among
men as a *haereticus*, rather than to live quietly as a Christian
under the eye of God.[29] Berengar set the tone of the controversy,
then, by raising difficulties which were conceived of from the first
in dialectical terms.

It was certainly the dialectical complexion of the debate which
lent the topic its persistent interest among scholars throughout
the century which followed, for as knowledge of dialectic pro-
gressed, new aspects began to become apparent to succeeding
generations of scholars. It was this which helped to keep it alive
as an issue in the schools, even after it had ceased to be a focal
point of controversy, and which principally concerns Alan in his
Contra Haereticos.

The problems which the debate with Berengar put into circulation were not so clearly formulated by Lanfranc, when he wrote
his *Liber de Corpore et Sanguine Domini*, as they were by
Guitmund, who was able to stand back a little, and see Berengar's
views in the longer perspective which a few decades had given.
A significant development in Guitmund's treatise is the recog-
nition that there is a division among Berengar's followers,[30] for,
as Alan points out in his own Prologue, one of the signs of heresy
is a tendency to fragment into break-away groups or sects.
Already, a proliferation of opinions was making the problem
noticeably more complex. Some heretics say that there is nothing
at all of Christ in the consecrated bread;[31] others that there is
truly something there, but that it is hidden[32] in the bread, which
continues to be fully bread; others concede that a change takes
place, but say that when the unworthy come to take the sacrament, the bread changes back and ceases to be the body of
Christ.[33] These new questions are not all of the same kind, and
not all of them lend themselves readily to dialectical treatment,
but in general, the tendency for a long time was for new issues to
be identified in dialectical terms, and for each new issue to
generate further problems in its turn.

Guitmund is still able to speak of 'reasons' as though they were of relatively little account. He calls them 'little reasons',[34] and implies that the most helpful procedure may be to dispose of these rational arguments before turning to the authorities. For Paschasius Radbertus and the Carolingians,[35] proof was almost entirely a matter of adducing authorities. Lanfranc tried hard to maintain this position; he did his best to confine the use of reason to the minimum in the *De Corpore et Sanguine Domini*. Most of the argumentation is to be found in Chapters 7 and 8, where Lanfranc protests as he argues that he would rather 'hide his art'.[36] He accuses Berengar of 'running to dialectic'.[37] His successors were conscious of the existence of a tension here, as Guitmund shows in his opening remarks. Gilbert Crispin, for example, opens his treatise on the Eucharist of the 1090s with a lengthy discussion of the respective merits of proof by reason and proof by authority in such matters. He himself has no objection to the use of reason, but he insists that there are matters in which authority alone can afford a proof. 'Since Truth says that it is true that (the bread) is the body of Christ, it cannot be established by any other argument.'[38] It is proof enough, on this view of things, that Christ himself said: *Hoc est corpus meum.*

The arguments from reason were the trouble-makers in the long term. Some scholars felt a general sense of affront to their common-sense in the orthodox account of the Eucharist. Berengar seems to have shared this sense of outrage. He held that if we adhere to the view that the bread literally becomes the body of Christ we shall be obliged to believe things which common-sense cannot accept – that what we chew is not divided up by the chewing, that what we swallow is not digested, that, contrary to all appearances, what still looks and tastes like bread and wine is now bread and wine only in outward form. 'Nature does not allow such a change', says Guitmund, and in any case it is not conceivable that it is right for Christ to be torn by human teeth. The sense of outrage which moved the heretics is, then, given a certain passion by a sense of affront to reverence; but the intellectual basis on which it rests is the insult to common-sense.

The art of dialectic fastens upon technical and detailed aspects of this insult to reason. In an attempt to understand what exactly is meant by the assertion that the bread does not merely stand for the body of Christ as a sign, but is truly and substantially the body of Christ itself, Lanfranc emphasises the point at length. The bread is substantially changed into true (*vera*), proper (*propria*), life-giving (*vivificatrix*) body and blood, and after consecration it is the true body of Christ, not merely through the sign and power of the sacrament, but in property of nature and truth of substance.[39] Guitmund distinguishes between the notion that the bread is *substantialiter* the body of Christ and the view that it is called so in name only.[40] Gilbert Crispin employs the same vocabulary in his opening statement of the orthodox position.[41] The technical vocabulary of the eucharistic controversy grew, but the focus of the argument continued to lie in the notion of 'substance' to be found in Aristotle's *Categories*, its alternative meanings, and the words which might be appropriate for describing what remained of the bread and wine when the substance was changed.

What, then, were the problems which presented themselves to Alan for solution when he surveyed the heretical notions about transubstantiation which were abroad in his own day? First, the main issue. The heretics say that the bread is not changed in substance into the body of Christ by the words which are said by the priest in the Mass. Now what do we mean by 'change' says Alan? He is able to point to six types of *mutatio* recognised in the dialecticians in framing his reply. Thierry of Chartres sums them up for us conveniently: *generatio, corruptio, augmentum, diminutio, alteratio, secundum locum mutatio*.[42] In theology we have a special list of types of change, applicable to the peculiar circumstances of the alteration which takes place in the consecration, or in several places in Scripture where a miraculous change is described. There may be an alteration of the accidents in the same subject, as when something which is white becomes black. This is *alteratio*. *Alteritas* involves a change in the *substantialia*, where the *materia* remains the same. This is what happened when the water was changed into wine at the marriage at Cana. *Transubstantiatio*, the change which takes place at the consecration in the Eucharist, means a change in both the *materia* and the *substantialis forma*; nothing remains of the matter of the bread, nor of its substance, but certain accidents remain, such as roundness, whiteness, flavour.[43] The change involved is of the sort

Alan describes in the opening of his theological dictionary – a reversal of familiar changes (of accidents in created things where the substance is unaltered). It would surprise no-one if the bread grew mouldy but remained bread, because that would be a change in accident only, but it is an affront to common experience if the substance alters but the bread looks and tastes the same.

It is out of this difficulty that the heretics raise the further points which trouble them. If the form of the bread has somehow been detached from its substance, we may reasonably ask in what it now resides (*in quo sit*). Surely the accidents of the original bread do not any longer really exist, for there is nothing for them to exist in? At best they can be no more than appearances. Orthodox doctrine teaches that they are as real as they were before, and unaltered in any way, for it is only the substance of the bread that has changed.

The heretics have more difficulties to raise. If, day by day, in Masses all over the world, bread is being changed into the body of Christ, it would seem that the 'quantity' of his body is being increased. Again, we must first marshal the meanings of the word 'increase' as they are used of things in the created world, and then ask what special meaning may be applicable in this 'theological' context. Normally we increase something by extending its parts[44] as when a plant grows; or we add to it,[45] as when we make a heap of things by adding more items to it. Neither of these methods of increase applies here, for at the consecration nothing is added to the body of Christ; nor are its parts extended. In no sense which applies to the physical world is there any increase, and so the heretics' objection, which is a purely physical one, is seen to be no objection at all.

Next the heretics object that if, as a result of the act of consecration, the bread ceases to be, it must have been corrupted. Here we can resolve the problem by looking carefully at the terms we are using. The bread does not 'begin to be' the body of Christ,[46] which would imply that it abruptly stopped being bread; it 'becomes' the body of Christ,[47] and so we should say that it ceases to be[48] but not in such a way that it is corrupted.[49] Alan points out that since no natural process of decay is involved,[50] but a miracle,[51] there is no reason to introduce the notion of decay into the discussion. Again, his argument turns on a refutation of the truth of the heretics' claim for the things in the natural world. If we recognise that *naturalia* and *theologicalia* obey different laws, the difficulty disappears. It is, as he had explained at length in the Preface to the *Summa Quoniam Homines,* precisely because they try to apply the laws of the natural world outside that world that the over-confident masters of the *artes* fall into heresy. There could scarcely be a clearer instance of the way in which this may happen.

In the same spirit the heretics enquire how a body of such a size as the body of Christ must be (if we are to believe in the literalness of the change) can possibly enter in through the mouth of a man. Here again, natural or literal-mindedness has created a difficulty. The body of Christ in the Eucharist, Alan explains, is the body of Christ *cum iam sit glorificatum,* not the physical body he had on earth. In relation to that glorified body, questions of size and distance and space and location are irrelevant.[52] Likewise, in objecting that the body of Christ cannot be torn by teeth and broken into parts, the heretics are thinking of the body Christ had on earth. What is 'divided' or 'broken' visibly when the Host is masticated, is the *forma panis,* the outward form of the bread, for there can be no *fractio* or *divisio* in the body of Christ *iam glorificatum.*[53]

The heretics maintain that if the bread becomes the body of Christ, then it becomes something other than it is (*aliud quam sit*). There is a contradiction in its very existence. Alan is able to meet the objection on the heretics' own terms, by pointing to a parallel in the natural world. If wine is changed into vinegar, some of the properties of the wine remain. The vinegar is liquid, just as the wine was liquid. Similarly, the bread of the Eucharist retains some of its properties even when it has been changed into the body of Christ. Another parallel with a change in created things suggests itself, too. If we read that an angel has taken human form, we understand that the angel is somehow hidden under the human form. Similarly, when the consecration takes place the body of Christ takes the form of bread and is hidden under the bread.

Alan cannot meet all the heretics' points in this way. In more than one instance he is obliged to resort to the view that it is by a miracle that the change takes place. The heretics said that if only the accidents of the bread remained after the consecration, they would have nothing in which to inhere. It would be as though some part of the air was rounded, flavoursome, white, and that part changing continually as the 'form' of the bread was moved from place to place. Moreover, there would then be *soliditas* in the air, for solidity is one of the accidents of the bread which remains.[54] Alan can only say that the *color* and *sapor* are, 'miraculously', in the form of bread. The resort to mystery is not, however, a sign of defeat. Alan can always give a 'reason for the mystery' which will show off its glory. Where are Christ's head and feet in this 'body', ask the heretics? This is a matter of divinely ordained 'deceiving appearance', Alan explains. William of St Thierry had earlier made the point that we must distinguish between the illusions by which magicians deceive the eye, and the way in which the miracle of the Eucharist deceives the eyes without falsehood.[55] Alan goes further, describing three kinds of *fallacie visus*, an inability to see what is before our eyes, the *prestigium* or trick of the *ars magica*, which is intended to deceive, and the vision sent from God, whose purpose it is to instruct. The appearance of the bread in the Eucharist is not designed to deceive but to edify. There are three good reasons why the appearance is retained (reasons to be found in Peter Lombard and elsewhere).[56] The body of Christ continues to look like bread so as to prove the faith of those who eat it; so as to avoid causing repugnance to the faithful, who might find the eating of raw meat distasteful; and so as to avoid the risk that unbelievers might mock at Christians when they saw them eating the flesh of their Lord. This is a mystery with good reason behind it, and Alan is impatient with the heretics who are forcing him to explain what had much better be worshipped as a mystery, and treated with respect.

Indeed, some of their objections are utterly trivial. If a mouse stole a piece of consecrated bread, would it eat the body of Christ? Why can no more liquid be poured into a full chalice of consecrated wine if only the appearance of wine is there? The mouse, says Alan impatiently, would be miraculously nourished by the appearance of the bread, as though it were bread in substance, much as a man may be made drunk by the fumes of wine.[57] The *species vini* fills the space in the chalice miraculously, just to the top and no further.

This, then, is the difficulty Alan has in mind when he speaks of the 'multiplicity of objections'. Heretics are devious and inventive. If orthodoxy of faith is to be defended against them the apologist must have his wits about him. He must have a knowledge of the objections and responses in detail, a skill in putting his arguments, and an overall understanding of the problem of heresy; he must be both a theorist and a practical man.

AGAINST THE HERETICS

Alan made an art of preaching – not too much of an art, for, he says, 'Preaching should not glitter with verbal trappings and purple garments of colours.' On the other hand, it ought not to be too lowly in style, 'with bloodless words'. If it were to be too obviously indebted to art, too highly decorated, it would seem as if it had been elaborated to win admiration for the preacher's skill with words, rather than designed to teach his fellow men about the faith, or exhort them to live virtuous lives. Too studied a presentation will defeat its own end, for such preaching will be unlikely to move the listener, Alan explains.[58] The listener he has in mind here seems to be the believer rather than the heretic.

Preaching should be persuasive, certainly, and in this it is rhetorical, but the *Orator,* says Cicero,[59] has a threefold purpose: to teach, to give pleasure and to move men's hearts: *ut doceat, ut delectet, ut flectat.* Augustine explores the implications of this in the *De Doctrina Christiana.*[60] His emphasis, like Alan's is upon the prime importance of teaching, solid instruction in the faith. 'The weight of preaching should be in the meaning, so that by the power of its meaning it may soften the minds of the listeners, excite the mind, evoke contrition, rain down doctrines, thunder warnings, caress with promises, and so tend wholly towards the benefit of the listeners.'[61] Showy preaching, which is all surface glamour, may give pleasure, but it will be the wrong kind of pleasure. Fallacious arguments may move men's hearts, but not to any good. The preacher must first of all seek to teach, on solid authority and with sound arguments. Again, Alan is explaining how to preach to the faithful. This task of teaching has two aspects, according to Alan's own definition of preaching: the preacher must teach sound doctrine and he must encourage the

living of a good Christian life. For purposes of *moralis instructio*
certain passages of the Bible are more helpful than others. The
preacher should search the Gospels, the Psalms, the Pauline
Epistles, the Books of Solomon especially.[62]

But what is the preacher to do when his task of instruction in
the faith involves, not explanation to the faithful, but an attempt
to convert unbelievers and heretics to the true view? Alan has
nothing to say in *The Art of Preaching* about the special needs of
the missionary preacher, although he is conscious enough of the
existence of heresy to rail against the heretics' own method of
preaching in his preface.[63] The heretics preach in secret, and
therefore the honest Christian should always preach in public to
show that he has nothing to hide.[64] The heretics put forward false
arguments, which are like the monsters of Lamentations,[65] which
have the faces of young girls, the feet of horses and the tails of
scorpions. They begin from true propositions and draw false conclusions from them.[66] Special measures are required if heretics
are to be converted to the truth. Merely moving his hearers will
not win the missionary converts. The art of rhetoric gives way to
hard argument, which alone will lead to the firm intellectual
conviction of the truth which is required.

In the *Summa Quoniam Homines* Alan compares the position
of Theologia in his own day with that of Philosophia in Boethius'
Consolation of Philosophy. There, he remembers, Philosophia
complains that the *familiares* of her own household, the Stoics and
Epicureans who call themselves philosophers, have formed break-
away sects, and tried to claim philosophy for their own. In Alan's
time, it is Theologia who complains that her own kith and kin are
separating themselves from her, and disporting themselves among
their errors[67] in their heretical sects. The task of reclamation must
fall to the scholar who can win over these defectives from the
truth by argument, by his skill in dialectic.

In his four books against the heretics, Alan sets about the task
systematically, with, it seems, the intention of providing his
readers with a handbook in which they could look up answers to
any difficulty the heretics might raise in a disputation. It is not
easy to determine who these 'heretics' were. The village people
who followed the leaders of popular heresy were not theologians,
and it is doubtful whether the demagogues, such as Peter of

Bruys, who won their loyalty were very much better equipped to
defend their faith in argument, although Abelard's pupil Arnold
of Breschia and others were thoroughly competent. It may be that
many of the objections Alan considers were raised in the schoolroom as academic questions, which, as it were, rationalised and
made technical the half-formulated objections of simpler men.
The interest of Alan's rejoinders lies, not so much in what they
have to tell us about the realities of popular heresy, but in the way
they complete his own theological system.

That is not to say that he had no contact with heretics; there
is every reason to suppose that he was involved in preaching
against the Cathars and the Waldensians, too, perhaps a little
later. But Alan was above all an academic. In his treatise against
the heretics the procedure throughout is to discuss 'the opinion of
those who say...'; he is not interested in heretical practices, but
in heretical beliefs.

What, then, were the heretics saying, inside the schools or
outside?

1 *Against the Cathars*

If Alan was to begin at the beginning, it might be said that the
Cathars of the south of France whom he identified as latter-day
dualists forced him to begin, as it were, at two beginnings. 'They
say that God is the beginning of light, from whom are spiritual
things, that is, souls and angels; the beginning of darkness is
Lucifer, from whom come temporal things.'[68] In support of this
contention they cite: 'A good tree cannot bring forth evil fruit, nor
an evil tree good fruit.'[69] Since God is the highest good, they
argue, evil does not come from him; but evils exist, and so they
must come from some other source. Therefore, since God is the
beginning of good things there must be another beginning of evil
things. Now in Genesis 1.2, we read that 'darkness was upon the
face of the deep'. So the world had its beginning from the darkness. The creator of the world was the beginning of darkness, and
thus the *auctor mundi* was evil. Christ himself says in the Gospel,
'The prince of this world is coming, and he has nothing in me.'[70]
There he calls Lucifer the prince of the world rather than himself
and so it was he who was the author of the world rather than
Christ, and elsewhere it is written 'No-one can serve two masters'

that is, God and Mammon.[71] There Christ calls himself and 'Mammon', that is, the Devil, 'masters', but Christ is not called 'Lord' except because he is Creator. Therefore, similarly, the Devil is called 'Lord' because he, too, is a creator. The chapter goes on in similar vein, until Alan has set out the Cathar position in full, citing the authorities on which they rest their case, and explaining how they interpret them.[72] In the next chapter he turns from 'authorities' to 'reasons', and treats the philosophical arguments the heretics advance with equal clarity and brevity. They say that if God made visible things, he could either have made them corruptible or not. If he could not, he was lacking in power. If he did not wish to although he could, he was envious. Again, if a cause is immutable, its effect is immutable, but it is agreed that corporeal things are mutable, and therefore their cause is mutable.[73]

It is not difficult to imagine how helpful it would be to a missionary preacher to have these abstruse and complex matters made plain for him. Alan has made an economical summary for him of a great deal of material in the Fathers – and no doubt of contemporary heretical discussion, too. He also provides answers to all the heretics' points. The remark about the tree, for example, is not to be taken to refer to good and evil in the way the Cathars suggest. The word 'evil' in the expression 'evil action' may be taken to refer to the wickedness of the action, rather than to the action itself. The wickedness or *deformitas* itself is nothing, for evil is nothing. If reference is made to the action, something which really exists is under discussion. The action itself comes from God, as do all things which exist, but if the reference is made to the wickedness of the action, which is 'nothing', then the evil cannot be said to come from God. If in other words, we accept with Augustine that evil is nothing, there is no need to postulate the existence of an evil source from which bad actions, or 'bad fruit' must come. In a similar way, we say that the word 'darkness' refers to the absence of light rather than to something with an independent existence, and so the world did not have its very beginning from the darkness. The 'darkness' of Genesis 1.2 is not something in its own right, but merely an absence of light. The Devil is not called 'the prince of this world' because he created it, but because he is the prince of worldly men, and rules in their hearts through their worldly appetites. For the same reason he is called 'master' of the world.[74] Alan has philosophical arguments for the heretics, too. God could indeed have made the world immutable; he did not lack the power. Nor was he envious. He permitted it to be mutable, so that through the mutable we might become immutable. For every changeable thing hints at the unchangeable; every movement speaks of stillness. As to the question of causation: an efficient cause is one thing, a formal cause another. Nor is it necessarily the case that what is predicated of the Creator must be true also of his creation. God is the efficient cause which gives created things a beginning, and having a beginning they must also have an end. It follows that they must be mutable.[75]

We might pursue these arguments, but perhaps enough has been said to indicate Alan's combination of brevity with thoroughness. He gives each point no more space than is absolutely necessary but he allows himself time to make it clear, at least to the reader trained in the schools, exactly what line of argument is likely to prove fruitful. It is an unfortunate but perhaps unavoidable feature of his explanations that the heretics' viewpoint often seems common-sense, and Alan's attempt to explain it away, contrived and requiring the splitting of hairs. This comes about partly because he is always in the position of the man who speaks second in a debate. He is not free, as he had been in the *Summa Quoniam Homines,* to put the orthodox view straightforwardly. He looks at the 'Manichees' more than once there, commenting that it is worthwhile to show where they are in error 'for that opinion is still very much alive in many men's minds'.[76] In dealing with the same argument in the *Contra Haereticos* he can present it only piecemeal, in reply to specific points raised against it. Moreover, it is to be expected that the argument which wins popular support among heretics will have a ready appeal to common-sense. Heresies may accumulate accretions of elaborate explanation, but when the initial idea is stripped down to its essentials it is likely to prove an attractive one, for that is why it gained currency in the first place. Alan is engaged in the *Contra Haereticos* in exactly this task of stripping down ideas to make them easy to grasp.

His approach is theoretical, although his purpose is practical.

A scholar capable of expanding Alan's embryo arguments could make ready enough use of them in the formal disputations which were sometimes held with heretics, but it is likely that this vast corpus of material was intended chiefly to form a reference-book in which Alan arranged topics in a logical order, so that the user could quickly find the passage he needed, for a sermon perhaps, or for use in a public disputation. There is an academic dryness about the presentation which is very different from the vigorous, earthy practicality of the *Ars Praedicandi*.

The question of the two *principia* is not relinquished until Alan has shown exhaustively that the good God made the material as well as the spiritual world, that a single, omnipotent God made visible as well as invisible things, that on no grounds at all need we postulate the existence of a second, evil power who made the visible world.[77] Then he turns to a second prominent belief of the dualists, that human souls are in fact nothing but fallen angels, sent to dwell in human bodies eight times in succession, so that if they cannot purge their sin in the first they may have seven more chances. They have an authority for that in Matthew's gospel,[78] which Alan discounts. He explains that the heretics are mistaken in thinking that the fallen angels are to be saved; not all the angels fell and some remain in heaven, but those who sinned are lost for all eternity.

In keeping with their view that material things are evil, the heretics refuse to accept that Christ really became man, and ate and drank and grew up and suffered pain and death.[79] Alan insists that it makes nonsense of Scripture and of reason to take this view, for much hangs upon it, not only with respect to the Incarnation and Redemption, but also in connection with the future of mankind. If Christ was merely a phantom human being, what reason have we to believe in the resurrection of the body? The heretics pour scorn on the idea, saying that flesh which is reduced to ashes or to dust is not capable of being resurrected. Some would go so far as to say that the soul perishes with the body: Alan is able to marshall arguments here from named 'philosophers of the gentiles', Mercurius in the *Asclepius*, Virgil, Cicero, Plato in the *Timaeus* and the *Phaedo*,[80] to prove that the human soul is immortal.

In keeping with their belief that the Old Testament was

inspired by the Devil, the heretics claim that the Mosaic Law was given by Satan, that the Old Testament Fathers were evil and are damned.[81] The heretics have no time for the sacraments of the Church, either. They say that baptism profits no-one in infancy, some holding that infants are without sin, and dismissing the idea of original sin, and others accepting the existence of original sin, but questioning the efficacy of baptism where the infant is too young to have faith. Similarly, many heretics dispute the need for any sacraments at all, or those of less extreme persuasion point to particular difficulties. Is there any place for repentance after the remission of sin which takes place in baptism? Why are some sacraments repeated (penance, the Eucharist) and others administered only once (baptism, extreme unction)? Why is it not enough merely to confess to God, without benefit of sacraments?[82]

What picture of the Cathars emerges from these chapters? They will not allow that it is possible for God to be responsible for evil, however obliquely. They would like to think the fallen angels might be saved, and they find in the paradoxical condition of humanity, man's curiously compound being, ample evidence for the view that man is an angelic being trapped for a time in a lump of clay. The tone of the Old Testament, its tales of war and revenge, seems to them so out of keeping with the message of peace in the New Testament, that they can only conclude that the prince of this world is the author of the Old and the good God the author of the New. They react strongly against the Church's claim to a monopoly of the path to salvation, its looming physical presence. There is, they say, no *locus materialis*, no place on earth which is the Church. The prayers of the saints do not benefit the living. The sacraments are not necessary to salvation, or even helpful. All the good man needs to know is that the spiritual is good and the physical evil. He must abstain from meat and keep himself unspotted from a world in which, as a spiritual being, he has no place.[83]

2 *Against the Waldensians*

The Waldensians, whose leader was fired by an anger against what he saw as clerical abuses, take the Cathar disquiet about the authority of the Church a great deal further. Indeed, this is their principal concern as heretics. Valdès 'led by his own spirit, and not sent by God', began a 'new sect', presuming to preach without priestly authority, without divine inspiration, without knowledge, without textual authority, without reason, without prophetic vision, without apostolic mission, without even a teacher.[84] His followers are leading simple people astray all over the world with their seductive promises. They are telling people that it is not their duty to obey man, but only God.[85] In particular, they need take no notice of what the priests of the Church tell them, for they do not necessarily have the power of binding and loosing which would enable them to remit men's sins. Only the true followers of the Apostles have that, and not all the Church's priests are true followers. Ordination confers no automatic power. No-one is bound to confess to a priest if there is a layman to hand to listen. General absolutions pronounced by bishops are valueless. All this strikes at the very foundation of the Church's authority in the world, even more directly perhaps than the Cathars' teaching.[86]

More: the Waldensians set up standards of personal morality higher than those the Church exacts. Every lie is a mortal sin, they say. In no circumstances is it right to swear an oath. It is never right to kill a man.[87] They are, in effect, separating themselves from the Church on the grounds that it is setting too low a standard; they claim to be more orthodox than the ordinary Christian, more Christian than the Church itself. While the Cathars dispute the need for the sacraments on the ground that they are intrinsically ineffective and meet no real need, the Waldensians dispute the Church's power to administer sacraments by ministers who are unworthy.[88] The appeal to the populace was perhaps much the same in both cases. The ecclesiastical monolith, the power which governed life now and life to come alike, was being challenged. There was liberation from a felt tyranny in both Cathar and Waldensian viewpoints.

3 *Against the Jews*

The Jews are a very different matter. These are not members of a new sect, but the holders of old-established positions. They attack Christianity at its foundations, not as the Cathars do, but from another angle. There is no difficulty here about the existence of two *principia*. The Jews press so hard for the existence of only one God that they will not allow the doctrine of the three Persons a foothold.[89] It is to this difference of opinion that Alan addresses himself first. Then he looks at the Jews' claim that the Mosaic Law has been in no way changed or superseded, for the commands of God can never alter. Alan tries to show that *quantum ad litteram*, as to the letter of its observance, the law is dead. Then the Jews seek to show that the Messiah has not come, and that Christ himself was not God. They will not allow that Christ was conceived by a Virgin.[90] In settling this question and its implications, Alan repeats some of the arguments he has advanced against the Cathars. He demonstrates that it was necessary for God to redeem the human race by becoming man himself and submitting to death, that Christ not only suffered to save us, but truly rose from the dead and ascended to heaven.

It is a mark of his time perhaps that Alan gives the Jews such short shrift. When Gilbert Crispin wrote the *Disputatio Judei et Christiani* on which Alan relies to the extent of several substantial borrowings,[91] he was one of the first Christian scholars of his day to hold systematic discussions with the Jews about the differences between Judaism and the Christian faith. His abbey of Westminster was being extended in the 1090s, and it may be that he came into contact with his 'Jew of Mainz' in the course of business concerned with the building work.[92] Jews and Christians appear to have been mixing socially with considerable freedom, and there are other cases of attempts at conversion: the most notable perhaps those of Petrus Alphonsus and Hermann, the Jew who wrote an account of the process of his conversion by Rupert, abbot of Deutz.[93] During the middle years of the twelfth century, Jewish scholars were sometimes consulted by Christian theologians anxious to clarify the meaning of a Hebrew word.[94] But towards the end of the century the Christian heretics attracted so much attention and appeared so much the more urgent a problem, that the Jews seem to have diminished in importance to Christian apologists, and we find Alan tucking them in after the Cathars and Waldensians almost as an afterthought.

4   *Against the Moslems*

What do the Moslems claim? They allow that Christ was conceived by the Spirit of the Virgin Mary, but they do not believe
the Spirit to be the Holy Spirit, the third Person of the Trinity,
'but rather a natural *flatus*', the breath of life we find in every
living thing, and in man himself. It was with such a 'breath' that
God breathed upon the Virgin so that she conceived.[95] If the
flatus materialis stirs the earth to life, so that plants sprout from
it, how should we wonder if a divine breath made Mary bear
Christ? This view takes away Christ's divinity, for there is then
nothing of the divine substance in him. The *flatus* is some 'inter-
mediary between God and man'.[96] Thus the Moslems, every bit
as much as the Jews, deny Christ his rightful place among the
Persons of the Trinity. Nor will they concede him his full
humanity. Because he was conceived by the breath of God he
must have been incapable of suffering, and immortal, too, they
claim.

The Moslems also see heaven in very different terms from the
Christians. In heaven the blessed will eat and drink bodily food.
In their lives on earth they maintain different practices. They see
no objection to having several wives, but on the other hand, they
object strongly to the use of images in worship; the statues in
Christian churches seem to them no better than idols. Mere
washing in water is enough, they think, for the remission of sins,
for was not Naaman the leper cured of his leprosy merely by
washing in the Jordan? Above all, they are convinced that no-one
but they and their followers are to be saved.[97]

It is, on the face of it, a little surprising to find the Moslems
treated even more briefly than the Jews. The Moslems were by
no means a sect to be regarded as thoroughly understood and to
be put on one side for the moment.[98] On the contrary, Peter the
Venerable, abbot of Cluny, had, barely half a century earlier,
made the first serious attempt to discover what they believed,[99]
and much of the lore which was in general circulation was misleading and even fantastical. Peter the Venerable had pressed
scholars travelling in Spain in search of scientific works of the
Arabs to seek out someone who could help them translate the
Koran into Latin and to make a collection of materials relating

to Moslem beliefs, so that he could inform himself how best to set about converting them. If Alan knew this collection, he made little use of it, it seems. We can only conclude that the urgency of the Cathar and Waldensian problem occupied him almost to the exclusion of the Jews and the Moslems. The Cathars and Waldensians were renegade Christians, a threat to the Christian faith from inside it. The Jews offered little in the way of a threat, after so many centuries; there were few converts from Christianity to Judaism. The Moslems were, in a sense, geographically contained. The Cathars and Waldensians were spreading like wildfire within Christendom itself.

THE GRAND VIEW

In writing an up-to-date account of the beliefs of heretics so as to set out the orthodox case against them, Alan was doing nothing new. By the 1180s or 1190s, when his four books *Contra Haereticos* were composed, there were many such treatises in existence. Peter the Venerable, abbot of Cluny, who commissioned the first Latin translation of the Koran, together with the other Moslem writings, had himself written against the Petrobrusians. Hugh of Amiens, abbot of Reading, and then bishop of Rouen, wrote three books against the heretics; Gerhoch of Reichersberg composed a treatise against two kinds of heretic.[100] Alan attempted something at once more systematic and more comprehensive. His series of four books were intended to form a *summa* when taken together.[101] He tried to avoid repetition of material which arose in connection with more than one 'heresy'. The book against the Moslems, for example, must be read in conjunction with the book against the Jews, for Alan says that what he has written against the Jews on the subject of the Trinity must suffice for the Moslems, too. In its attempt at completeness, Alan's treatise has some claim to be a forerunner of Aquinas' *Summa contra Gentiles*,[102] and also in the way it confronts the requirements of an apologetic or polemical theology. Alan never loses sight of the *impedimenta* in his systematic theology, but here they are in the forefront of his mind.

It might almost be said that Alan anticipates Aquinas directly in his classification of the two tasks of theology. Medicine, says

Aquinas, brings about health and drives out sickness. Similarly, the theologian must cater for the needs of the faithful and strive to bring them to spiritual health, and at the same time seek to drive out the spiritual sickness of heresy. Alan's treatise against the heretics has the same double purpose; he entitled it *De Fide Catholica* and its subtitle, which identifies it as a polemical work, seems to have been added later.[103]

The faithful will learn to avoid error best if they know where it lies:[104] 'We should not avoid evil if we did not know what it was'.[105] Exactly the same principle applies to the *inferior theologia,* moral theology, where we must learn to recognise those things which should put us to flight (*fuga*), that is, the vices, and those things which should draw us to choose them (*electio*), such as the virtues.[106] The *impedimenta* are to be studied, then, not only so that the apologist can counter the arguments of the heretics, but also because there is a positive benefit to the faithful in understanding where error lies.

Alan's instinct is to regard the problem of heresy as a single problem – without ignoring the substantial differences which exist between the errors of different sects. He defines a heretic in the *Two Questions on the Faith* as one who, while calling himself a Christian,[107] creates or follows a new sect, from the worst of motives: for the sake of the money he can make out of it, or to seek human favour, or for some other worldly reason.[108] There is no question in Alan's mind of honest disagreement, for a heretic like all the Devil's brood is a deceiver. The heretic deliberately misrepresents the truth as he sees it.

It was something of a commonplace among twelfth-century writers against the heretics to describe the 'novelties' of contemporary heresy. Alan draws comparisons between those *antiqua dogmata* against which the Fathers had written, and the *novae haereses* of his own day, which left contemporary scholars with a task for which the Fathers had not prepared them. It was the cumulative effect of these recent changes which led Aquinas, too, to the conclusion that it was no longer possible to proceed *contra singulorum errores* as the Fathers had done, that a comprehensive approach was now required. To put it at its simplest, the problem had grown bigger. Heretics were now disporting themselves (*debacchantes* is a favourite word of Alan's here) among the very oldest and the very newest heresies; they had all the errors of the past to add to their novelties.[109] The result has been the creation of a universal heresy.[110] It is as though the heretics had made 'one idol out of different idols, one monster out of different monsters, one common poison out of different poisonous herbs'.[111]

Will this paradoxical tendency for modern heresy to be at the same time divisive and united (for heretics form sects, not a single body) stretch to cover those who do not call themselves Christians, and who thus fall outside the terms of reference of Alan's definition? Alan describes the Cathars as *haeretici temporis nostri*;[112] the Waldensians are *haeretici* and their leader is a *haeresiarcha*,[113] but the Jews and the Moslems are not strictly heretics. They do not call themselves Christians and Alan refers to the Jews as *Judaei* as though no further comment was required. The Moslems, he tells us, are called, vulgarly, *saraceni vel pagani*.[114] Alan would not, then, want to call all the unbelievers to whom he addresses himself in the *Contra Haereticos* 'heretics'. Indeed he is hard put to it to find a generally applicable term. Aquinas speaks of the *gentiles* in the title of his *Summa contra Gentiles,* but Alan uses *gentilis* more naturally to refer to the classical authors. He says, for example, in the *Art of Preaching* that the preacher may legitimately introduce *dicta gentilium,* just as Paul sanctions the use of the sayings of the philosophers in his Epistles.[115]

There was, however, a distinction which Alan found helpful and which enabled him to group together all unbelievers for purposes of *impedimentum* theology. In a sermon addressed to priests, he separates the *populus* and the *gens*; the *gentes,* he explains, are merely 'begotten' (*geniti*). They are not distinguished by any *character*, of circumcision or baptism. A *populus,* on the other hand, is united by more than birth. A 'people' is a company of men who live in one place under a single law.[116] We may therefore speak of a *fidelis populus,* he suggests in another sermon.[117] This 'faithful people' excludes all kinds of *infideles*. If in order to write a *Summa contra Gentiles* or a *Summa contra Haereticos* it is necessary to identify a single enemy, then both Alan and Aquinas may be said to have found it in the failure of all 'unbelievers' to belong to the *fidelis populus*. Unbelievers are foreigners, non-citizens of the City of God.

There is no question, then, of Alan's having blurred the distinctions between the groups he considers. Indeed he treats each sect separately in a book of its own. He emphasises that Valdès founded a new sect,[118] and that Mahomet was the founder of a sect, too.[119] He goes to some trouble to explain how the Moslems differ from the Jews and from Christians. They agree with the Christians that one God is the creator of all things; they agree with the Jews in denying the doctrine of the Trinity.[120] They do not agree with the Jews over all points of Mosaic law, but at their own whim, as it seems to Alan, they accept some points and not others. They say that Christ was born of a Virgin, and conceived by the Spirit of God, but they do not accept that the Spirit is the third Person of the Trinity. It is rather, they believe, a *naturalis flatus,* such as is found in men and in all living things.[121] But the most important thing from the point of view of the theologian is what true heretics and other kinds of unbelievers have in common: their need to be taught the true faith.

Alan was not the only scholar of his day to try to take a whole view of the problem. Nicholas of Amiens looks east and sees the *ridiculosa Mahometi doctrina* holding sway,[122] and he surveys the Western world and sees all its parts corrupted by the presence of so many heretical sects.[123] Like Alan, he asked himself how they were all to be convinced of the truth when all they have in common is their rational minds. There is no text they will all accept as authoritative. Gilbert Crispin had already pointed out in his *Disputatio Judei et Christiani,* a seminal work of the last decade of the eleventh century, that the apologist must accept as a limitation upon the range of his arguments the fact that the Jew will accept only the authority of the Old Testament.[124] Gilbert does use New Testament authorities, but sparingly, and in his *Disputatio cum Gentili* he is obliged, as he recognises, to do without authorities altogether, for the pagan philosopher accepts no authority at all. In seeing the difficulty so clearly, Gilbert was ahead of his time. Twelfth-century authors, on the whole, kept the authorities in their arguments, for two compelling reasons. Firstly, they were uneasy about the lengths to which unbridled reason might take them or their readers, if it was not balanced by authority. Gilbert Crispin himself emphasises in the treatise on the Eucharist that there are truths which authority alone can

establish, and which cannot be supported by reason. This preference for argument by authority is particularly pronounced among
monastic writers, as distinct from those who did their work in the
open forum of the schools. Secondly, and here the heretics themselves exerted a direct influence, the popular heresies of the
Cathars and Waldensians were founded on what the orthodox
saw as misreadings of Scriptural texts. It was therefore felt to be
necessary – certainly by Alan himself – to show them their error
by meeting their texts with other texts, so that they might understand what they had misunderstood.

Peter of Blois, writer of some of the most admired letters of his
time, composed a *De Fide* in which he tried to bring together all
the textual authorities which might be used in establishing the
orthodox doctrine against the heretics.[125] Nicholas of Amiens
prefers to confine himself to reasoning for, as he says, 'It is not
enough to conquer the heretics to bring in authorities, for the
heretics of today either deny them or pervert them.'[126] Peter is
more optimistic, although as he surveys the scene he reflects sadly
upon the wickedness of heretics, who fabricate false doctrine from
motives of greed or vainglory, or out of hatred of the faith,
pretending to knowledge and leading many with them into error,
but he is sure that the best method of refuting them is to have
ready a collection of Scriptural *auctoritates, in promptum,* so
that he can meet the heretics and the Jews well-armed. To use
formal reasoning, discussing the Trinity with the aid of the arts
of the *trivium*,[127] is a mistake. Alan's *Summa* makes use of both
reasons and authorities, giving equal weight to each, and it is thus
a more comprehensive work, methodologically speaking, than
either of the others. Throughout the work he alternates *rationes*
and *auctoritates* marshalled by the heretics with the *rationes*
and *auctoritates* the Christian may employ against them. He has,
moreover, separated the reasons from the authorities, so that the
user of the handbook may conveniently find his way to whichever
form of proof he needs in dealing with a particular case.

Both Alan and Aquinas have something to say about their
mode of proceeding. Alan thought that the reason for the vitality
of the heresies in his own day was the fact that the *fides catholica*
rests not only on 'divine reasons', but also on 'human foundations'. It is, despite the liability of human institutions to collapse,

in the last resort impregnable because it is fortified by *auctoritates theologicae* and *irrefragibiles maximae*, and those earlier heretics who attacked the faith with their human reasonings could be shown, reasonably, that they were wrong. Modern heretics, however, are restrained neither by divine nor by human reasons; they let their imaginations run riot, and create monsters out of their philosophical speculations and their failure to realise that their insights are bounded by the limited perceptions of their senses.[128] In order to combat them, we must use the old authorities, certainly, but we must also fashion new arguments which will meet them on their own ground. Modern heretics are, in their foolhardiness, all the same. We have seen how, out of so many heresies, old and new, they make 'one general heresy'. There is, then, a unity in the task, but there is also great diversity, and Alan sets about combating this deceptively united front among the heretics by breaking down their beliefs into their component parts, and marshalling first reasons, then authorities against them, point by point. In an early manuscript of Book I, the copyist has marked in the margin each *oppositio hereticorum* and each *solutio magistri,* each authority, as it is brought in against them.[129]

Aquinas devotes a chapter to the question of the 'order and mode of proceeding in this work'. There is, he believes, a twofold truth of things divine, a truth which can be attained by reason, and a truth which lies beyond the reach of reason. The first is available to the apologist who wants to refute the heretics; the second is not, for all it is accessible only through faith. 'Therefore we must proceed to the demonstration of the first truth by demonstrative reasons, with which an adversary can be convinced.' He places proofs by authority in the higher category of proofs which lie beyond the reach of human reason. There is nothing to be gained by using them until the heretic has been brought round; then he may be open to conviction by such means. Therefore, 'Let us proceed from the more obvious to the less obvious which go beyond reason.'[130] If Aquinas really has the *gentilis,* the pagan, in mind, then he has no choice but to go about his task in this way. Alan's 'heretics', however, are all sects whose members are willing to accept some authorities, the Cathars that of the New Testament, the Jews that of the Old, and he proceeds accordingly, by giving first reasons and then authorities. In the main – and this is significant – he confines himself to the 'authorities' the pagans themselves have suggested and explains where they have misinterpreted them.

Alan has thus arrived at a suitable method of proceeding in disputations with heretics, on the most practical of grounds: the grounds that these techniques are likely to work. This has been the purpose of his grand stock-taking. He has been searching for the common factor which makes all heresy ultimately one, so that he can advise the missionary preacher and the scholar how best to go about the task which is indispensable if their theology is not to be one-sided: if their *expedimenta* theology is to be complemented as it should by *impedimenta* theology.

6 Making Man Anew

THE BACKGROUND

Among Thierry of Chartres' friends and pupils was a scholar much like Alan in his interests and in his cast of mind. Bernard Silvestris has been credited with commentaries on Plato's *Timaeus*, on Martianus Capella, on the first six books of Virgil's *Aeneid*,[1] and with the translation of an Arabic astrological treatise. He was a poet and teacher of rhetoric, too. Matthew of Vendôme, his pupil, calls him 'the glory of Tours, the gem of scholarship, the pride of the schools'.[2] Bernard's *Cosmographia* and his *Mathematicus,* a tale of the fate of a perfect man and his sorry experiences in the world, provided Alan with models for his own *De Planctu Naturae* and the *Anticlaudianus,* and showed him what might be done by a latter-day Martianus Capella. Calcidius on the *Timaeus,* the *Asclepius,* the *Mathesis* of Firmeus Maternus, all went into the composition of the *Cosmographia* or *De Mundi Universitate,* which was dedicated to Thierry and read before Pope Eugenius III in 1147.[3]

The *Mathematicus* tells of a splendid, upright Roman soldier, with a wife of uncommon beauty and breeding, modest and virtuous, who, blessed in everything, except that he is childless, goes to seek the advice of an astrologer. He learns that he is to have a son, but that his son will kill his father. He tells his wife that she must make sure that no child of hers is allowed to grow up, but the child which is born to her is of such beauty and has such winning ways, that he demands to be loved. He is sent away to be nursed, unknown to his father. His name is Patricida, and he represents human perfection in natural endowments, in learning, in political and military excellence. He grows up knowledgeable in all the liberal arts, and his learning is described in some detail. The rest of the story relates the unfolding of the fateful prophecy.[4]

The technical exploration of the ways in which words may have literal or 'transferred', figurative meanings reflects in miniature a universal mediaeval habit of mind: of looking for hidden meanings under the surface of the words and events of a story. Alan's readers would not have found the symbolic characters of the *Anticlaudianus* or the *Mathematicus* strange. An earlier generation would have heard St Bernard's parables, stories which he used to tell when he preached in Cistercian houses and elsewhere, in several of which the virtues and vices fight a battle for the hero's soul and rescue him from Satan.[5] In the interpretation of Scripture it had been the custom to look for allegorical meanings from the days of Origen in the third century, and before him, Philo of Alexandria, a contemporary of Paul, had attempted to explain difficult passages and apparent contradictions in the Old Testament in this way for the edification of his fellow Hellenist Jews in Alexandria.[6] The device not only served the purpose of *translatio* in getting over difficulties of exegesis. It also made it possible to see the Bible as a whole, in which every part prefigured or echoed another. In Alan's own day Joachim of Fiore was putting forward elaborate schemes of correspondences between Old Testament and New Testament figures.[7] In Alan's mind, and in that of Bernard Silvestris, the patterns of correspondence between symbolic figures and the abstract ideas for which they stand were clear and natural and entirely appropriate to the storyteller's art.

The *Cosmographia* might be regarded almost as a preface to the *Anticlaudianus*. It tells the story of Nature's first making of the man whom she is obliged to remake in the *Anticlaudianus*. Before the beginning of time, Nature approaches *Nous*, Divine Providence, to plead for Silva, the material of created life, who is longing to come into existence.[8] Accordingly, Nous creates the universe and covers the earth with animal and vegetable creation.[9] Then she instructs Nature to call together Urania (Heavenly Reason) and Physis, who are to make man.[10] Urania is responsible for his soul, and Physis for his body. Nature's task is to join body and soul together. It is an allegory of creation, set in a Neoplatonic universe, comparing the great cosmos with the little universe of man himself, the *microcosmos* of the human body and soul. The account of events in the megacosmos in Part I is complemented by the story of the fashioning of the human body or lesser universe in the second part.

The plot of the *Anticlaudianus* is considerably more complicated than that of the *Cosmographia*, but Alan's debt to Bernard is plain enough. He writes a sequel. Nature contemplates her achievement and sees what man has become. Looking at him, Nature is dissatisfied with her work. The man she made has proved a sorry disappointment. She calls a heavenly council of the Virtues to help her repair her bad workmanship by fashioning a perfect man. The Virtues are eminently realistic. Prudence (*Phronesis*), who is human wisdom, reminds Nature and her sisters that they have only limited powers. They can make a perfect body, but they cannot make a soul. Reason (*Ratio*) makes the sensible suggestion that Phronesis should travel to heaven and ask God to create a perfect soul for Nature's new Man. She designs a vehicle, and the seven Liberal Arts, daughters of Phronesis, construct it. Concordia joins the parts together and the chariot sets off for heaven, bearing Ratio and Phronesis and drawn by the five horses of the five senses.

Reason can go no further than the stars, but when they reach the borders of heaven, a guide appears, in the form of Theologia. She leads Phronesis onward, riding a single horse (the horse of hearing) into the lower heaven. There, when she sees the angels, the saints, the Virgin and Christ, and all the wonders that are there, she faints. She does not possess the power to see beyond the reach of human reason, and so she is dazed by the sight. Only Faith, sister of speculative Theologia, can revive her. She provides her with a mirror, in which she can look at heaven in reflection, and so avoid being blinded by the reality. Faith then takes Phronesis on into highest heaven, into the very presence of God. God grants her request for a soul, and asks Nous to provide an archetype.

The soul is made in the image of the archetype. Phronesis takes the soul back to earth, and nature constructs a body from the four elements. Concordia binds body and soul together. The Virtues bestow their gifts on the new man, and he proves himself in the ensuing *Psychomachia*, or battle of virtues and vices, where the Vices attack him under the leadership of the Fury Allecto, and Nature and the Virtues help him to rout them. The New Man becomes ruler of an earth restored.

This story has a number of meanings. Alan says in his Prologue that he intended it to have, like Holy Scripture, a literal sense,[11] a moral sense and an allegorical sense. The first is for simple men and boys, the second for those more advanced in the faith[12] and the third for the man who is nearer perfection.[13] He himself clearly regards the highest of these senses as the most important, the 'proper' sense, and he wants it to be protected from the gaze of the unworthy. That is why he has made it hard to find.

The only reader who will be likely to arrive at it is the man who understands the difference between the ordinary meanings of words (which are perfectly proper in their way) and the higher, theological meanings; he who does not press the senses beyond their proper bounds, who does not over-extend reason. The rules of grammar, logic and rhetoric, arithmetic, astronomy and music are all to be found in operation here, but also the laws of the heavenly science,[14] theology itself. With an arrogance founded upon his confidence that only the true theologian will appreciate the work, Alan says that he does not fear criticism, for it can come only from those who are unworthy to understand his message.

The poem, for all its secular trappings, is a theological work. There was ample precedent for Alan's confidence in the allegorical possibilities of poetry. Some lines of the sixth Book of Virgil's *Aeneid* were frequently cited as evidence that secular writers may bear witness to Christian truth in this way:

> Principio celum terras camposque liquentes...
> Spiritus alit...

Thierry of Chartres mentions them in his treatise on the six days of Creation, and the author of the commentary on the *Aeneid* refers to them, too; Alan himself quotes the same lines in his sermon on the Trinity. 'Our Virgil', says Alan, 'makes mention of the Holy Spirit.'[15] There was no objection in principle to using an ostensibly secular world-picture in a Christian allegory in the minds of many twelfth-century writers, although the Christian is, of course, in a quite different position from Virgil. He can choose to write plainly about Christian truth, or to cloak the truth in allegory.

If we ask why Alan chose this form, we can only answer that he found in poetry a vehicle for the expression of the ineffable which prose could not give him. He could not quite achieve what he wanted, but he stretches his powers of expression to the limit in the *Anticlaudianus*; he marshals a rich vocabulary: *altiloquus, ciclicus, debriare, intersigna, mollicies, obaudio, pigmeus, sacies, soporare, tenor, umbratilis, ydropicare.*[16] If he occasionally makes himself almost incomprehensible, that is because he is trying so hard to make the most of the licence poetry gives him to exploit all the figurative possibilities of language. Here is part of the description of Logica, in which, if we look at it in the Latin, the strain on his resources can clearly be seen.

> Cur decurtati species nascatur elenchi,
> Quando vel afferesis vel sincopa curtat elenchum;
> Qualiter, usurpans vires et robur elenchi,
> Singula percurrit inductio, colligit omne,
> Sed tamen inferior sese summittit elenche.[17]

THE COSMOS

In the *Cosmographia* Bernard Silvestris describes how Physis constructs the human body. Out of the four elements she fashions the human constitution, so as to make each man's nature conform to the elements from which it is made. In the perfect man she sets these elements or humours in balance, so that he will be neither too choleric nor too melancholy, neither too volatile nor too phlegmatic. When she has the material properly adjusted, she divides the lump into three parts, so as to make head, breast and loins.[18] Physis knew what to do because she had looked for a model in the structure of the universe. 'Physis knew that she would not make a mistake in creating the lesser universe of man if she took as her pattern the structure of the greater universe.'[19] For example, a man ought to have a head to rule his body, just as the Godhead rules and disposes the 'body' of the universe.

It was something new for mediaeval scholars to see the universe in this way. It is not without significance that astronomy was for many centuries the most neglected of the little-studied *quadrivium* subjects, and that Boethius' *Astronomia*, if he ever completed it, was lost. In the earlier Middle Ages, cosmology was not a matter of much interest except to the computists. Bede wrote treatises on time and *On the Nature of Things*, whose primary purpose is to teach the reader how to equip himself to calculate the date of Easter, rather than encourage him to speculate about the structure of the universe.[20] In the twelfth century, with the rediscovery of Ptolemy's *Almagest,* in the far more speculative climate of the day, cosmology took on a fresh interest.

Parallel with the study of the physical universe which became popular now, lay another interest which seems to have revived in the twelfth century: in the notion of hierarchy. This owed a great deal to the work of the fifth century Pseudo-Dionysius, which had inspired John Scotus Eriugena's scheme of a hierarchy of natures.[21] It is not, strictly, an astronomical system, but it can without undue difficulty be married with the astronomical scheme, the angelic orders allotted a sphere each, and the precise mathematical relationship of one sphere to another worked out in harmonic proportions. Dante was to celebrate such a marriage at its most splendid in the *Divina Commedia*.

As astronomy and the philosophical and mystical systems of Pseudo-Dionysius, the *Timaeus*, Martianus Capella's *De Nuptiis Philologiae et Mercurii*, Macrobius' *Commentary on the Dream of Scipio* were brought together in the twelfth century, so a *philosophia mundi* evolved. Honorius Augustodunensis' *Clavis Physicae* was one of the first attempts to write about the universe in this way. Thierry of Chartres tried to reconcile the *Timaeus* and the Genesis account of creation in his book on the 'Six Days'. Bernardus wrote his *Cosmographia*.[22] The cosmos was mapped.

Thierry's discussions are concerned with the *minutiae* of the discrepancies between Plato and Scripture, not with a grand new view of the universe. The new picture of the cosmos inched its way into existence, as comparisons were drawn between texts. It was indeed not entirely new, but rather a change of emphasis. The idea of placing man as a microcosm within the macrocosm was encouraged by Macrobius's remarks on the littleness of man in the universe, in his commentary on the *Somnium Scipionis*. The picture of the human soul descending from its natural heavenly habitat into the body – a neoplatonic commonplace – is in the *Asclepius*, and we have seen something of what twelfth-century authors made of it. Virgil has something to say on the matter, too. In Bernard's commentary on the *Aeneid*, Book VI, the author moves from allegorical interpretation to word-by-word commentary because this, he thinks, is the book in which Virgil is at his most philosophical. The *descensus ad inferos*, Virgil's descent into hell, is said by professors of theology to be nothing less than this descent of the soul into the body.[23] With the aid of philosophical speculation – as the *Asclepius* teaches – the soul may raise itself up to contemplation of the heights from which it came, and thus return to heaven. The study of the universe and especially of the heavens, is thus an antidote to the *malitia* which weakens all human nature because of man's bodily condition. From the *Asclepius*, too, Bernard drew ideas about the relations of macrocosm and microcosm, which encourage him to take the view that Physis could not go wrong in taking the cosmos for her pattern when she set about making man.[24]

THE BODY PUBLIC

Another comparison between the human body and that larger organization of things within which the human body itself has a place, was being developed in the twelfth century: the analogy between the body of a man and a body of people, where each member has a proper place and function. The image is found everywhere in the Pauline Epistles. St Paul describes the faithful Christian as a member of the body of Christ.[25] There, he has a place and function allotted him by God, and it would be as absurd for him to try to change it as it would be for the foot to try to behave like the ear, or the eye like the shoulder. He exists to serve the good of the whole body of Christians, the *congregatio fidelium*, the *universitas fidelium*.

This picture of the individual as an inseparable part of a whole, provided an apt analogy when mediaeval writers began to think about the secular community. It proved adaptable in exactly the ways which were needed. John of Salisbury explores its possibilities in the *Policraticus,* drawing, he says, upon a work of Plutarch's, the *Institutio Trajani,* in which Plutarch compares the *res publica* to a body. The head of the republic, the prince, is like the bodily head, subject to God alone; the senate is like the heart, from which proceed good and evil impulses; the eyes and ears and tongue do the work of judges and provincial governors; officials and soldiers are the hands; the feet are the agricultural labourers.[26] It was not difficult by means of this analogy to establish the importance of the whole body's welfare in comparison with that of the individual, and to show that the individual was valuable insofar as he served the community.[27] It was equally plain that just as the head, the seat of reason, controlled the body, so the ruler rightly controls the community.[28] John of Salisbury's classical authority gives him all the assistance he needs in developing the Pauline analogy to make it fit the civil community, but no doubt the image was acceptable principally because it was familiar from Scripture. That gave it a force it might not otherwise have had, for analogy is a notoriously debatable method of 'proof'. The notion of the individual as part of a larger organism, however readily it fitted the secular community, was never to be entirely separated from its Scriptural associations in mediaeval writers.

The habit of most mediaeval scholars was to look for consensus everywhere in their reading, and when they found discrepancy they tried to mend it. The effrontery of Peter Abelard's *Sic et Non* lay in his challenge to the assumption that any discrepancy among the authorities could be explained away if the text was studied carefully enough. Once the idea of comparing the body of the faithful with the secular or public body, the microcosm of the individual with the macrocosm, became current, more and more authors were brought in to provide material for comparisons and extensions. That is what has happened in the composition of Bernard's *Cosmographia* and Alan of Lille's *Anticlaudianus*. Biblical and secular sources could be shown to work together magnificently here, by the exercise of a little poetical ingenuity.

Augustine had held that society is nothing more than the sum of the individuals who compose it; it has no independent existence as a body in its own right. Things looked rather different in the twelfth century. The public authority or government was a force to be reckoned with;[29] more, it was interesting to scholars as a subject of study. Masters like Peter the Chanter did not confine themselves to the schoolroom. They tried to make their learning relevant to the needs of men in the world.[30] It is not without significance that the new schools throve in urban centres where there was business to be done, and not in monastic seclusion. Bernard of Clairvaux admonishes his Cistercian protegé Eugenius

III for giving too much time and energy to the hearing of litiga-
tion, but he himself was obliged to live very much in the world.[31]
The first book of his *De Consideratione* describes graphically how
much of the rush of business in the papal court was being initiated
and conducted by men whose only interest was to get themselves
into the public eye.

The energies of some of the best minds of the day were going,
not into the cultivation of inward and private virtues, but into the
outward activities which define a man's place in the world of
commerce and law and civic government. But the effort to
'locate' man in the universe encouraged much scholarly industry
designed to 'place' him minutely within his family, his village, his
city, his kingdom, too, as well as within the Church; and to show
how all these 'placings' displayed similar characteristics, how the
pattern of microcosm-in-macrocosm was to be found everywhere.[32]

When technical terminology is relatively undeveloped and
abstract ideas have not yet been clearly formulated, pictures are
helpful. The organological analogy is a picture. It lends itself to
the poet's colouring better than to philosophical analysis. The
heart of man, says Bernard in Chapter 14 of the *Microcosmos*, is
the animating spark, the king, governor, creator, 'It is a noble
lord, journeying about through all the kingdom of the body, to
the limbs and the senses as they administer, and it sustains each
of them in the task assigned to it... Its royal palace and imperial
throne is in the breast.'[33] John of Salisbury, too, is attracted into
figurative by-ways; he exploits all his resources of Scriptural
and classical illustrations, in his attempt to make his image of the
state clear and convincing. The *Policraticus* is something new in
prose, just as the *Cosmographia* and the *Anticlaudianus* are
something new in verse. John even coined a new word for his
title.[34]

Perhaps the most striking indication of the familiarity the
'body public' idea achieved in the twelfth century is Alan's choice
of the *res publica* as a model to help his readers understand how
the universe works in the *De Planctu Naturae*. To compare the
body public or the universe with the human body is one thing;
everyone understands how the parts of his body serve one
another's needs; but to compare the universe with the kingdom or
other secular community argues a ready comprehension of these

nascent 'political' theories on the part of Alan's readers. First the motion of the planets is compared with opposing armies:

Just as the army of the planets opposes with contrary motion the fixed rolling of the firmament, so in man is found a continual hostility between lust and reason.

Reason, which comes from heaven, turns towards heaven when it concentrates upon heavenly things. The activities of lust draw man the opposite way, into wilfulness and waywardness, and make him move the opposite way to the firmament of reason, so that he turns and slips down into the declivity of earthly things. Next, man is compared to a foreigner or stranger, who lives on the outskirts of the universe like the inhabitant of the suburbs of a city. In the universe 'as in a great city', order is established by the control of the government. The heavens are like the citadel of a human city, where the ruler lives; the air above the earth is like the middle of the city, where the heavenly army of angels does its work of administration. Man, the foreigner, lives in the suburbs. The ruler rules; the angel administers; man is ruled. The comparison can be made threefold, extended to man himself, whose head is his citadel of wisdom, his heart the seat of his magnanimity, his loins, like outlying districts, given over to pleasures not fitting for the members of the city. Man may also be compared with the universe. The sun's heat is like the warmth of the heart; the moon, mother of humours, like the liver, from which the humours of the body arise; the changing seasons are like the ages of man. Microcosm and macrocosm, man, universe, city, are all one.[35] Man is so fully set in context that he can only be understood properly by the study of the context in which he lives, and Alan accordingly sets out parallels between universe, the body public and the human body.

THE NEW MAN

There is little of what we should now recognise as 'humanity' in this man; he is entirely a symbolic being. The words *humanitas, personalitas, individualitas* were the subject of great interest in the twelfth century, but they were discussed largely in abstract terms. It was, for example, a matter of debate whether it was the possession of a body which made a man human, as St Paul seems to be suggesting in Romans 6.19 (*humanum dico propter infirmitatem carnis vestrae*).[36]

When Otto of Freising discusses the nature of 'humanity' as it affects the course of history he considers *personalitas* and *individualitas*, and he hits upon a new view of the historical process as something in which the actions of the individual may have a conspicuous effect.[37] Yet, historian though he was, Otto has the twelfth-century scholar's habit of thinking in philosophical terms. The highly abstract nature of his conception of *humanitas* and *individualitas* is clear enough if we look at Otto's finer distinctions: 'the individual and the single are not interchangeable', he says, 'for every individual is single, but not every single thing is an individual'.[38] The term *humanitas* has not yet acquired the associations which allow us to call a man 'humane'; nor can we yet move from *individualitas* to 'individualist', from *personalitas* to the notion of having a distinctive personality or character, in the modern sense. Otto's 'individual' is not far removed from Boethius or Porphyry,[39] an element in dialectic, a mere notion, not a man.

If we contrast with this Thomas Browne's consoling words *To a friend upon occasion of the death of his intimate friend* in the seventeenth century, it is clear how far the idea of human individuality still had to go in Otto's day. 'So intrinsical is man unto himself', says Browne, that 'Some doubt may be made, whether any would exchange his Being, or substantially become another Man.'[40] These are not twelfth-century sentiments. In the twelfth century the generality is still present in the particular, the type in the individual. We still find that concern with the ideal which characterises earlier descriptions of saints and princes. The interest in the individual gave a new depth and roundness to the rather two-dimensional sketches of eleventh-century hagiographers, but the most urgent need was to define the perfect man. The 'renaissance'[41] prince[42] figures in the literature of the day, but he is an ideal not an actual man. The principal reason for this perhaps is that twelfth-century thinking about human perfection is predominantly academic, in its philosopher's concern with abstractions especially.

For all their inventiveness and adventurousness, the scholars of the day questioned the old authorities reverently, on the whole, expecting to find that the points which troubled them were points at which they had misunderstood the author's meaning. They rarely challenged the fundamental assumptions which underlie the old teaching, as thinkers of later generations were to do. They did not question whether man is indeed a sinful being, at present far from perfect. There is no sign yet of the great change which had taken place by the time Alexander Pope wrote his *Essay on Man*:

> Then say not man's imperfect, Heaven in fault;
> Say, rather, man's as perfect as he ought.[43]

A number of fundamental questions about the nature and way of life of the perfect man had been asked by theologians from the first Christian centuries. The questions implied in Pope's brisk resolution of the difficulty were not new to scholars of the eleventh and twelfth centuries, but they saw them in a fresh light. The air of all these discussions of man, like so much of the thought of the day, has the peculiar freshness which it gains from the very juxtaposition of the old and familiar with the adventurous and new. Whether they were writing about the individual or about the ideal, or about the perfect man in whom both are fully realised, contemporary scholars were able to draw on a considerable literature, and they rarely attempt to express a new view without making copious reference to the old, and setting it carefully in context. These habits bred in them by their scholarly training give a flavour to their reflections which we shall not find in Pope and his contemporaries. It is the flavour of the schoolroom, but it is something more. A real, pioneering theological investigation was going on into the question of the *perfectus homo*.

It has been suggested that the discussion of the topic in the schools was largely prompted by Boethius' treatment of the humanity of Christ in the *Contra Eutychen*.[44] It clearly lies behind Otto of Freising's analysis. In some scholars' hands, this, together with Boethius' other *opuscula sacra*, gave rise to the kind of controversial discussion which brought men to trial for heresy,[45] but it also encouraged the development of techniques of intensive analysis which went beyond the traditional methods of Scriptural exposition by reference to patristic authority, which earlier scholars chiefly favoured. The study of Boethius' theological tractates made even those scholars who were especially well-versed in the liberal arts think hard. The very limitations and restrictions of approach and method against which they laboured so vigorously struck sparks from their minds.

In the *Contra Eutychen* Boethius tries to meet the objections of Eutyches and Nestorius to the orthodox doctrine that in Christ there were two natures, human and divine, in a single person. He asks what exactly we mean by 'nature' and 'person', and how the two components together make up man. He makes use of the term *humanitas*, although with little of the range of associations *humanitas* has had in Cicero, or even Cassian or Augustine – and as the term came to have in our own word 'humanity'.[46] Thierry and his pupils were looking for something philosophically more restricted in their exploration of Boethius' term. What do we mean when we say that man is 'human'? they ask, and they answer in the most austere of terms by defining 'humanity' as that which all men have in common;[47] indeed, it is the 'one thing' all men have in common.[48] The difficulty lies in showing how this may be; now, although a man is not humanity,[49] humanity is the essence of man.[50]

In Gilbert of Poitiers' commentaries the discussion is no less technical. Gilbert was famous for his unwillingness to simplify his teaching for beginners.[51] Everything turns on the application of Aristotelian teaching on *genus* and *species* and *differentia* (and of the laws of the philosophy of language of the day) to a theological problem. It has little to do explicitly with the concept of the perfect man, but it has a good deal to do with it implicitly – indeed it is indispensable to twelfth-century thinking on the subject to try to understand by such means what is the essence of man, the *humanitas*, which must in some sense be distilled in the perfect man. The study of the *Contra Eutychen* suggested one means of approach, and an eminently satisfactory one to scholars who liked to wrestle with a subject, to find it difficult, to feel that they had won an intellectual battle when they arrived at a working solution. The twelfth-century study of *perfectus homo* was firstly theological, and its 'theological' direction was laid down by the study of the liberal arts. One of the values of

Bernard Silvestris' *Mathematicus* lies in the illustration it provides of the place the study of the liberal arts was coming to occupy in the minds of twelfth-century scholars.[52] Even a *perfectus homo* sprung from knightly stock, whose future prowess is to be largely on the battlefield, is credited with a knowledge of the *artes*. From the eleventh century it is common for the lives of saints to include some reference to the outstanding performance of their subjects in the liberal arts[53] – even though they are usually reported to have given up such studies in order to devote themselves to *lectio divina*.

Into this context of increasingly technical theological speculation we must put the familiar questions of earlier Biblical exegesis, the question which arose from the study of Genesis in particular, for Genesis was a great focus of interest in the twelfth century as it is in every scientifically-minded age.

Did God create perfect man in Adam? If so, how was it possible for him to fall? Can it be God's fault that he fell, because he failed to make Adam perfect? How could a perfectly good and all-powerful God create a being with so tragic a flaw? And what are we to say of the state of man now? Did the redeeming work of Christ restore him to the condition of unfallen Adam? In that case, why is there so much sin in the world? Perhaps, some suggested, Adam was created with, as it were, a perfection not fully realised, a potential for perfection. Could he, then, achieve perfection by his own unaided efforts, or did he need the help of divine grace? One question follows from another. These questions are directly prompted by an examination of the teaching of Genesis. Underlying them are ancient paradoxes and classical problems of theology and philosophy: the problem of evil, the paradox of perfection apparently giving rise to imperfection.

In the face of man's obvious present imperfection, who are we to blame? Is 'Heaven in fault'? We must look beyond the Middle Ages here: Pope suggests an answer. Man is not imperfect, but exactly what he was meant to be, a creature of limited powers, to whom limited aspirations are appropriate:

> His knowledge measured to his state and place;
> His time a moment and a point his space.[54]

Some of the ancient problems could be set aside in this way in the eighteenth century, but Pope's mediaeval predecessors could not avoid them so easily. When they asked themselves what man was created for, they looked for an answer in different terms. In their view of things, the whole universe awaited the perfecting of a certain number of human beings, who were to take the place of the fallen angels in the heavenly city (as well as the places already allocated to mankind in his own right, before the angels fell, some said). The end of the world and of time could then take place, and eternity begin. At another level, we might answer the question as St Bernard does, in the *De Diligendo Deo*, by saying that man was made to love God, and that the business of his life is to grow as close to God in love as the limitations of his nature permit.[55] Such perfect beings must have more of heaven in them than Pope allows, and his argument that the ills of mankind have proceeded largely from excessive aspirations after higher things would have been quite unacceptable to mediaeval scholars. All their habits of thought, all the assumptions with which they approached their reading, encouraged them to look to a perfection of the very highest in man.

The wealth of both tradition and innovation in the theological background is impressive, but it has received little attention in the study of perhaps the most adventurous attempt of the twelfth century to describe the perfect man and the task he ought to carry out (his *officium*): Alan's *Anticlaudianus*. It has been suggested that the poem is a *Summa de Virtutibus et Vitiis*, a *Psychomachia*, an epic poem of adventure and warrior prowess, a scholastic treatise in verse, an allegory.[56] It is all these things, but it also is a most audacious piece of theology.

A THEOLOGICAL EXPERIMENT

P. G. Walsh remarks that Alan 'promotes an unorthodox doctrine' in the *Anticlaudianus* 'which fascinated the imagination of many twelfth century intellectuals'.[57] This he identifies as a kind of millenarianism, the prospect of a golden age on earth, with which the poem ends. Only in passing does he comment on the fact that 'the notion of the perfect man regarded literally runs into difficulties with the doctrine of original sin'.[58] This is the crux of the matter. In the *Anticlaudianus* Alan describes Nature's plan to redeem her earlier failures by fashioning a perfect man, who will have no cause to reproach her for any shortcomings in her work. He will not fall victim to temptation; he will show that it is possible for a man to live a perfect life. The vices will be conquered, and mankind will return to the state of Adam before the Fall. Alan thus puts forward a scheme for the 'redemption' of mankind which amounts to an alternative to the Incarnation.

In the thirteenth century, the French adaptation of the poem by Ellebaut tries to put this dubious theology right by making the 'perfect man' Christ himself. This, as Ellebaut's editor points out, is 'an extremely free adaptation, not a translation',[59] and his version is certainly not what Alan intended. Ellebaut inserts passages describing the incarnation of Christ through a virgin; the angels figure largely in the poem, and there are explicit Scriptural references, all of which are conspicuously absent from Alan's original. Alan himself mentions Christ only briefly,[60] and as a quite distinct being from the *perfectus homo*. Yet he himself firmly believed that Christ was supremely and solely the Perfect Man. He berates the heretics of the twelfth century who believe that Christ was not a real man, but a *phantasticus homo*, only apparently a man.[61] So far was Christ really man, he argues, that he assumed with his humanity all the defects of human nature (*defectus humanae naturae*) except *ignorantia* and *peccatum*. It was only fitting (*decuit*) that he should assume our limitations if he was to free us from them.[62] There can, then, be no question of Alan's intending to take up a heretical position in the *Anticlaudianus*.

He makes, in fact, rather modest claims for his hero.[63] Alan's perfect man is a work of Nature, but Nature and her sisters have to ask for God's help because she cannot give him the soul which is the essential component of manhood. Alan emphasises on several occasions that no-one but God can create a soul.[64] Nature must work even in her humbler role of maker of his body, with the materials God has created *ex nihilo*, and given her to work with:

Divinum creat ex nichilo, Natura caduca Procreat ex aliquo.[65]

The Divine creates from nothing; fallen Nature procreates from something.

In his *Sermon on the Holy Spirit* Alan explains that 'Nature, so to speak, makes everything, but she does not perfect anything; she procreates but she does not create or fill; to the Holy Spirit alone does it belong to perfect, create, fill.'[66] In the *Anticlaudianus* man's present imperfection is not ascribed to any fault on the part of 'Heaven'. It is seen as the result of Nature's incompetence.[67] Nature concedes, in her long opening speech, that there is nothing among her works which has not a right to accuse her and her sisters of some fault in its making. Alan's hero is to be the only perfect work of Nature. Nature is, as a rule, only too subject to error. Nevertheless, this new being is to be what man ought to have been if Adam had not sinned. He is man before the Fall. He is free of the taint of original sin, because he is not of the stock of Adam.

Alan takes a bold step in suggesting that God would approve, or even countenance, the making of such a man. Anselm had argued two generations earlier, in the *Cur Deus Homo,* that if God had made new human beings who were not of the stock of Adam – as he certainly could have done – he would have conceded defeat at Satan's hands. His original plan for Adam and his progeny would have been thwarted. 'For the human race, so precious a work of his, would have perished entirely, and it was not fitting that what God had planned concerning man should be altogether wiped out; nor could his plan be put into effect unless the race of men were liberated by the Creator himself.'[68] Alan's proposed alternative is therefore a topic of some philosophical and theological daring, and one which he himself would appear to reject in the *Contra Haereticos*: 'For it was fitting that just as the human race was lost through a man, so its redemption should be brought about by a man...but a mere man could not redeem; for if he had been a mere man, he would have been infected with the corruption of human nature.'[69] If Alan's scheme in the *Anticlaudianus* provides an acceptable alternative, then the Incarnation was not the absolute necessity which Anselm argues that it was. Nature herself could have saved mankind.

Alan makes God a willing enough participant in the plan. In Ellebaut's version, Prudence intercedes with God on behalf of man, and begs him to save mankind. God grants her request, and proposes that the Perfect Man shall be born of a Virgin; he sets out, in some detail, the plan of the Incarnation. In Alan's version, the emphasis is significantly different. The plan is put by Reason, and her suggestion is not the same as that of Ellebaut's Prudence. 'Reason', God says, 'has already put it to me that I should...bless the world with the divine presence (*numen*) of a heavenly man.'[70] This *celestis homo* is not Christ, but the being on whom Nature, with Prudence, Reason, Concord, Plenty, Youth, Laughter, Temperance, Moderation and all her other sisters, proposes to confer every gift, and for whom they request God to give them a soul of matching perfection. He is not God made man, although Alan consistently describes him as *divinus homo*. He is in some other manner a 'heavenly man', a man whose perfection of nature is completed by the gift of a soul more perfect than other human souls, but still a merely human soul. Thus Alan conforms with Christian orthodoxy up to a point by making his power to withstand the vices and live a perfect human life come from God, not from Nature or from within himself. It is a gift of grace. The redemption this man is to confer on the rest of mankind by proving that it is possible for man to live perfectly, is, indirectly, the work of God, but it is not a redemption brought about by God's becoming himself that perfect man.

In the years between Anselm's writing of the *Cur Deus Homo* and Alan's composition of the *Anticlaudianus* there had been a shift of emphasis among scholars. The view that the Incarnation was necessary, because it was the only possible way for God to redeem the world which was entirely in keeping with his power and his goodness, had given way in Peter Abelard to the view that Christ became man principally to demonstrate that it was possible to live a perfect human life. Christ came, in other words, to set an example.[71] Alan's allegory appears less startling when it is set against this background. His hero is to set an example to the rest of mankind. The redeeming act is to show that sin need not be triumphant over humanity, but Alan's hero is simply and solely man.

He sets an example of a unique kind, however, in reflecting something of God which man has not been able to show since the Fall, except while Jesus was on earth among men. He is a man in whom Nature and her sisters are mirrored,[72] but also the God in whose image and likeness man was made.[73] In this mirror other men may learn what human nature ought to be, rather as Alan himself says in his *Art of Preaching* that man may see his condition, in the mirror of Scripture, his wretchedness in the mirror of creation, his guilt in the mirror of Nature.[74] In his *De Incarnatione Christi* he suggests that everything in the created world is a book or a picture or a mirror for man, in which he may behold his own condition:

Omnis mundi creatura	Every creature in the world
Quasi liber, et pictura	Is like a book and a picture
Nobis est, et speculum.	To us, and a mirror.
Nostrae vitae, nostrae mortis,	A faithful representation
Nostrae status, nostrae sortis.	Of our life, our death,
Fidele signaculum.	Our condition, our end.[75]

The mirror of creation, full of Nature's errors, damaged by Adam's Fall, shows man only the horrors of his state. In the mirror of this man he will see Nature and her sisters at their best; he will see what will give him hope and inspiration. He will see perfection mirrored, not imperfection, and thus, in the limited way in which He can be reflected in creation, he will see God mirrored.

Alan's choice of a poetical form as a vehicle for this curious piece of theology cannot be without significance. He was master of a vast range of *genres* of composition, as his surviving works amply demonstrate, and he deliberately fixed on this one for his purposes here. Perhaps he was anxious to cloak the audacity of his theological innovation a little. He deliberately makes it far from easy for his readers to follow him, by choosing uncommon words, and by elaborating his conceits. The literal sense of the poem will, he promises, please the ears of boys (*puerilem demulcebit auditum*) and the moral sense will inspire those who are trying to make themselves perfect (*perficientem imbuet sensum*), but the greater subtlety of the allegorical sense will make the understanding of the advanced student more acute. Only the reader who is prepared to wrestle with the technicalities of the liberal arts in the poem, the hard theology, will really understand it. The work is to be approached by a narrow way, and only those who are ambitious to grasp what is above the heavens (*intuitum supercelestium...audent attollere*)[76] will derive full benefit from reading it. This, in Boethian terms, is exactly the difficulty theology ought to put in the way of the idle and unworthy.

He puts difficulties in his own way. The form he chooses is a far from convenient vehicle for his thoughts, and it is doubtful whether it would have allowed him to express himself quite clearly even if that had been his wish. Yet he contends with the problems it raises, because it allows him to dress up his hypothesis of an alternative redemption in colourful robes, to juxtapose a variety of ideas current in his day, to bring the notion forward for inspection in a bright dress, and thus to stimulate his readers to think afresh.

Why did he choose to put forward, even in allegory, a view at variance with the principle that Christ is the Perfect Man – and at variance with it in such signal ways? We know that he had no quarrel with the doctrine of the Incarnation. Perhaps there is an element of sheer intellectual curiosity in the attempt to explore the possibility that a perfect man might be created who was not Christ, and not Adam, not even of the stock of Adam – a fresh start embodied in a new creation. That is exactly what his hero is.

This is, above all, a poem of ideas. But Alan's ideas are theological rather than philosophical; that is to say, they carry with them the baggage of associations and the many devotional and spiritual dimensions which distinguish such ideas from more strictly philosophical problems. The form he chose had the advantage for his purposes of allowing him to treat ideas associatively in ways to which poetical images lend themselves. What he has to say in the *Anticlaudianus* provides a framework for a discussion of the state of contemporary thinking on the subject of the perfect man. The *Anticlaudianus* was written in the 1180s, when many of the stirrings of new ideas of the earlier part of the century had become more settled patterns of thought among scholars. Alan gives us his new, challenging idea, in terms he and the scholars of his day could grasp readily, because they were familiar. He brings together traditional and new ideas, and tries to describe a man who is more than a type, and at the same time more than an individual (he has none of the quirks and peculiarities and *differentia* which make Peter different from Paul), but he is less than Christ. He is human perfection without being also divine. He is not God but entirely man, where Christ is both fully God and fully man. He is *purus homo* made a redeemer.

THE ACHIEVEMENT OF PERFECTION

A poem like the *Anticlaudianus,* in which the philosophical content is heavily overlaid by plot and imagery, is not perhaps the place for a discussion of the nature of perfection.[77] Certainly Alan seems to have thought so, but Peter Lombard provides a distinction in his *Sentences* which may have been in Alan's mind as he wrote. Peter Lombard distinguishes between a temporal perfection (the perfection of created nature), the perfection which nature has when grace works on it[78] and the perfection which belongs to God alone.[79] Alan's hero is to have the second perfection, the perfection of nature raised to its greatest heights. He is to have all the perfections of twelfth-century thought, for example: the perfection of completeness (Anselm's favourite sense of the term); the perfection of being perfectly fitted for his work; the perfection of sinlessness. As Fortune says, he does not need her gifts, for what can chance do when nothing in him is subject to chance?[80] He cannot fail because nothing is lacking for his success. To borrow a definition which became a standard one (Aquinas makes use of it) that which 'attains its proper end, which is its ultimate perfection',[81] may be said to be perfect. Alan's *perfectus homo* fulfils perfectly the purpose for which he was brought into being.

According to Genesis, God made man in his own image and likeness.[82] When Alan described his perfect man as *divinus homo* he had in mind the principle that the perfect man must be as like his divine original as possible, but his choice of a poetical vehicle for his description allowed him to avoid entering fully into the conventional discussions which engaged other twelfth-century scholars. Hugh of St Victor, a generation earlier, asked whether the image and likeness of God resides in man's soul alone, or in the body, too. He concludes that bodily nature[83] is incapable of imitating the divine nature[84] and so the likeness is[85] in the soul alone. Hugh's contemporary, the Benedictine scholar Rupert of Deutz, also asks in what sense man may be said to be made in the image of God. It cannot, he argues, be merely a matter of 'living'; even beasts are living things. Nor can it be a matter of being rational; even wicked men and devils are reasonable beings, and they cannot be said to be like God, but the holy and righteous are like God; these qualities belong to the sons of God alone.[86]

For his own purposes, Alan needs to make only one thing clear. Perfect man (like all men) is made up of body and soul, and it is in his soul that he is godlike. His soul belongs to heaven, his body to earth. On earth he will be human; among the stars he will be divine:[87] and so he will be both man and God. In this way, the roles of God and of Nature in making the perfect man are kept quite distinct, and Alan is able to concentrate upon the work of Nature, where the greater part of the traditional literature confines itself to the work of God in creation. In this he was attempting something not entirely original, for Thierry of Chartres and others before him had attempted to set science and Genesis side by side and to reconcile their two accounts of creation; the originality of Alan's approach is that it allows him, within the confines of the literary *genre* he has chosen, to examine what we might call the 'natural causes' of perfection in man. He considers, with only the barest nod to Genesis, what goes into the making of a perfect man, and in order to do this he has to distinguish the two principal components: body and soul. This composite, dual nature of man is a sustained theme of the poem.

It is a common theme in other writers, too. Peter Lombard points to the *duplex natura* the twofold nature of body and spirit, which distinguishes mankind.[88] Alan speaks of the twofold being of man,[89] but Alan's emphasis is different. It is not making the distinction, but in the use he puts it to, that his thinking is his own. He explores the implications of this compositeness. Body and soul themselves are composite, for nothing is truly *simplex* but God himself. In the *Anticlaudianus* God asks Nous to prepare an exemplar, an ideal pattern for the soul,[90] which may serve as a model for the forming of a spirit rich in every gift of virtue. Nous brings together the beauty of Joseph, the wisdom of Judith, the patience of Job, and so on.[91] In making the body of the perfect man, Nature, too selects her materials (this time from the four elements) and then mingles and shapes them. Honorius Augustodunensis describes the process briefly and prosaically,[92] Alan more exuberantly, as he explains how Nature separates her materials from the body of formless matter, then brings together again what she has separated, and forms it into the body of a man.[93]

So mixed a thing is man that we may even speak of the process of 'joining' body and soul together. As a rule, Reason claims in the *Anticlaudianus,* she unites body and soul, or the soul would refuse to stay in the body, and would return to its own proper sphere.[94] In the case of perfect man, Concord joins them in a bond of peace,[95] and there is no battle of flesh and spirit.[96] The two parts of man are in perfect balance. If there were no soul, man would be a mere animal. If there were no body, he would be an angel or a devil. Alan describes the sequence of uniting the component parts of man graphically. An almost mechanical process of manufacture goes into the making of his *perfectus homo.*

It should perhaps be noted in passing that Alan's perfect man, like Adam, stands for perfect woman, too. Twelfth-century discussions of Adam include Eve, implicitly. Abelard explains in his commentary on Romans that 'Adam', like *homo,* is a name used commonly for both men and women.[97] Alan has, nevertheless, something to say about the Virgin's exemplification of perfect womanhood. For Alan, as for Newman, 'Mary...is a specimen, and more than a specimen, in the purity of her soul and body, of what man was before his fall, and what he would have been, had he risen to his full perfection.'[98] Alan describes Mary as the daughter who brings about the rebirth of her mother Eve, who restores woman to what she was before the Fall, and in whom woman as she ought to have been, perfect woman, is exemplified,[99] but he gives no more prominence to Mary in the poem than he gives to her Son, and for the most part the *perfectus homo* of the *Anticlaudianus* is taken to represent the perfection of both sexes simultaneously.

Let us return to the perfect man. What of his dwelling-place? Here again, Alan's scheme obliges him to be unconventional. Adam was first given a home in paradise, but he was intended for heaven. As Peter Lombard says, Genesis relates that he was created outside paradise and then put into it;[100] he was not created within it because it was not to be his eternal home. He was not to remain there (*permansurus*).[101] This raises, for Alan and his contemporaries, a question whose answer Peter Lombard says that it is useful to know, even though it is often asked out of mere curiosity. If Adam was not to remain in paradise for ever, how was he to be transferred from his first home to heaven? What was to be the end of his *inferior vita* and what the mode of his *transitus ad superiorem*?[102] On the basis of their reading of Augustine, Peter Lombard and others suggest that Adam was in some way both mortal and immortal before the Fall. If he did not sin, he would not die; if he sinned he would die. The choice was his own. Philip of Havelberg says that if he had behaved well, in due time 'without the intervention of death, he would have been carried into the company of the angels'.[103]

All this implies that there was a potential rather than a fully realised perfection in unfallen Adam. Honorius Augustodunensis tries to answer the question, 'Why did not God make him perfect and incapable of sin in the beginning?' There is, he says, greater merit in the harder way.[104] Hugh of St Victor argues in his *De Sacramentis* that God cannot have made man imperfect;[105] yet it is not until after the resurrection from the dead that man will be perfectly (*perfecte*) free from both sin and the penalty of sin.[106] Adam's perfection was not inevitable. Like formless matter in Thierry of Chartres' commentary on Boethius, he had the potential to become different things, for 'possibility is the capacity for receiving different conditions'.[107] The possibility of perfection is only one among them.

In his *Complaint of Nature*, Alan sees the two principal possibilities still open to man after the Fall, in terms of one of his favourite images: sensuality leads the human mind to fall into vice; reason leads it towards virtue. The one turns a man into a beast; the other transfigures him *potentialiter* into a God.[108] Peter the Chanter describes the result. If a man behaves as though he were no more than a body, and commits fornication, he goes on all fours like a beast, and his face looks downwards. If he keeps a proper balance, and looks up towards God, as only man amongst all the animals is designed to do, his will be the *facies gratiae*, the face full of grace.[109] Progress may be positive, or it may be negative. Man may move upwards towards perfection, or downwards towards a sub-human state.

Contemporary writers have a good deal to say about the progressive positive achievement of perfection. Bernard writes of the *gradus humilitatis,* the steps of humility.[110] Honorius Augustodunensis describes the journey of the soul in its exile, towards its native land,[111] and the ladder to heaven which the Christian soul must

climb.[112] Human perfection, for Adam as he was first created and
for the rest of humanity still, is something to be realised pro-
gressively; it is not a fixed and static condition. Even the *perfectus
homo* of the *Anticlaudianus* has a battle to fight with the vices to
prove himself perfect. When he wins, earth itself is made perfect.
The virtues come to dwell on earth, and earth vies with heaven in
beauty and fertility and peace. Earth becomes the paradise it was
before the Fall, and the ante-room of heaven it was first intended
to be. Perfect man dwells in a land made perfect; man's Fall
brought death and destruction and disharmony to Nature. In the
Anticlaudianus Nature's efforts to find a means of putting things
right are rewarded, and she sees her realm perfected.[113]

Nevertheless, the conclusion of the *Anticlaudianus* cannot be
regarded as the final end. Perfect man is meant for heaven.
There was extensive discussion from the end of the eleventh
century (in the school of Laon, for example) of the question how
long Adam was to remain in paradise if he did not sin, and of the
paradox of his mortality-in-immortality.[114] Peter of Poitiers looks
at all sorts of related questions. Was unfallen Adam subject to
disease? Did he need food to sustain him?[115] Simon of Tournai
sees it as a 'possibility' from the first that Adam could die.[116]
The stronger probability in the beginning was that God's plan for
the progressive perfecting of Adam would mature as it was intended to do, and he would be translated to heaven. Alan's New
Man is given advice on how to behave by each of Nature's sisters
in turn. He is taught how he should wear his hair and choose his
clothes, as well as how he should conduct himself, but that is
before he is declared finished and ready. As a completed piece of
creation Lille's New Man is already a *divinus homo*, already
perfect (though untried until after the battle between good and
evil), a man of heaven. He comes from his homeland to save the
earth. He is not a toiling soul making his way to heaven. The
Anticlaudianus does not speak of his pilgrimage, nor of his taking
his place in the heavenly city. We leave him ruling a happy earth.

There is, however, an equivalent to the work of grace which
was widely argued to be necessary to Adam's perfecting. All the
hero's friends align themselves with him in battle, and they carry
out the work of grace in perfecting Adam. Adam was, says Simon
of Tournai, in a double *status* or condition before the Fall.

He had all the blessings of nature[117] but he was also able to take advantage of the free gifts of grace which were freely given him.[118] These he lost by sinning, so that he was despoiled of grace.[119] This was grace which he would have had if he had stood firm in what he knew to be right (by the light of nature).[120] Peter Lombard agrees that man could not be perfected by nature alone, but that he needed grace, too.[121] Here again we can see Alan nodding to a conventional area of argument, but avoiding any detailed or direct treatment of it. He never considers explicitly the problem of the respective roles of nature and grace in the perfecting of man, but he makes it clear that his hero cannot save the world by living a perfect life by his own unaided efforts. He needs the help of the virtues and the powers which made him. His perfection is fortified by both Nature and grace. In the *Psychomachia* the *impedimenta* of the vices are finally routed by the *expedimenta* of the virtues in a grand display of practical moral theology in action.

The problem of the relationship between nature and grace had a wider context for contemporary scholars than its most important connection with the perfection and perfecting of man. The twelfth century saw the first full-scale systematic attempts in mediaeval times to reconcile two accounts of creation, that of Genesis and that of the ancient philosophers who tried to explain the beginning of the world in terms of natural causes. There is, perhaps, a loose parallel in recent times in the problem of reconciliation which Darwin posed for Biblical theology in the nineteenth century. The twelfth century produced no Darwin. The scientific ideas which were being compared with the Genesis account of creation were not new, and no single scholar was responsible for bringing them back into fashion. They came to notice as a result of a growing general interest in the textbooks which contained them, especially perhaps the *Timaeus* commentary of Calcidius. What was new was the systematic comparison of the two accounts. Thierry of Chartres' treatise *On the Work of the Six Days* takes the Scriptural text as its basis, and interprets it point by point according to scientific principles. Thierry's purpose is to show that the process of creation can be explained entirely in terms of what we might call 'natural causes'; he looks for an existing rational and scientific method in Scripture's account. He says that

Genesis shows the causes which brought the world into existence and the order of its creation in time *rationaliter*,[122] according to reason. He himself proposes to 'try to show by physical *reasons* how heaven and earth were made'.[123] He wants to make it clear that science does not challenge theology but rather supports it. In so doing, he does something to eliminate the role of grace from his scheme of explanations, and to bring into prominence that of Nature. Unfortunately, the treatise is unfinished, and Thierry does not reach the creation of Adam in his story. It is impossible to tell how he would have dealt with the creation and perfecting of man. It is unlikely that he meant to rule out grace altogether. His views on the respective roles of grace and human merit in his treatise on Boethius' *De Trinitate* are orthodox enough.[124] But implicit in his attempt to explain the making of the world scientifically is the view that God normally works in creation according to natural laws, not by direct intervention.

Thierry is careful to keep as close as possible to Scripture throughout, to exploit every possible point of contact between the tradition of the secular philosophers and that of the Bible. There are, he explains, four causes of the world, efficient, formal, final and material. God the Father is the efficient cause; God's Wisdom, the Word, is the formal cause; God's benevolence, the Holy Spirit, is the final cause. The material cause is matter, or the four elements.[125] Thierry takes this traditional explanation and applies it point by point to Genesis. *In principio creavit Deus* refers to the efficient cause. Whenever we meet: 'God said' we are to take it to refer to the work of God the Word, the Son who is the formal cause. Wherever the text says: 'And God saw that it was good' it refers to the *benignitas* of God, the final cause.[126] Thierry takes this attempt at reconciliation further than most. There were many among his contemporaries who thought the attempt misguided, but, controversial or not, there was a widespread notion that such a unity of science and theology, of natural explanations of the creation of the world, and those which have recourse to something beyond nature, might be achieved. Divine and natural causes might be shown to work side by side towards the same end, but they were not, in the last analysis, a single cause.

Thierry concedes as much. Alan's first distinction remains

absolute. Nature may make the body, but God creates the soul; nature cannot achieve perfection unaided by grace, and science cannot explain creation without allowing for the work of the First Cause. Adam would not have got to heaven without God's help,[127] and Alan's hero, too, requires divine assistance and the aid of the virtues in his battle with the vices.

Alan does not attempt to give his perfect man individuality. The allegorical figures with which he peoples his poem made any thing of the kind inappropriate. His hero is a mere puppet of God and Nature. His will, presumably, is free, but we see nothing of an inward struggle for the right. The battle takes place externally. His will does not bend; but we cannot think it might. There is no warmth in the man, none of what a modern writer might call 'human interest'. Alan's hero is unutterably dull in his perfection. Alan himself appears to lose interest in him as the poem draws to an end. The quality he lacks is that of attractiveness. He is not, like Gerard Manley Hopkins' Christ, a hero to be emulated, 'a hero all the world wants'.[128] It is to be assumed that, if he is truly perfect man, he does in fact possess the beauty of body, mind and character which would make all men love him, but it is beyond Alan's powers – or perhaps beyond his immediate purposes – to portray a living perfection. Hildegard had seen the more than human glory of the human faces of the Trinity in her vision of the *simplex homo*: 'I saw...a beautiful and wonderful image...like the form of a man, whose face was of such beauty and brilliance that I could look at the sun more easily.'[129] This was not Alan's view.

1   *The Body*

Alan perhaps drew on Thierry's teaching, or on that of Gilbert of Poitiers, or on Bernard Silvestris, but in any case, he writes within the tradition of the day in outlining the composition of the hero's body. Fire, in him, does not disturb or excite the body, as is its usual way. His blood draws its components from the air; water supplies him with a digestive tract.[130] The result is beauty. The face of the perfect man is that of another Narcissus or Adonis. It would arouse passion in Venus if she saw it,[131] but Alan does not dwell on its beauty, because he is concerned to emphasise that even a perfect human body is profoundly inferior to the soul. It is first and foremost a dwelling-place for the soul: 'a hospice, and a fleshly home which the spirit may enter'.[132]

The soul does not find it distasteful to live in so perfect a body, but that is as far as Alan is able to go, and many of his contemporaries would not have been prepared to go so far. Alan himself has the double standard which was a legacy of both Platonism and Manicheeism. In the collections of topical material which he assembles in the *Ars Praedicandi* he describes the foulness of the body, and the dangers to the soul of giving way to the lusts of the senses. He writes against gluttony, against luxury.[133] In the *Contra Haereses* he argues against the Manichean view that there are two separate *principia,* because the Cathars, the latter-day Manichees, must be persuaded to abandon their view that the material world cannot have been made by a good God who is pure spirit. Christ, they assert, did not have a real body.[134] The incarnation of God himself is hard to grasp. But in the *Anti-claudianus* he gives praise to the perfection of the human body, even if he does so grudgingly.

2 *The Mind*

The perfect man is intelligent, but again, Alan has little to say about this, under the heading of his mind or *animus.* He emphasises, not knowledge, but wisdom, not intellectual power, but force of character.[135] By far the most important thing is the character of the perfect man. He is a being in whom there is no excess. Chastity moderates *luxuria.* Even modesty, surely in itself a gift of moderation, is given in 'due measure': *nec in dando mensuram deserit.*[136] Constancy forbids both over-exuberant gestures and too sober a demeanour.[137] She even arranges the hero's hair and dress, so that neither shall make him seem either effeminate or drab.[138] Reason teaches him not to act precipitately, not to experiment with uncertain remedies, not to be too easily led.[139] Honesty, too, teaches moderation.[140]

3 *Character*

The gifts of Phronesis are the most significant because they bind together character and intellect. She gives a treasure-house of a mind,[141] all the riches of mind.[142] In particular, she gives a thorough understanding of grammar, logic and rhetoric, and of the four mathematical arts of the *quadrivium*. Each of these is to be made to serve the purposes of virtuous and edifying thought and utterance. The furniture of the mind becomes the furniture of the soul. We move on next to what are purely and most evidently gifts of character: piety (*pietas*), faith (*fides*) and generosity (*largitas*). Thus Alan encapsulates the gifts of the mind within the gifts of character, and pays more than lip-service to contemporary conventions about vices and virtues – on which there is abundant literature.

We see, then, what are to be the characteristics of the perfect man, in body, mind and character, but he still does not appear a fully developed human being; he is not attractive because he lacks, in the modern sense of the term, the *personalitas* which was being so widely discussed in Alan's century in connection with Boethius' *Contra Eutychen*. By comparison, Alan's perfect man is a mechanical figure, a puppet of God and Nature. His perfections are coldly itemised, in terms little more evocative than Hugh of St Victor's comment that Adam was made perfect in body and mind, as far as was fitting,[143] or Gunzo's remarks of an earlier century on the wisdom of Adam, who was able to name the animals by the light perhaps of some innate knowledge of the liberal arts.[144]

4 Man in the World

One of the reasons for the failure of Alan's hero to come alive, metaphorically speaking, is his solitude. There are no other men, no angels, no animals in the *Anticlaudianus*. The *perfectus homo* stands for all mankind and there are no comparisons with the relative perfections of angels or of animals. Yet Alan was deeply interested in angelology. In his *Expositio Prosae de Angelis* he considers what an angel ought to be, his duty to love God, the different *officia* of the various orders, rather as in the *Anticlaudianus* he asks himself what man should be.[145] In the *Anticlaudianus* he is much more interested in the implications of the idea that man is a whole company in himself, that he is not only a compound, but also a corporate being. A man is a world in himself, a microcosm. In a sermon for Palm Sunday Alan speaks of the citadel of man, fortified and defended by the virtues.[146] In a sermon on the Holy Spirit he speaks of man as a world,[147] who has something in common with all created things, in existing, with stones, in living, with trees, in feeling, with brute beasts, in reasoning, with spiritual beings.[148] Like his contemporaries, Alan goes further: we have seen that man is not only a world in himself, but also a tiny kingdom, in his very composition. In a noble city, there is a ruler, a body of men who administer and carry out the business of the city, and another body who have to obey the laws. Similarly, in the *respublica* of the universe, God rules, the angelic army carries out his orders, and man, 'like a stranger, dwelling in the suburbs of the world', ought to obey. In man himself there is a similar pattern. The head rules,[149] with its wit and power of reasoning[150] and memory.[151] The heart carries out the orders of the head, with a *magnanimitas* governed by prudence. The desires of the flesh ought to obey.[152] The *topos* of man as a miniature world or microcosm of the state has become a rhetorical commonplace.

Even though it is a commonplace, it has something of importance to tell us about the twelfth-century view of the organic relation of man and the rest of creation. When Adam fell, death and destruction entered not only his own life, but the life of the whole world. When Alan of Lille's *perfectus homo* wins the battle against sin, the whole world becomes verdantly beautiful and everything in it full of peace and well-being. In the Arthurian cycle, the Fisher King's sickness is reflected in the famine and desolation of his country, and his recovery makes it flourish. Alan's hero is a warrior prince who fights for the welfare of his lands.[153]

This is an aspect of that 'community-language' which Colin Morris identifies in the New Testament. He has in mind the idea that the Perfect Man, Christ, 'was regarded not as another human being, separate from (though greater and better than) the believer' but as the means by which the believer, through identification with him, is 'identified also with all other believers'.[154] This notion that the perfect man is, in some sense, all men at once, is to be found quite explicitly in the *Anticlaudianus*. 'He will possess in himself alone whatever we all possess. Thus all men will be one and all will be as one; one in his being, he will nevertheless be all in his virtues.'[155]

Such a man will be 'all men' in another sense, too. To borrow an image Alan himself uses in the *Sententiae*, Adam was a tree from which came many branches, some green, some bare, who are the posterity of Adam. From its root came forth the rod (*virga*) or Virgo Maria.[156] The conception of the whole of mankind as a unity of so literally an organic kind is infinitely adaptable. In his *Sermon on the Holy Spirit* Alan says that the Church may fitly be said to be the world;[157] or again, man himself may be said to be the world.[158] It is adaptable because its elements are interchangeable. Man is a social being; he is society itself; he has a place in the world; he is the world itself. Alan's hero is not, in this sense, alone in the *Anticlaudianus*; the whole human race is in him, as it was in Adam.

Nevertheless, he is not the New Adam of orthodox Christian doctrine. In the *Book of Sentences* he wrote at the end of the eleventh or the beginning of the twelfth century, Bruno of Segni describes the new heavens and the new earth which are to come when the old have passed away; he writes of the new world, the new heavens, the new clouds, the new mountains and trees and animals and powers and sea, and fishes and birds. He begins like this: 'A new man (*novus homo*) has come into the world, who made the new world and the old. For he came from the Father, and he came into the world so that he might make the unclean clean...But how has he come, who is everywhere, and who was already in the world, and the world was made by him?'[159] This New Man is indubitably Christ. He came from the Father, and he came into the world and restored it. In some sense, Alan's perfect man has done as much, but he is not Christ. This, then, is the paradox of Alan's *perfectus homo*. Alan brings together a comprehensive knowledge of traditional teaching, a sound Christian faith of impeccable orthodoxy, a thorough understanding of the technicalities of the liberal arts of his day, and writes a poem about a perfect man in whom all the qualities of the ideal are realised, and who is the sum of all possible human individuals. He stands for the perfection of man *purus*, man alone. His hero is not unaided by God, but he is solely man, not both God and man. Theologically this is astonishing in its daring, and its implications for the valuing of man in his own right are considerable. It is understandable that Ellebaut was embarrassed and tried to put Alan back on the right track, by making the hero Christ himself.[160] The challenge was not taken up directly, but it has something of importance to say about the twelfth-century view of man which has not perhaps been given the attention it deserves.

Conclusion

Stephen Langton, later archbishop of Canterbury, was outstanding among the masters of theology at Paris at the turn of the century. His inaugural lecture survives,[1] and it is evident that from the very beginning of his career he set a standard of thorough competence, in the mainstream of contemporary Biblical scholarship. He takes as his text Exodus 12.34, 39 and 16. The Children of Israel set out from Egypt with sacks of meal on their backs. With these they made bread in the glowing embers of the fire when they camped for the night; then, in the desert, they received heavenly manna; later still, when they had arrived in the Promised Land, they ate the fruit of that land. Here Stephen undoubtedly has a good story, full of narrative interest, and likely to whet the listener's desire to know what these three kinds of food represent in his own life, and to understand what are the individual grains which fill the sacks. Stephen does not disappoint them of answers. 'We, like true Children of Israel, before we come to the land of heavenly promise and eat the fruit of that land, ought to eat a twofold spiritual food in the present, taking grain from Egypt and tasting the heavenly manna.' We may learn from studying the ten plagues of Egypt what 'grains' are to make up the meal. He ventures a scholarly joke: 'let the deceitfulness (*fallacia*) of the world be brought to nothing, for a sophism perishes when it is detected'.[2] No point of exposition is neglected: 'Now let us look at'; 'Now let us consider', says Stephen.[3]

It is not easy to compare like with like, for we have no inaugural lecture from Alan, but he gave a sermon to priests assembled in synod which would have had a not dissimilar audience. Alan takes as his theme the bed of Solomon. The text survives in what may be a compressed form, but even so, the high colouring of Alan's language is unmistakeable: 'We read that our

Solomon, that is Jesus Christ (who is thought to be referred to in a spiritual sense) lay on a threefold bed. The first bed is purple, the second gold, the third a bed of flowers.'[4] A liveliness animates the conventional *distinctiones*, and it is as though Alan leans over the edge of his pulpit to take his listeners into his confidence. Alan had gifts as a writer – for all his faults of stylistic over-contrivance and his frequent preference for a hard word where an easy one would do – which make him outstanding among his contemporaries. He had all the skills of a Stephen Langton in exposition, together with, in a degree beyond most masters of the day, the instinct of a poet. He turns a sentence round to obtain the maximum effect of climax: 'By foxes, which are deceitful animals who live in holes in the ground, are understood the heretics.'[5] Before he tells the listener who the foxes are, he makes it clear what is to be inferred from the comparison. Elsewhere in the *Elucidatio* on the Song of Songs he contrives a rhyme:

Haec sunt verba coelestis sponsi consortium postulantis verba matris ad praesentiam filii suspirantis.[6]

There is nothing peculiar to Alan in all this, for these devices are common enough among his contemporaries, but the cumulative effect of his consistent concern for fine writing, his consciousness of the need to fit his style to his purpose, makes his work distinctive.

What were Alan's special qualities as a master? He was certainly a painstaking teacher, going to endless trouble to explain what he is about: 'We must deal with prudence in this order', he says in the treatise on the virtues and vices and the gifts of the Holy Spirit, considering what prudence is, in what it consists, and how many kinds of prudence there are. He evidently prepared carefully and always had plentiful material, which he put into order so as not to confuse his listeners. In Chapter 2 of the same treatise, he sets out his order of treatment; *quid sit virtus genere*; *quid sit usus*; what is the difference between catholic and political virtues, and so on; whether every virtue has its opposing vice and whether he who has one virtue has them all.[7] In his commentary on the Song of Songs he comes some way to meet his pupils, leaning forward again, but this time over the lectern not the pulpit. 'It is as if the Holy Fathers said...'; 'It is as if he said...', he explains, paraphrasing. 'Notice that above the Virgin is called the fairest of women.'[8]

This solid common-sense as a teacher and the ability to moderate his style to fit the task in hand, balances the intellectual passion and the taste for the obscure in Alan. He himself advises the priest who hears confession to strive for a sensible balance, neither heaping up the penance out of hatred, nor diminishing it unduly out of love.[9] (Nor, he advises, with a wry touch of worldly wisdom, must the priest allow himself to be bribed.) His approach to theology is confident. He is sure that everything will work together, not in the large calm way St Anselm thought, but with the assurance of the man who has read everything and found what may be trusted to forward the cause of orthodoxy and what may impede it.

Alan was undoubtedly one of the most talented writers of his day, and one of the most prolific, but something must be said on the negative side. His writings were much celebrated in his own day and they have continued to be read in every century since, but the poems have not proved to possess the qualities which make the works of Chaucer or Dante still speak directly to their readers. He is disappointing as a philosopher, too. He did not advance the technical resources of the grammarian or the dialectician, as a number of nameless and quite humble masters did, by working away at technical difficulties. He had a thorough mastery of common doctrine in these matters, and that is all. He is not to be compared with Abelard as a problem-solver, either in dialectic or in theology. He did not have Robert Grosseteste's capacity for sitting down quietly with a problem and working it out step by step. He lacks Aquinas' power of seeing complex problems clearly mapped out, and a direct road to a solution lying open before him. When Alan meets something he cannot understand, he is inclined to take refuge in a cloud of words. His mind shies at difficulties, and yet he is attracted by difficulty; he loves to talk about it. Again, despite his wide knowledge of the sources, Alan was not in the first rank as a Platonist, if we compare him with Augustine or Anselm. His Platonism is all pictures. He had flair, but not brilliance, persistence, but not depth, a taste for novelty, but no real originality.

Wherein, then, lies his undoubted importance among the

masters of the second half of the twelfth century? It is partly a matter of scale; he wrote so much on so many subjects that he made a considerable quantitative contribution. But more important perhaps is his very confidence, his willingness to try to climb heights too great for him. In his (sometimes misconceived) enterprises he pressed the developments of the first half of the twelfth century as far as he could, and made some of their limitations plain. The first half of the century had been a time of optimism in philosophy and theology. Everything seemed possible, and developments looked promising, but although Alan was, in some respects, a scholar better suited to the atmosphere of the earlier generation in which he was born and educated than to that of the schools of the end of the century, his writing lacks the simplicity and clarity which marks the best work of the period. When he tried to pursue these discoveries with his peculiar combination of boldness and intricacy, he showed that he lacked the qualities which might have enabled him to make a real advance, but he also showed that the possibilities of expansion along these lines were less than had been thought.

Alan's contemporaries called him *doctor universalis*, by which they meant no more than to express their admiration for the range and depth of his learning as it manifested itself in his teaching.[10] Few can have been able to read his collected works and judge him on his range as a writer. To the modern reader the scope of his surviving writings is undeniably impressive, but his darting eye for a new word or a fresh author, his apparently boundless enthusiasm for novel ideas and new kinds of book or study-aid, belies his single-mindedness. He consistently strove to draw all his learning together in the service of theology.

That the *Anticlaudianus* has received so much attention as a work of literature, and a secular one at that, has tended to create a false perspective. 'The title, the chosen medium, the initial invocation, the poetic texture, all proclaim Alan's determination to visualise the world with secular eyes', says P. G. Walsh.[11] Although he points out that Alan's work 'overwhelmingly consists' of 'treatises of theological and devotional learning' he sets these aside and looks at the *Anticlaudianus* without further reference to them, as if it stood apart in its author's mind as it has tended to do for his modern readers,[12] but the *Anticlaudianus* is not the work of a young man still disporting himself among the liberal arts and the classics, and not yet a serious theologian. Alan wrote it about 1183, when he was probably in his sixties, and it had behind it several of his most substantial theological writings, some years of teaching in Paris and perhaps elsewhere. Alan was already an established theologian. The hero of the *Anticlaudianus* is Nature's child, but he is above all a man under God. Although he has help from the secular handmaids of theology, the liberal arts, Alan is himself guided principally by *Phronesis* or *Prudentia* and *Ratio* (for 'rational theology'), the Virtues (for 'moral theology') and *Theologia* and *Fides*, Theology and Faith themselves, in recounting the tale. The *Anticlaudianus* is a Christian allegory for all its classical dress. Unless we look at it in the context of Alan's intellectual passion for theology we shall not understand Alan's purpose in writing it.

In another recent article, Michael Wilks has suggested that perhaps 'the *Anticlaudianus* is really a species of Court Poetry, combining both the form of the panegyric with a *vademecum* to aid the instruction of a Christian prince'.[13] He goes on to suggest that perhaps Philip Augustus is the prince in question, and that Alan may have written the *Anticlaudianus* specifically for the occasion of the Coronation in 1179 or that of Philip Augustus' marriage to Isabella of Hainault in 1180.[14] Now there is no doubt that Alan intended different readers to derive different kinds of enjoyment and illumination from the work, burying *secreta* deep within it for those with eyes to see them, and presenting at the same time a good, gripping story for those of immature tastes,[15] but there is nothing to suggest that he meant, late in life, to imitate the writing of a John of Salisbury. For all his powers of entertaining his readers, Alan was a man of great seriousness who never gave his energies seriously to any piece of work which would not ultimately forward the theologian's task. He dedicated to William VIII of Montpellier, not a courtly compliment, but four books against the heretics, which might be expected to be useful to a prince in that part of France.[16]

Because he found it stretched him beyond his capacities, Alan found theology intellectually far more exciting than secular studies. He was attracted equally by its challenge and its mystery. The episode of Prudentia's stupefaction as she enters the realm of

Theologia is a dramatic image of his own sense that that which lay beyond the reach of reason and the ordinary procedures of the *artes* was infinitely desirable because it so far outshines what they can show to him. In the commentary on the Lord's Prayer he distinguishes between the grammarian's *oratio* and the theologian's *oratio* in terms which make it plain how dull he found the former and how exciting he found the latter:

The grammarian describes an *oratio* thus: an *oratio* is a fitting ordering of words[17] but in theology an *oratio* is said to be a disposition of the mind, which is often stirred by words when it is sluggish.[18]

This deep, vibrant excitement of the mind in prayer sweeps up the emotional and spiritual elements in devotion into an intellectual aspiration after God which is characteristic of Alan.

Like any clever man of the world, he could no doubt have turned his hand to light verse and the 'trifles' which easily pleased courtiers (as John of Salisbury complains at the beginning of his *Metalogicon*), but his writing would perhaps always have had too much intensity and too much heat for such tastes. For all his wit and sparkle and humour, Alan was intensely serious. The two are not necessarily incompatible; combined in Alan they make for a kind of uncommon, if sometimes misdirected, vitality.

APPENDIX 1

A NOTE ON THE AUTHORSHIP OF THE
'DE ARTE CATHOLICAE FIDEI'

The question of authorship has given rise to a lengthy controversy[1] which has perhaps helped to divert attention from the important differences of method between the *De Arte Catholicae Fidei* and the *Regulae Theologicae*. The greater part of the discussion has turned on the evidence of the manuscripts. The majority of the rubrics and the ancient catalogues give the piece to Nicholas of Amiens. In the preface to his continuation of the Chronicle of Sigebert of Gembloux (dealing, as does the first book of the *De Arte,* with the first cause of all things) Nicholas covers some of the same ground as the *De Arte*, in remarkably similar terms. Some manuscripts name Alan of Lille as the author, however, and it has been suggested, on the basis of a Zagreb manuscript, that he is the author of the first five books, while Nicholas of Amiens added a sixth, which is found under his name in this instance.[2]

P. Glorieux suggested some years ago that it might be helpful to look at the internal evidence. He makes some brief comparisons between the two treatises, chiefly on matters of style and the use of typical expressions and formulas, and he finds no stylistic grounds for giving the *De Arte* to Alan,[3] but he did not consider the differences of method and content. The comparison of the use made in the *Regulae* and the *De Arte* of what has often been taken to be a single axiomatic method will not settle the question of authorship, but it bears out Glorieux's view that the internal evidence does not justify us in attributing the piece to Alan against the consensus of so many manuscripts which credit Nicholas with its composition. As to content, two further indications which emerge from a comparison of the two treatises, and which appear not to have been noticed, would seem to settle the question of authorship in favour of Nicholas. The *De Arte Catholicae Fidei* was composed *Contra Haereticos*. The author says at the beginning that he sees no point in employing authorities against *moderni heretici,* since they distort or deny them. He will argue with reasons only.[4] Alan of Lille's four books *Against the Heretics*[5] consistently make use of both reasons and authorities. Mlle d'Alverny suggests that Alan's work is to be dated between 1185 and 1200.[6] It is difficult to believe that a piece so closely contemporaneous with the *De Arte Catholicae Fidei* could have been composed by Alan on a basis which he himself had rejected in the dedication of the *De Arte Catholicae Fidei* to Clement III between 1187 and 1191.

Secondly, Alan describes in the exposition of *Regula* II how in the highest heaven there is only unity, God himself. In the heavens, where the angels dwell, there is 'otherness' (*alteritas*) but not *varietas*, that is, the beginning of number, but not true number or plurality. Only under the heavens is there true number or plurality. It is clear that he adheres to the view that two is not a number and the first number is three.[7] In the *De Arte,* by contrast, the author shows that there cannot be two First Causes, by an argument which depends for its force upon the idea that if there were two, they would fall into the province of number.[8] They would then differ, for he has shown in a previous theorem that things which fall into the province of number either differ or cause to differ, but things which differ are compound things, made up of forms and properties, for it is properties and forms which distinguish things which are different from one another. The First Cause cannot be compound, for Nicholas has shown that every compound thing has a cause higher than itself. These hypothetical First Causes would not then be First Causes at all.[9] It seems unlikely that the same author is responsible for two arguments which rest upon such incompatible first principles.

Perhaps the strongest piece of evidence that the author of the *Regulae Theologicae* is not the author of the *De Arte Catholicae Fidei* is the difference between the 'axiomatic' methods employed in the two works. Alan of Lille borrows his method from that employed by Boethius in the *De Hebdomadibus*. He readily acknowledges his debt to Boethius' in the Preface to the *Regulae*. It is clear that he has studied Boethius' introductory remarks about method in the *De Hebdomadibus* minutely, and the work of the twelfth-century commentators – particularly Gilbert of Poitiers.[10] He has gone much further than Boethius, adapting Boethius' method to cover the whole of theology (he extends Boethius' modest series of nine axioms to a hundred and thirty-four, at least). He has gone beyond Boethius, too, in beginning with 'the most general maxim'[11] and systematically deriving all his other laws from it, but nowhere is there any indication that his development of the Boethian axiomatic method owes anything to Euclid. His maxims are *communes animi conceptiones,* but not *theoremata.*[12] The author of the *De Arte,* on the other hand, begins in the manner of Euclid's *Elements* by listing a series of definitions, *petitiones* and *communes animi conceptiones.* The 'maxims' which he groups in his five books are called *proposita* before they are proved, and once he has reached the point with each where he can say: *et sic patet propositum* he describes it as a *theorema,* and introduces it as the equivalent of a *communis animi conceptio,* a self-evident principle or a principle which requires no proof, in later demonstrations. The definitions and postulates and axioms are brought in systematically where they are needed throughout the treatise, and a fresh set of definitions is given at the beginning of the second and the fourth books, to meet the needs of the new subject-matter with which they deal. The structure of the whole treatise is clearly Euclidean. Even if we allow for the possibility that during the ten years which probably elapsed between the composition of the *Regulae Theologiae,*[13] and that of the *De Arte,* Alan of Lille saw the possibilities of a second axiomatic method based on Euclid's *Elements* which had not been clear to him when he wrote the *Regulae* there is nothing to suggest that this in fact happened. The two works are quite independent in conception and execution and their methods are technically so distinct that it is hard to believe that Alan of Lille can have been responsible for both, even if the weight of the evidence did not suggest so strongly that the *De Arte* is the work of Nicholas of Amiens.

C. Balić proposed a solution on the basis of a group of manuscripts which include a sixth book. Of these, one attributes the first five books to Alan, the sixth to Nicholas,[14] and Balić suggests that this is the answer to the difficulty posed by the discrepancy in attribution which is to be found among the manuscripts of the *De Arte*. Nicholas wrote only the sixth book, and copyists credited him with the others by mistake, but if we can state with confidence that Nicholas of Amiens is the author of the five books of the *De Arte* which are listed in the preface to the work, after the dedication to Pope Clement,[15] it begins to seem likely that Balić is wrong on two counts. Not only was Alan of Lille not the author of the first five books, but Nicholas of Amiens was probably not the author of the sixth book. It is unlikely that the author who says that he has divided his *opus* into five books added a sixth without making some comment on the addition and his reasons for it. There can be no question of the extra book having been written earlier, since it makes use of theorems demonstrated in the first five books, and gives their book and number in each case. The sixth book was certainly written to go with the first five. Nicholas of Amiens is therefore the least likely, not the most likely candidate for the authorship of Book VI.

The strongest indication that the author of the additional book is not the author of the first five is the content of Book VI itself. It deals with the topics briefly covered in Book I of the *De Arte*, *proposita* XXIV–XXX, and concerned with the Trinity, but whereas the governing principle of the discussions of Book I is that in the creation of every substance there is matter, form and their bringing-together (compare Book I, *propositum* VI), Book VI is concerned with the roles of *potentia, sapientia, bonitas* as the cause of all things, and with the way in which Father, Son and Holy Spirit are to be regarded as one Cause, not three. A fresh set of definitions is given at the beginning, of *potentia, scientia, sapientia, voluntas, bonitas, procedere, discretio,* none of which has been given before, although *bonum* and *discretum* have been previously defined, in rather different terms. The sixth book was clearly thought by its author to fill a gap in the coverage of the first five, and he set about adding material on the Trinity in a manner out of keeping with the tight-knit argument of Nicholas' original treatise. His material could not be inserted into Nicholas' sequence of argument as it stands, and although he has made use of Nicholas' method, his work is quite independent. There is, unfortunately, no indication in the manuscripts to suggest the identity of the author.[16]

The *Regulae* itself has what may be an additional section. It is, superficially at least, a less shapely work than the *De Arte*. There is no division into books, although it is possible to distinguish some topical arrangement of the subject-matter and a *summa*-like progression from God to sacraments which parallels that of the *De Arte*. The text reproduced in Migne from Mingarellius' edition of 1756 gives only 125 *regulae*. The printed texts of 1492 and 1497 give 134. The manuscripts are divided, ending, sometimes it seems quite arbitrarily, after Rule 111 (MS. Bodl. 136, ff.31ᵛ–41ᵛ, Bodleian Library) or after Rule 113 (MS. Royal 9 E XII, f.216ʳ–226ʳ, British Library). Rule 124 (MS. Bodl. 550, ff.119ʳ–137ᵛ, Bodleian Library) brings the treatise to an end in one manuscript, although the last rubric is for Rule 120, and the last four *regulae* run on afterwards without distinction, as if they belonged to Rule 120. MS. Egerton 832, f.270–318ᵛ (British Library) gives the full 134 *regulae* as they appear in the Basle printed text of 1492. The numbering of the *regulae* is made uncertain by the fact that, although in some instances they are numbered in the margin, sometimes the first rule to be set out in red or as a heading is Alan's citation in the Prologue of the first axiom of Boethius' *De Hebdomadibus*:

Communis animi conceptio est enuntiatio quam quisque intelligens probat auditam.[17]

The first difficulty presented by the manuscripts, then, is that of determining where the author intended the treatise to end.

After Rule 115 there occurs a comment which indicates a change of direction if not a change of author:

Pertractatis regulis que theologice facultati specialiter sunt accomode, agendum est de his que ad naturalem pertinent facultatem.

Having dealt with the *regulae* which belong properly to theology, the author intends to turn to those which are proper to natural science, but he intends to do so in such a way that the reader will realise how they are related: 'because those do not wander from theology, which are truly common to both subjects'.[18] This passage is heralded by a red capital and a new paragraph, or by underlining in red, in a number of manuscripts. There can be no doubt that although Migne prints it as part of the text of Rule 115, it constitutes a new beginning. There is no reason to postulate an author other than Alan of Lille for these last *regulae*, but it is important that the difference between the main body of the work and the section on natural laws should not go unrecognised. The Prologue describes the special character- istics of theological *regulae* and Alan has something to say there about the *regulae* of the liberal arts, but nothing at all about *regulae naturales*. If Alan himself composed the last few *regulae* he certainly did so as an afterthought, for there is no indication in his outline of his plan for the work that he intended to continue along these lines.

Alan has given an almost complete systematic theology up to Rule 115, beginning with the Divine Nature and going on to Man, Incarnation and the Sacraments. Now, instead of using the technical principles of the secular arts to illuminate and help him interpret, and sometimes to frame, his *regulae,* as he has done up to now, he allows the principles of secular learning to work as they were designed to do, upon problems which arise in con- nection with the natural world. But at each stage he looks at the implication of the principle in question for theology. To take an example: in Rule 122, Alan explains that there are both first and second causes (*Causarum alia prima, alia secunda*). In the natural world, the first kind is that by which a man is a man; *in divinis* it is that by which God is God. In the natural world, the second kind of cause is that by which he who is a man is capable of laughter; *in divinis* it is that by which the Father is the Father and the Son is the Son. Parallels of this kind are carefully drawn throughout the *regulae* of this final section.

Mlle d'Alverny has discussed the evidence of the manuscripts as to the circumstances of composition of this last section of the *Regulae Theologicae*.[19] There can be no doubt that it was com- posed as an afterthought and added to the work as it was first conceived, but there is nothing to indicate how long a period may have elapsed. What is important for our purposes, however, is the fact that the piece is an appendix or addition, and that, like the sixth book of the *De Arte* it cannot be inserted into the existing sequence of demonstration of the main body of the work. Like the sixth book of the *De Arte,* Alan's appendix is concerned with causation, and with aspects of causation which are not covered in the earlier work. In view of the puzzling relationship between the two treatises and the *Liber de Causis,* and the surprising range of notions about causation which are touched upon in the course of the *De Arte* and the *Regulae Theologicae* and their appendices, the theme is clearly one which would repay detailed investigation. It is of some importance in the speculative theology of the group of 'axiom' treatises to which the *De Arte* and the *Regulae Theologicae* belong.

Robert of Melun, a theologian of the school of Peter Abelard, emphasises the importance of distinguishing between different kinds of causes.[20] He himself gives only three: *suprema, ultima* and *media,* but he would have been familiar with a wide range of meanings of *causa*: with the Ciceronian usage of *causa* in connection with forensic rhetoric, for example;[21] with the idea, developed by Boethius, that a 'cause' may provide a definition, as when we say that a 'day' is 'the sun on the earth' and thus explain a day by describing its cause; with the dialectician's propositional *causa,* which, on its own, or together with another, leads to a conclusion;[22] with the distinction of final, formal, efficient and material causes in the creation of the world.[23] Yet Robert of Melun has a far less developed theory of causation than that which Nicholas of Amiens displays in the *De Arte.* Robert explains that supreme causes are not themselves effects,[24] but that other kinds of causes lie along a line of causation, where intermediate causes are causes of more things than they are themselves effects of, while ultimate causes are causes of relatively few things, but effects of many causes. The central notion here is that a cause is something which has an effect: *est autem causa omne illud quod aliquid efficit.* Nicholas' definition makes a cause that which brings something into existence, and it equates a 'thing caused' (i.e., an effect) with a created thing.[25] Robert's definition, although it fits Christian theology well enough, and indeed he goes on to deal with the question in strictly theological terms, is essentially a philosopher's definition. Nicholas' is designed especially for use by the Christian theologian who wants to discuss the relationship between causation and creation which shows the Supreme Cause to be God himself. Nicholas adds to his definition two *communes animi conceptiones* connected with causation among the preliminary apparatus with which he prefaces Book I of the *De Arte*. Here again, it is clear that philosophical principles are being tailored to the needs of the speculative theologian. The first is a restatement of the definition of *causa*. Everything has its existence through that cause which brings it into existence. The second makes use of the hierarchical principle we have already seen in Robert of Melun.[26] A cause must be higher than its effect. There is nothing startling in any of Nicholas' definitions of axioms, nor in the theorems of the first book in which he shows that there must be one *suprema causa*, in which there can be nothing compound, but only perfect unity and simplicity,[27] and that there are *inferior* and *superior causae*.[28] Such notions, although they can be traced back to Pseudo-Dionysius or to other *auctoritates* which were available to twelfth-century scholars, were commonplace, the stuff of the very habits of thought of Nicholas' contemporaries.

The same might be said for the discussions of formal, final, efficient causes in Alan's *Regulae Theologicae*,[29] or of the idea of primary and secondary causes in Rules 122, 123, 124 of the appendix to the *Regulae*. When Nicholas' continuator discusses *bonitas* and so on as 'causes' in the sixth book of the *De Arte* he uses *causa* in much the same way as Robert of Melun in a similar discussion in his *Sentences*.[30] When in Book IV of the *De Arte* Nicholas himself speaks of the *causa baptismi* and the *causae* of the other sacraments, he makes the same use of *causa* in this connection as Peter Lombard. In rather the same spirit, Alan of Lille describes *charitas* as the prior *causa* among the virtues in Rule 91.[31] It is not so much in their habit of extending and adapting the sense of *causa* to so many purposes, nor in their particular usages that Alan of Lille and Nicholas of Amiens appear to be thinking about causation in a rather different light from the majority of the scholars of the day; it is rather in their heightened interest in the subject that the influence of the *Liber de Causis* makes itself felt.

A number of complications arise if we attempt to trace that influence in detail. Several maxims which are to be found in Proclus' *Elements of Theology* but not in the selection which makes up the *Liber de Causis* appear to have found their way into the *Regulae Theologicae* and the *De Arte Fidei Catholicae*. Various explanations might be put forward to explain this curious anomaly. Some of the parallels are slight, and may be no more than chance resemblances. Proclus, for example, states in Proposition 14 that everything is unmoved, intrinsically moved or extrinsically moved. In Rule 120 of the appendix to the *Regulae* Alan speaks of *causae* which are, respectively, *intrinseca* and *extrinseca*. He does not have anything to say about movement here, and the technical terms are most probably drawn from Cicero's distinction between intrinsic and extrinsic arguments in *Topics* 11.8. Other items, such as the notion that everything which in any way participates the good is subordinate to the primal good, which is nothing else but good (Proclus, Axiom 8),[32] are to be found in Boethius' *De Hebdomadibus* or elsewhere, or in Pseudo-Dionysius, another transmitter of Proclus' thought to the Middle Ages. We need not look directly to Proclus for a source of the starting-point of Nicholas' discussions of the divine goodness in Book II of the *De Arte*. Pseudo-Dionysian material, rather than the first five axioms of Proclus' *Elements*, almost certainly provided Alan of Lille with his first few *regulae* on the divine unity.

With Nicholas' first theorem: *Quidquid est causa causae est causa causati* we come to another possibility. The axiom is very like the seventy-fifth axiom of Proclus' *Elements*, but it is also to be found in exactly the form Nicholas gives it, in a *florilegium* collection known as the *Auctoritates Aristotelis* which was in circulation in the thirteenth and fourteenth centuries.[33] It resembles a passage in Aristotle's *Posterior Analytics*. In a number of cases we are presented with the possibility that some such collection of *Auctoritates Aristotelis* was already available when Alan and Nicholas were searching for their axioms; but where the source-text itself may have been available to them, as was certainly the case with the *Posterior Analytics*, it may be that we need look no further. Nicholas' *nihil est causa sui* of *De Arte* I.viii may echo the *nihil est sine causa* of the *Auctoritates*;[34] a number of passages among the *Auctoritates* touch on the discussions of *De Arte* I.iv–vii about the way in which a substance may be said to be 'caused' by matter and form and their bringing-together.[35] Several *Auctoritates* items convey the substance of the axiom: *omnis causa prior et dignior est suo causato*,[36] or the postulate:

nullius rei causam in infinitum ascendere.[37] Again and again echoes of the *Auctoritates Aristotelis* suggest that we should look to a *florilegium* source rather than to the *Liber de Causis* itself for Alan's and Nicholas' sources of axioms concerned with causation. The very 'axiomatic' appearance of many of the *florilegium* statements would encourage such borrowing. Even the discussion of the *causa dicendi* which occupies Rules 116–19 and 124–5 of the appendix to the *Regulae* could have been inspired by the statement, found in the *Auctoritates* as well as in the *De Causis*,[38] that the *causa prima* is above every name which can be named (*super omne nomen quod nominari potest*), although the notice is clearly Pseudo-Dionysian, too.

There remains the possibility that other items from Proclus' *Elements* may have found their way into circulation in the twelfth century apart from those which are collected together in the *De Causis*. Proclus' *Elements of Physics* was translated from the Greek in Sicily in the mid-twelfth century.[39] William of Morbecca's translation of the *Elements of Theology* of 1268 was based on a text of some antiquity, which is not the same as that of any of the existing earliest manuscripts of the Greek version.[40] It is possible that portions of the *Elements* were available in Latin in the twelfth century, if not the whole. A striking resemblance between Proposition 98 and the famous dictum concerning the sphere whose centre is everywhere and whose circumference is nowhere is perhaps worth noting in this connection: Proclus says that every cause which is separate from its effects exists at once everywhere.

Enough has been said to indicate the enormous complexity of the problems which surround the relationship between the *Liber de Causis* and the treatment of causation in the *De Arte Fidei Catholicae*, the *Regulae Theologicae* and their appendices. A great deal of work remains to be done in this area; but the indications that at least one author may be added to Alan of Lille and Nicholas of Amiens, Gerard of Cremona and the author of the *Liber XXIV Philosophorum* (to enlarge the group of scholars who had a special interest in 'axiomatic theology') suggest that the use of *regulae* and self-evident principles in theological demonstration was not confined to so small a band as has hitherto seemed likely. The role of the *florilegia* may then be of some importance, not only in furnishing some of the axioms themselves, but also in encouraging a certain 'axiom-mindedness' among our authors, an interest in such laws. Without it axiomatic theology could not have developed as far as it did in the second half of the twelfth century.

THE EUCLIDEAN AXIOMATIC METHOD OF THE 'DE ARTE CATHOLICAE FIDEI'

Like the *De Hebdomadibus* and the *Regulae Theologicae*, Nicholas of Amiens' treatise employs *communes animi conceptiones* but in a very different way, and the use to which he puts them, together with a series of definitions and *petitions*, identifies his axiomatic method as Euclidean in inspiration. The laws which are demonstrated point by point throughout the treatise are called *theoremata*, not *regulae*, and they are brought in freely to support further arguments, in much the same way as Euclid's theorems. Like Euclid, Nicholas provides a fresh set of definitions when they are needed – at the beginnings of Books II and IV (and Book VI, which is found as an addition in some manuscripts, but whose authorship is open to question).[41] Nicholas' three *petitiones* and seven *communes animi conceptiones* apply throughout. Theorems introduced later as established laws are carefully identified by the number of the book in which they were demonstrated and the number of the theorem itself. The arrangement is designed to ensure that the reader has always already been given a demonstration of any theorem he will need in order to understand the demonstration now before him, and that no *descriptio, petitio* or *communis animi conceptio* has to be introduced incidentally.

Nicholas describes his treatise as an *ars*. It is an 'art', not of grammar or dialectic or rhetoric, but of the catholic faith. It is something of a commonplace in contemporary discussions of the nature of an art to say that an art is a collection of principles or laws which serve the purpose of establishing a particular subject-matter.[42] In calling his book an *ars catholicae fidei* Nicholas is explaining the nature of its subject-matter. He tells us something about the method of such an art, its *modus*. It contains *diffinitiones* and *distinctiones* and *propositiones artificioso successu propositum comprobantes*.[43] These terms alone are not enough to identify the method as Euclidean, but they contain nothing which is out of keeping with the idea that it is so. Euclid himself begins with a series of definitions, and the Latin term commonly used to describe them in the translations of the *Elements* made in the twelfth century is *definitio*. The author of an introduction to one of the versions attributed to Adelard of Bath speaks of *anxiomata,* but he qualifies the statement by saying that Euclid 'explains the definitions of things'.[44] The *distinctiones* are perhaps chapters or sections, or more probably, in a Euclidean context, the theorems and their demonstrations which are so well marked off from one another in the manuscripts not only of Euclid's *Elements*, but also of Alan's *Regulae Theologicae* and the *De Arte Catholicae Fidei* itself. The *propositiones,* we are told, prove when taken together (*comprobantes*). Nicholas speaks a little earlier of the degree to which matters of faith are *probabiles,* 'provable', and there is an interesting negative form in Book I, theorem xvi, where Nicholas describes as *prius improbatum* something which has earlier been disproved.[45] The function of the propositions, then, is to prove, not individually, but when they are set beside one another and adduced collectively. It begins to look as though the 'propositions' may be the petitions and self-evident notions which, apart from the preliminary definitions, constitute the apparatus with which the *ars* is provided. What they prove is the *propositum*.[46] Again and again Nicholas ends the demonstration of a theorem with: *Et sic patet propositum.* Until it is proved, then, a statement is a *propositum.* Once it is proved, it is added to the initial petitions and self-evident notions as a *propositio* which may, in its turn, be used to prove further *proposita.* The author of the introduction to the Adelard of Bath Euclid tries to save his readers confusion by explaining that 'propositions are explained in the indicative and *proposita* in the infinitive'.[47] Propositions put it that something is or is not, but *proposita* are concerned with whether something is to be done or not in a given situation: *ubi aliquod est faciendum, vel non.* This scarcely illuminating explanation is all we are given. Another version, Gerard of Cremona's Euclid, opens with a less extensive discussion of Euclid's intentions. The *propositum* here is that which prefaces[48] or goes before the exposition.[49] This exposition, according to Nicholas of Amiens, proceeds by 'artificial arguments'. There is a parallel in Gilbert of Poitiers' use of *artificiose transit*,[50] and Nicholas would perhaps have had in mind here the distinction Cicero makes between intrinsic arguments, which must as a rule be worked out by art, and thus 'artificially', and extrinsic arguments, or evidence, which are not, in this sense, 'artificial', because they are not a matter of art.[51] The arguments of Euclid are 'artificial', because they are a matter of art.

These, then, are the general terms in which Nicholas describes his *ars*. If they stood alone, they would not be enough to place its Euclidean inspiration beyond doubt, but Nicholas goes on to list a number of definitions of terms, which he calls *descriptiones*, three *petitiones* and seven *communis animi conceptiones*. He explains what purpose each of these is designed to serve. The *descriptiones* are given 'so that it may be clear in what sense the terms appropriate to this art are to be used'. They are, in other words, definitions. The *petitiones* are statements which, although they resemble maxims, or self-evident propositions, in not being susceptible of proof by anything outside themselves, are not in fact self-evident, and must be conceded by the reader for purposes of discussion. The 'common conceptions of the mind' are statements which are self-evident, so that as soon as anyone hears them he grasps that they are true. Out of these are to be drawn the proofs or demonstrations which follow. The parallel with Euclid's opening definitions, postulates and axioms is clear enough.

If we compare Nicholas's choice of technical terms with the Latin renderings of Euclid made by Adelard of Bath, Gerard of Cremona and Hermann of Carinthia, we find that where translation of, or commentary on, Book I of the *Elements* survives, *petitio* is consistently used for ΑΙΤΗΜΑΤΑ and *communis animi conceptio* for ΚΟΙΝΑΙ ΕΝΝΟΙΑΙ, but for Euclid's definitions the most usual term is *diffinitio*. If we are to argue that Nicholas of Amiens is drawing directly upon his study of Euclid, this presents a worrying discrepancy, but the term *descriptio* does occur, in the passage *Deinde ex circuli descriptione argumentum elicito* in Adelard of Bath, for example, and if we look at Boethius' distinction between description and definition in the commentary on the *Categories* and in the *De Differentiis Topicis,* it begins to seem as though Nicholas is in fact selecting his technical terms with precision. Boethius explains that a definition is made by means of *genus* and *species* and *differentia*; but if we want to define something which is itself a genus the method cannot be applied. The terms Nicholas wants to 'define', *substantia, forma, materia,* require *descriptiones,* not *definitiones.*[52]

If we want to argue that Nicholas is drawing on Euclid, *petitio* presents no difficulties, but it might be objected that the phrase *communis animi conceptio* is used by Boethius in the *De Hebdomadibus,* too, and that Nicholas's definition of it may echo that of Boethius. Compare: *adeo sunt evidentes, quod eas auditas statim animus concipit esse veras* from the *De Arte,* with Boethius': *est enuntiatio quam quisque probat auditam.*[53] The echo is slight, however (*auditam*; *auditas*) and the evidence, not only of the use of Euclidean terms, but also of recognisably Euclidean methods of argument, weighs heavily in favour of the view that the *communis animi conceptio* of the *De Arte* is Euclidean rather than Boethian in inspiration.

What, then, is the structure and method of Nicholas' arguments in the *De Arte Catholicae Fidei*? He avoids the overwhelming emphasis upon the *communis animi conceptiones* to the exclusion of definitions and petitions, which is characteristic of the axiomatic method which belongs to the Boethian tradition of the *De Hebdomadibus.* The whole Euclidean apparatus is brought into play. Like Euclid himself, at the beginning of Book x of the *Elements,* for example, Nicholas introduces fresh definitions when he needs them, in Books II and IV. He consistently refers his readers back to demonstrations already made, and uses theorems as established truths in later demonstrations. In the first theorem he employs a, b and c, not perhaps in imitation of Euclid (the device is more likely to have been adapted from the *Prior* or the *Posterior Analytics* of Aristotle) but nevertheless, the procedure is entirely in keeping with that of Euclid. He is systematic in the arrangement of the *petitiones* and *communis animi conceptiones* at the beginning. They follow the order in which they first appear in the text. The definitions, too, are given roughly in the order in which they appear in the text, although Nicholas has not been so meticulous here. All the petitions are used in Book I, and they are treated as though they were axioms in their power of commanding assent, even though Nicholas has conceded that they must be granted voluntarily by the reader. The *petitiones* are 'The cause of every composite thing compounds': 'The cause of nothing can be traced back indefinitely'; the third is perhaps best understood by means of an example which Nicholas gives when he introduces this petition in Book 1.xix: God is said to be good through cause and effect, because all good proceeds from him and he effects every good (*et ipse efficit omnem bonum*).[54]

The first of these is used in the demonstration of theorems 5, 6, 10, 18; the second appears in the demonstration of theorem 9, and the third in 19. Of the *communis animi conceptiones,* only the first three appear in Book 1; 4 and 5 appear in Book 11, 6 in Book 111, and 7 in Book 1v. This distribution reflects their subject-matter. The first three have a bearing upon the discussions of causation in Book 1: 'Everything has its existence through that which causes it to come into existence'; 'Every cause is prior to and higher than what it has caused'; 'Nothing is prior to or higher than itself.'[55] The fourth and the fifth have to do with the subject-matter of Book 11, the creation of man and angel, and free will. 'If anyone greater possesses one lesser than himself, the lesser, and those things which are his, is bound to act for the honour and according to the will of the greater.'[56] 'He who does injury deserves a greater penalty according to the greatness of him who is injured.' The sixth *communis animi conceptio* is concerned with the subject-matter of Book 111, the Incarnation of the Son of God for the redemption of mankind. 'According to the importance of him against whom the sin is committed, ought the satisfaction to be adjusted.'[57] The seventh concerns the subject-matter of Book 1v: 'things heard move men's souls effectively, things seen more effectively'.

Of the definitions, those given at the beginning of Book 1 are supplemented at the beginning of Book 11 by definitions of *bonum, malum, utile, iustitia, bene mereri, male mereri, humilitas, misericordia, gloria, gratia, satisfactio peccati.* Book 1v opens with definitions of *praedicatio, sacramentum, baptismus, eucharistia, matrimonium, poenitentia, dedicatio basilicarum, chrismatis et olei inunctio, ecclesia.* The definitions needed for the first book are those of technical terms of the liberal arts – especially of dialectic – and of natural science (*naturalis* or *physica*). When, in the second and third books, we move on to the subject of sin and redemption, a fresh set of definitions is needed. The fourth and fifth books deal with the sacraments and the last judgment; for the fourth book, new definitions are again needed; the fifth draws in part upon the discussions of the second and third books.

Like Alan of Lille in the *Regulae Theologicae*, Nicholas of Amiens has moved a long way from the beginning of his treatise, where his subject-matter lends itself fairly readily to treatment by 'axiomatic' means; but, like Alan, he has kept to his method throughout, as closely as his subject-matter permits. The whole treatise is a masterpiece of contrivance, in which the mechanics of the Euclidean method are sustained throughout, and the terminology of *theoremata, propositiones, descriptiones, petitiones, communis animi conceptiones* is used consistently.

Alan of Lille's treatise cannot be dated precisely, although it seems likely that it was written in the 1170s. The *De Arte Catholicae Fidei* is dedicated to Pope Clement III, and can therefore be dated between 1187 and 1191.[58] It is not impossible that Nicholas of Amiens drew some inspiration from Alan of Lille. But his axiomatic method is quite distinct, far more sophisticated, and indebted to geometry in a more direct way than the method of the *Regulae Theologicae*. We must speak, not of one, but two kinds of 'axiomatic theology' in these decades of the later twelfth century.

APPENDIX 2

Peter the Chanter's *'De Tropis Loquendi'*

THE PROBLEM OF THE TEXT

Peter the Chanter's *Verbum Abbreviatum*, the *Summa de Sacramentis* and the *De Tropis Loquendi* present almost insuperable problems to the editor. Like his commentaries on the Bible and the *Summa Abel*, they were all delivered in the first instance as lectures. They all survive in several forms, at least one of which is probably based directly on the *reportatio*. This method of composition, where the master worked from notes made by a student at his own request, revising and polishing, lent itself to an almost organic process of growth and development in the work. The author himself might make repeated modifications, especially if he gave the same lecture-course more than once. Copyists of the 'published' version (or versions) too, seem to have felt free to make their own adaptations and abbreviations, omitting or inserting examples as they chose.

Not only is it difficult to establish a text which we can be reasonably confident that Peter himself would have approved, but it is hard to say what status should be accorded to the other versions of each treatise. In a parallel case – that of Peter of Poitiers' *Distinctiones super Psalterium* – P. S. Moore concludes that it is likely that the longer version is closer to the lectures, and that the abbreviation came later.[1] It has been suggested that Peter the Chanter, too, began to abbreviate his works, or at least to re-edit them, towards the end of his life, but in some passages of the shorter version the abbreviation has been made so unintelligently that it is difficult to believe that it can be Peter's work as it stands.

The manuscript tradition of Peter the Chanter's *Summa de Sacramentis* has been closely studied by J. A. Dugauquier in the introduction to his edition of the *Summa*.[2] His conclusions are summarised by Baldwin.[3] He did not find a 'good' manuscript, and has been obliged to make do with the oldest as a base (Troyes 276, of the late twelfth century from Clairvaux). This is likely, on the grounds of its early date and its Cistercian provenance, to be the best available,[4] but the problem of the status of other versions remains.

Baldwin himself has examined the manuscripts of the *Verbum Abbreviatum* (written perhaps between 1191–2). He comments: 'When...the manuscripts of the *Verbum Abbreviatum* are investigated closely they show that, like the *Summa de Sacramentis,* this was not a simple work written in one form and at one time, but rather a treatise which evolved through a number of versions.'[5] He takes the view that there was first a long, rambling 'lecture' version of the *Verbum Abbreviatum,* and then a short, reference version.[6] He has distinguished four groups of manuscripts, a long version, a short version, a series of abridgements and some reorganised versions.[7] Again, we are left with not one, but several treatises.

In the case of the *De Tropis Loquendi* twenty-three manuscripts survive,[8] plus two fragments.

A   MS Avranches, Bibliothèque municipale 28, ff.93ra–115vb (s.xiii), from Mont St Michel

B   MS Cambridge, St John's College, B.8, ff.lra–25va (s.xiii inc.), from Christ Church Canterbury.

C   MS Cambridge, Corpus Christi College 217, ff.2ra–10va (s.xiv), from Worcester.

D   MS Cambridge, Jesus College Q.C. 18, ff.1ra–39rb (s.xiii[ex.]).

E   MS Cambridge, Trinity College R.14.40, ff.1a–43a (s.xiii [inc.]).

F   MS Cambridge, University Library Gg.4.17, ff.3ra–34ra (s.xiv), from Christ Church, Canterbury.

G   MS Cambridge, University Library 1 i.1.24, ff.184ra–204vb (s.xiv).

H   MS Cambridge, University Library Kk.1.28, ff.146vb–173rb (s.xiii).

I   MS London, British Library, Harley 3596, ff.67ra–82ra (s.xiv).

J   MS London, British Library, Royal 12 F XII, ff.76ra–102vb (s.xiii)

K   MS London, Lambeth Palace 122, ff.198vb–214vb (s.xiii[inc.]), from Lanthony.

L   MS Orléans, Bibliothèque municipale 199, ff.257a–285a (x.xiii), from St Benoît-sur-Loire.

M   MS Oxford, Bodleian Library, Rawlinson C 161, ff.169ra–188ra (s.xiii).

N   MS Paris, Bibliothèque Mazarine 298, ff.162ra–189vb (s.xiii), from St Victor.

O   MS Paris, Bibliothèque Mazarine 891, ff.132va–146rb (s.xiv^{ex.}), from Collège de Navarre.

P   MS Paris, Bibliothèque Nationale Lat. 3487 A, ff.133r–143v (s.xiii), from St Pierre, Conches-en-Ouche.

Q   MS Paris, Bibliothèque Nationale Lat. 14892, ff.89ra–126vb (s.xiii), from St Victor.

R   MS Rein, Stiftsbibliothek 61, ff.122r–146v (s.xiii^{ex.}).

S   MS Salisbury, Cathedral Library 171, ff.1r–42r (s.xiii), from Salisbury.

T   MS Troyes, Bibliothèque municipale 398, ff.89ra–115rb (s.xiii), from Clairvaux.

U   MS Troyes, Bibliothèque municipale 789, ff.112ra–124vb (s.xiii^{ex.}), from Clairvaux.

V   MS Vaticano, Regin. Lat. 1283, ff.37ra–55ra (s.xiii).

W   MS Worcester, Cathedral Library F 61, ff.154va–167ra (s.xiv), from Worcester.

X   MS Zürich, Zentralbibliothek C 97, ii, ff.86r–86v (fragment) (s.xiii).

Y   MS Bern, Stadtbibliothek AA 90 nr. 20, ff.1r–3v (fragment) (s.xii–xiii).

Z   MS Paris, Bibliothèque Nationale Lat. 14445, ff.270r–296v (burnt) (s.xiii).

An Analysis of the *De Tropis Loquendi*, from eleven samples of the text (made by the late F. Giusberti):

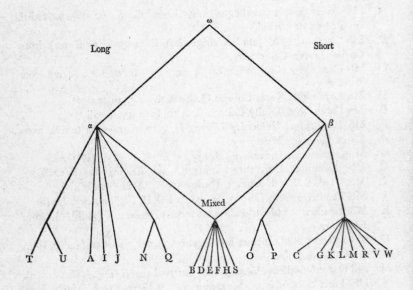

	Longer version		Shorter version	
(1)	A I J T U N Q		B D E F H S	C G K L M R V W O P
(2)	A I J T U	N Q	B D E F H S	C G K L M R V W O P
(3)	A I J T U N Q		B D E F H S	C G K L M R V W O P
(4)	A I J T U N Q B D E F H S			C G K L M R V W O P
(5)	A I J T U N Q B D E F H S			C G K L M R V W O P
(6)	A I J T U N Q B D E F H S			C G K L M R V W O P
(7)	A I J T U N Q B D E F H S			C G K L M R V W O P
(8)	A I J T U N Q B D E F H S			C G K L M R V W O P
(9)	A I J T U N Q B D E F H S			C G K L M R V W O P
(10)	A I J − − N Q B D E F H D	O −		C G K L M R V W
(11)	A I J − − N Q B D E F H S	O −		C G K L M R V W

Of these manuscripts, several contain other works of Peter the Chanter.

Z, now destroyed, contained the *Summa de Sacramentis.*

L (*Summa*) = I (*Trop.*) (MS London, British Library, Harley 3596).

R (*Summa*) = R (*Trop.*) (MS Rein, Stiftsbibliothek 61).

O (*Summa*) = K (*Trop.*) (London, Lambeth Palace 122. This manuscript also has the short version of *Verbum Abbreviatum* with marginalia incorporated into the text.) (See Baldwin II, 251).

P (*Trop.*) also has the *Verbum Abbreviatum* (short version, without marginalia, see Baldwin II, 250).

Of these L/I is fourteenth century and Dugauquier found it to diverge considerably from the group from which he selected his base manuscript (*Summa* I, xci and Baldwin II, 243).

R/R, of the later thirteenth century, also contains an inferior text of the *Summa.*

O/K is early thirteenth century, but it contains the 'popular' or 'vulgate' version of the *Verbum Abbreviatum* which Baldwin distinguishes from the longer version, closer to Peter himself, which circulated chiefly in the Paris region. It seems, then, that none of these manuscripts has anything to recommend it as a foundation for an edition of the *De Tropis* on the basis of the juxtaposition of the *De Tropis* with a good text of another of Peter's works.

The two manuscripts from Clairvaux, T and U, are both

thirteenth century copies. In T the *De Tropis* is accompanied by a *florilegium* compiled from the writings of Bernard, Hugh of St Victor, Anselm etc., by Ailred of Rievaulx's *De Spiritali Amicitia*, Odo of Cambrai's *De Peccato Originali* and a sermon. In U its companion-pieces are the *Sentences* of Master Martin, Alan of Lille's *Regulae Theologicae* and Rupert of Deutz's *De Divina Officia*. Both copies of the *De Tropis Loquendi* have the same explicit: *De schematibus et quod nichil in ipsis posset ostendi quod non precesserit scriptura divina confirmare exemplis*. Their Cistercian provenance and their relatively early date would recommend them strongly, but the text they preserve is incomplete.

Of the other identifiably French manuscripts, N and Q are related. Both come from St Victor and are therefore geographically close to Peter's activities as a master of theology in Paris. Both are of the thirteenth century, but they, too, diverge significantly from the bulk of the manuscripts, preserving a text in which the long version gives way to the short for a time.

From St Benoît-sur-Loire comes L, a thirteenth century manuscript but containing the short version of the treatise.

From Mont St Michel comes A, a thirteenth century manuscript containing the longer version.

O is a late fourteenth century manuscript from Collège de Navarre, and preserves the short version.

P is a thirteenth century manuscript, from St Pierre, Conches-en-Ouche, which is incomplete (*explicit: ergo in lege peccaverunt*), and preserves the short version.

The 'mixed' category of manuscripts probably have a common ancestor. They all have the same explicit, and those whose provenance can be established are all English: B and F from Christ Church, Canterbury, and S from Salisbury. B and E are early thirteenth century, and it seems likely that this conflation of the two main versions was made quite soon after Peter's death and that the first copy was made in England or taken to England at once. Every manuscript in this group is now in an English library. It is possible that William de Montibus is responsible for this version, or at least that he brought it to England when he returned to Lincoln. His own *Tropi* was probably composed in England, and he evidently had a copy of Peter's *De Tropis* to refer to as he worked. In an early thirteenth-century manuscript from Lanthony (K), now Lambeth Palace Library MS 122, William's *Tropi* is followed by Peter's *De Tropis Loquendi*, (ff.178–214ᵛ).

I have attempted to do no more here than call attention to the difficulties which present themselves if we wish to make use of this important and neglected work on one of the great masters of late twelfth-century Paris. There is, however, one characteristic of the work which may make it possible to draw upon Peter's teaching without misrepresenting him, and without awaiting a full edition. The scheme of the work, and the rules Peter gives for resolving contradictions in Holy Scripture, are remarkably consistent. The 'doctrine', in other words, is readily available, even if we cannot with confidence list the examples and their exposition exactly as Peter intended.

The Prologue, which was edited by the late Franco Giusberti, has now been published, in a collection of his works. I am indebted to his widow for permission to make use of his preliminary work on the manuscripts.

A COMPARISON OF PASSAGES FROM
THE 'LONG' AND THE 'SHORT' VERSION

Long Version*
    Legitur in Actibus Apostolorum quod omnes apostoli erant unanimiter perseverantes in oratione cum mulieribus et Maria matre Iesu et fratribus eius, id est contribulibus suis, scilicet Christi. Quidam tamen dixerunt relationem fieri ad hoc nomen Maria, non ad
5   hoc nomen Jesu, ne viderentur incidere in errorem Elvidii dicentis: *Post Christum natum eam cognitam fuisse a Joseph et peperisse ei filios fratres Iesu,* in quem invehitur Ieronymus dicens: *O pastorum idolum, sacerdos laicus.*
    Quandoque proprietas refertur in subiecto
10 Ut ibi: *Qui vult venire post me abneget semetipsum,* etc.
    id est maliciam suam, non seipsum substantialiter, quia id est impossibile. Deus autem nummum precipit impossibile. Maledictus enim homo qui, ut dicit auctoritas, putat Deum preceptorem esse impossibilium. Simile est Homo recedens a Deo se ipsum perdidit, et liberum arbitrium, quod sic
15 est intelligendum seipsum, id est bonitatem suam, qua indutus fuerat, et in qua integre consistere debuerat, et liberum arbitrium quod prius

habebat liberum. Sed post habuit arbitrium non liberum, sed quadam pronitate peccandi carni ancillatum.

Simile: *Quis fecit diabolum? Ipse fecit seipsum.* Non dico in
20 substantia, sed in malitia, cum Psalmista dicat: *Draco iste quem formasti ad illudendum ei*, quem, id est substantiam eius. Deus enim creavit substantiam diaboli, sed non eius malitiam.

Item cum indivisibilia sint opera Trinitatis quicquid fecit Pater fecit Filius et econverso. Autem carnem assumpsit, ergo et Pater. Quod non
25 est verum. Sed si quis diligenter inspiciat, quandam relationem implicitam inveniet, in hoc verbo assumpsi. Est enim sensus: Filius sumpsit carnem sibi, vel in se. Est ergo hic commutatio predicamenti, ut quemcunque hominem diligit Socrates diligit Plato, et econtrario Socrates diligit filium suum, ergo Plato suum. Quandoque et hoc relativum nomen aliud notat conicationem substantie
30 non proprietatis.

Ut hic: *Crucifixus est Christus, et cum eo alii duo nequam*, non communicato nequitia eorum, circa Christum, sed substantie conformitatem. Simile est: *Mittam vobis alium paraclitum.* Alium scilicet in persona non in substantia.
35 Item: *Alias oves habeo*, etc. Non dico nunc in ovina simplicitate existentes, sed alias in substantia, futuras tamen oves, et ad ecclesiasticam dignitatem revocandas.

Item et illud. *Ut congregaret filios Dei qui dispersi erant*, non qui tunc erant filii Dei, sed qui erant futuri. Apud Priscianum invenis
40 idem, hoc inter alias litteras, Sed de hoc alias.

* F.f.9ᵛ. This is the point where the short version breaks off and the longer version begins in the 'mixed' manuscripts.

1–3 Acts 1.14
5   Eluidius (?)
10   Mt. 16.24; Mk 8.34; Lk 9.23
15   Ps 103.126
30   Jn 14.16
35   Jn 10.16
38   Jn 11.52

IMPROPER USAGES;
'IN RELATIONE (NATURA AND PERSONA)'

Short Version*

Item Actus Apostolorum: *Erant autem omnes perseverantes in oratione cum mulieribus, Maria matre Iesu et fratribus eius.* Sed cuius eius? Non Marie sed Iesu.

Item regula: dictio quandoque refert accidens in subiecto,

5 quandoque subiectum in accidente.

Accidens in subiecto. Ut: *Qui vult me sequi abneget semetipsum.* Non quod facti sumus a Deo, sed quod nos ipsos fecimus per voluntatem propriam et carnalia desideria.

Item Augustus: *Homo recedens a Deo perdidit semetipsum*, id est talis est

10 in virtutibus qualis erat a Deo, *et liberum arbitrium*, id est facultatem liberi arbitrii, quasi illud non habuit a Deo liberum.

Item: *sedere a dextris meis non est meum dare vobis, sed quibus,* id est qualibus, *paratum est a patre.*

Item Augustus: *Quis fecit diabolum? Ipse semetipsum fecit.*

15 Econtra: *Dracoiste quem formasti ad illudendum,* etc. Sed relativum in prima refert accidens, in secunda substantiam que a Deo est.

Item substantiam in accidente refertur.

Ut: *crucifixi sunt cum eo alii duo nequam,* id est duo alii homines qui erant nequam.

20 *Et mittam vobis alium paraclitum.* Non dico alterius paraclitis et consolationis, sed alium eundem paraclitum.

Et alias oves habeo et cetera. Usque enim in finem seculi has oves nondum oves sed futuras oves adducet.

Et missus sum ut dispersos filios Dei aggregarem in unum, id est

25 futuros et nondum filios Dei.

Scilicet dicitur: Hec scribendi inter alias litteras.

* R. f. 128ᵛ

  1–2 Acts 1.14   16
    6 Mt 16.24; Mk 8.34; Lk 9.23
  12 Mt 20.23; Mk 10.40
  15 Ps 103.26
  18 Lk 23.32

    4 subiecto V) substantivo R.
    5 subiectum V, M) substantivo R.
    6 Accidens in subiecto)om. M, substantivo R.
  11 quod R
  20 Jn 14.16
  23 Jn 10.16

THE STRUCTURE OF THE TREATISE

In his Prologue Peter promises to deal first with *contraria,* so as to resolve them, then with things which 'seem alike' (*videntur similia*) so as to distinguish them from one another, and finally with those things which are truly alike, so as to demonstrate their likeness. He does not carry out his plan in its entirety, confining himself to *contraria*.

He sets out a scheme of subdivisions for *contrarietas superficialis,* that superficial contradiction which hides the profound agreement of everything in Scripture. This surface contradiction is found sometimes in one word, sometimes in different words. When it is in one word it sometimes occurs in the word itself, sometimes in the context in which the word is used. When it is in the word itself, it sometimes lies in the different meanings the word may have, sometimes in a difference of consignification, or of the time when the word is used, sometimes in other ways. In the case of difference of meaning, sometimes that occurs in 'proper' usages, sometimes in 'transferred' usages. The plan can be set out diagrammatically as follows:

A EQUIVOCATION

1 *Ex Varia Significatione*

(a) Proper Usages
(1) *Proper Names* i Cases where there is confusion between two men of the same name (Herod, Titus).
ii Cases where two different names are given for the same man (Salatiel, Phadaida).
(2) *Equivocation* i *Verbs* (*iurare*: to swear is to make a firm promise or to make a sacred vow. To swear lightly is forbidden, or to swear falsely).
ii *Nouns* (*homonyms*).
(*Pax* is sometimes a *carnalis affectus,* sometimes a *conscientiae tranquillitas*).

iii   *Adverbs (sicut, ut).*
iv   *Prepositions (de, secundum, preter, in).*
v   From the *coincidentia* of *two parts of speech*
      Noun and adverb (melius, tercio, used *nominaliter*
      or *adverbialiter* in different contexts).
vi   *Pronouns (hoc)*

(more cases of v, iv, iii, and cases involving conjunctions follow: *plus (nomen vel adverbium) pro, donec, ne, ab).*

vii   *Homonyms.*

(b)   Improper Usages
Cum Sacra Scriptura non habeat sermones de rebus celestibus, necesse est improprietate multiplici uti, que consistit

(1)   *tum in demonstratione*
(2)   *tum in relatione*
(3)   *tum in translatione*

For each of these, Peter considers the difficulties which arise in the case of:

i   *natura and persona*
ii   *subiectum and accidens*
iii   *materiatum and materia*
iv   *significans and significatum*
v   *continens and continentum*
vi   *totum and pars*

and some other types peculiar to each.

II   *Hyperbole, Ironia, Iocositas*

III   *Equivocatio ex varia consignificatione* (with a digression into *ex vario modo*)
IV   *Equivocatio ex varia appellatione*
V   *Equivocatio secundum diversos status*
VI   *Equivocatio secundum diversos intentiones*
VII   *Equivocatio secundum diversos respectus*

B   AMPHIBOLIA

i   *transitive*
ii   *intransitive*

C   EX DIVERSA SUPPLETIO

D   DICTIONES QUAE CADUNT   i   *in diversas species nominis*
                                ii   *in diversas partes orationis*
and miscellaneous items.

Notes

INTRODUCTION

1 Ralph's *In Anticlaudianum Alani Commentum* is edited by J. Sulowski (Warsaw, 1972). See, too, Adam de la Bassée (d. 1286), *Ludus super Anticlaudianum*, ed. P. Bayaert (Tourcoing, 1930); Ellebaut, *Anticlaudien*, ed. A. J. Creighton (Washington, 1944). For Ralph's testimony, see MS Paris BN lat. 8083, and see Hauréau, *Notices et extraits de quelques manuscrits latins de la bibliothèque nationale* (Paris 1891), vol. I, pp. 325ff.

2 *Textes*, pp. 11–29.

3 Sheridan, pp. 7–12. See, too, De Lage, and J. M. Trout, 'The Monastic vocation of Alan of Lille', *An. Cist.*, xxx (1974), 46–53. Sheridan gives a biography in his recent translation of the *Plaint of Nature* (Toronto, 1980), too.

4 John of Salisbury, *Metalogicon*, II.10, ed. C. C. J. Webb (Oxford, 1929); 1.5. For a recent study of John of Salisbury with a full bibliography, see K. Guth, *Johannes von Salisbury* (Munich, 1978).

5 M. Lebeau, 'Découverte du tombeau du bienheureux Alain de Lille', *Coll.*, xxIII (1961), 254–60 and MGH SS. xxIII, p. 881 (*Textes*, p. 22) on Alberic of Fontaines and the evidence that Alan died in 1202.

6 'Artium studiosissimus investigator', *Metalogicon*, II.10, p. 82. On the 'School of Chartres', see R. W. Southern, 'Humanism and the School of Chartres', in *Medieval Humanism* (Oxford, 1970), and N. M. Häring's reply in *Essays in honour of A. C. Pegis*, ed. J. R. O'Donnell (Toronto, 1974).

7 *Metalogicon*, II.10, p. 79.

8 'Ad omina scrupulosus, locum questionis inveniebat ubique...in questionibus subtilis et multus', *ibid.*, p. 79.

9 'Dedicit quod docuerat'; 'reversus dedocuit', *ibid.*, p. 79.

10 'Fisus lector sed obtusior disputator', *ibid.*, p. 82.

11 *Metalogicon*, II.10., p. 82.

12 *De Triumphis Ecclesiae Libri Octo*, ed. T. Wright (London, 1856), p. 74.

13 *Catalogus Virorum Illustrium*, ed. N. M. Häring, in 'Der Literaturkatalog von Affligem', *R. Bén*, LXXXI (1970), 82, cf. *Textes*, pp. 17–20.

14 PL 210.305–8; 332c; 334b; 685–8 and see Sheridan, pp. 8–9.

15 *Textes*, p. 21.

16 See *Textes*, pp. 12–14.

17 P. S. Moore, *The Works of Peter of Poitiers* (Washington, 1936), discusses Peter's *opera*.

18 For the benefit of monastic scholars, as well as those in the schools.

19 B. Smalley, *The study of the Bible in the Middle Ages*, 2nd ed. (Oxford, 1952), Chapter 2.

20 Baldwin, vol. I, p. 97, and vol. II, notes 43 and 52, pp. 66–7.

21 'Hodierna disputatio', Simon of Tournai, *Disputationes*, p. 237.

22 *Textes*, pp. 19–20, p. 63; *Quoniam Homines*, p. 116. For Otto of St Blaise's comment, see MGH SS, xx, p. 326.

23 'Glosa obscurior textu', Geoffrey of Auxerre, *Libellus* XL, PL 185.609B.

24 M. and C. Dickson, 'Le Cardinal Robert de Courson: sa vie', *AHDLMA,* IX (1934), 53–142.

25 J. W. Baldwin, *Masters, princes and merchants* (2 vols., Princeton, 1970). I have not attempted to go beyond his findings in the survey which follows.

26 His life is summarised in a sentence. Baldwin, vol. I, p. 43.

27 Warichez assembles the evidences for Simon's life in *Disputationes*, pp. x-xxxiii.

28 J. W. Baldwin, 'A Debate at Paris over Thomas Becket, between Master Roger and Master Peter the Chanter', *Studia Gratiana*, XI (1967), 125.

29 Baldwin, vol. II, p. 33, note 312.

30 D. Van den Eynde, 'Deux sources de la Somme théologique de Simon de Tournai', *Antonianum*, XXIV (1949), 19–42.

31 Peter of Poitiers' *Sententiae*, ed. P. S. Moore and M. Dulong (Notre Dame Indiana, 1950), II. xxxvi, xxxix, point out that sections 4–10 of the *Summa* are taken directly from Peter's *Sententiae*. For this passage, see Simon of Tournai, *Disputationes*, p. 47; Peter of Poitiers' *Sentences*, III.25; Peter Lombard, *Sentences*, II Dist. xxvi.2; Alan, *Reg. Theol.*, Rule 85, PL 210.664.

32 Moore, *Works of Peter of Poitiers,* pp. 38–9.

33 Baldwin, vol. I, p. 44.

34 Not to be confused with Peter of Poitiers of St Victor (see Baldwin, vol. I, pp. 32–4) or Peter of Poitiers of Cluny, see J. Kritzeck, *Peter the Venerable and Islam* (Princeton, 1964), pp. 31ff. On our Peter, see Moore, *Works of Peter of Poitiers*, pp. 1–24.

35 Baldwin, vol. II, p. 33, note 323.

36 Baldwin, vol. I, pp. 44–5.

37 A. M. Landgraf, 'Peter of Capua', *New Scholasticism*, XIV (1940), 57–74, and O. Lottin, *Psychologie et morale aux xiie et xiiie siècles* (Gembloux, 1959), IV, (2), p. 844.

38 *Textes*, p. 13. M. Wilks suggests that Alan had more of the courtier about him than his works immediately suggest. 'Alan of Lille and the New Man', *Studies in Church History*, XIV (1977), 117–36.

39 *Textes*, pp. 18–20.

40 C. Haskins, *Studies in the History of Mediaeval Science* (Cambridge, Mass., 1927), p. 96; Burgundius' phrase is a commonplace one, but it expresses his own view of what he was doing.

41 *Textes*, p. 13.

42 It is likely that Alan was connected at some time with the Benedictines. One sermon raises the possibility that he had links with the Augustinian canons. See *Textes*, p. 27, and P. Glorieux, 'Alain de Lille, le moine et l'abbaye du Bec', *RTAM*, XXXIX (1972), 51–62.

43 *Apostles' Creed*, p. 16. See, too, Baldwin, vol. I, pp. 88–116, on Peter the Chanter's use of the same division between 'celestial' and 'sub-celestial'. Baldwin's survey of schools and scholars in Chapter 3 makes it plain that Alan stands a little outside the circles he discusses.

44 *Quoniam Homines*, p. 20.

1. HANDMAIDS OF THEOLOGY

1 Peter's *Pantheologus* is in St John's College, Oxford, MS. 31, and see R. W. Hunt 'English learning in the late twelfth century', *Transactions of the Royal Historical Society*, XIX (1934), reprinted in *Essays in Mediaeval History*, ed. R. W. Southern (London, 1968), pp. 119–20, and B. Smalley, *The study of the Bible in the Middle Ages* (Oxford, 1952), p. 248. Selections from other *distinctiones* are edited by J. B. Pitra, *Spicilegium Solesmense* (Paris, 1855), vols. II and III¹. On the *distinctiones*, see P. S. Moore, *The Works of Peter of Poitiers* (Notre Dame, 1936), pp. 78ff., R. H. Rouse and M. A. Rouse, 'Biblical *Distinctiones* in the thirteenth century', *AHDLMA*, XLI (1974), 27–37, and cf. R. H. Rouse and M. A. Rouse 'The verbal concordance to the scriptures', *Archivum Fratrum Predicatorum*, XLIV (1974), 9.

2 'Et flosculis verborum et sententiarum depictus', St John's College, Oxford, MS 31, f.8.

3 Smalley, *The Study of the Bible*, pp. 246–8.

4 Rouse, 'The verbal concordance', pp. 1–30; see, too, D. A. Callus, 'The contribution to the study of the Fathers made by the thirteenth century Oxford School', *Journal of Ecclesiastical History*, V (1954), 139–48.

5 Cassiodorus, Preface to *Commentary on the Psalms*, CCSL, XCVII, p. 3.6.

6 Bede, *De Schematibus et Tropis*, PL 90.175A–B.

7 Peter Lombard, *Commentaries on the Pauline Epistles*, PL 191.1662 c.

8 'Quae fit translata dictione a propria significatione ad non propriam similitudinem.' PL 90.175A and 179B.

9 'Nimis videntur accommodae', p. 17.2, Chapter 10, and see Cassiodorus, *Institutiones*, ed. R. A. B. Mynors (Oxford, 1937), p. 42.11–12, I. XV. 2.

10 'Corporales imagines' is a commonplace in the *Confessions* and in the anti-Manichean writings.

11 'Nefas sit credere Scripturas divinas aliquid supervacuum continere', PL 70–17A, Chapter 10, cf. L. M. de Rijk, *Logica Modernorum* (2 vols., Assen, 1967), vol. I, pp. 51ff. and Boethius, PL 64.166–7.

12 'Licet obscure', PL 191.1662c.

13 'Aliqua similitudo', *ibid.*

14 'Videmus nunc per speculum in aenigmate', I Cor. 13.12.

15 'Videntur esse contraria', PL 191.1662c.

16 'Cum non sint', *ibid.*

17 'Artes enim liberales tanquam subsellia subserviunt theologie', F (= Cambridge, University Library, MS Gg. 4.17), f. 26. For a list of manuscripts and *sigla* see Appendix II.

18 F, f. 6 (Equivocation of Pronouns: *hoc*):

> Et notandum quod hoc pronomen hoc, sive aliud, demonstrativum quandoque demonstrat ypostasim, sive substantiam subiectam nature, circumscripta forma vel qualitate, per abstraentem intellectum vel spiritali statu indicans novam formam advenire.
>
> Ut: hoc lignum erit lapis; hoc fenum vitrum; hoc vinum acetum. Ut quasi circa quandam ilen [i.e. hylen] fiat ibi substantia alium statuum mutatio, sic dogmatizante phisico.
>
> Quandoque econtrario eo demonstratur sola forma substantialis circumscripta substantia subiecta sive ypostasi immo desitura esse.
>
> Ut: hic panis transubstantiatur in corpus Christi;
>
> Vel: hic panis erit corpus Christi, verum est.
>
> Verba mutationum substantie recipimus, non alia. Facta enim mutatione substantia panis et vini desinit esse. Non autem generalis forma adhuc enim ibi remanet panitas et unitas. Non sic in predictis, sed unitas adest, et perit fenitas. Substantia subiecta utrobique immobili manente. Sed huiusmodi demonstratio rara est, nec nisi in theologicis invenitur.

19 F, f.26.

20 'Ancilla domini', F, f.27.

21 PL 210.687–8.

22 *Logica Modernorum* II[11], 327.2.

23 On Roman and Carolingian *Differentiae*, see *De Proprietate*

Sermonum vel Rerum, ed. M. L. Uhlfelder, Papers and monographs of the American Academy in Rome, xv (Rome, 1954), introduction.

24 F. Giusberti's edition of the Prologue is published posthumously Naples, 1983). I am grateful to his widow for permission to make use of the text.

25 Matthew 2.19; Luke 3.1, 9, 21.

26 Matthew 5.34.

27 Matthew 5.33, Romans 1.9.

28 F, f.11, Q, f.101ᵛ II, T, f.94ᵛ. 'Restat ut dicamus de multiplicitate proveniente ex dictione vel oratione posita improprie, que translatio appellatur apud dialecticos.'

29 Matthew 1.1.

30 Isaiah 53.8, cf. Acts 8.33.

31 'Quam nullus potest verbo explicare', F, f. 16.

32 'Sed improprie dicitur generatio, quoniam non fuit ibi decisio carnis', *ibid.*

33 F, f.16.

34 On *translatio*, see, for example, John Scotus Eriugena, *De Prae-destinatione,* ed. G. Madec, CCCM, L (1978) Chapter 9, Peter Abelard *Logica Ingredientibus*, ed. B. Geyer, Beiträge, xxi, p. 399, and L. M. de Rijk, *Logica Modernorum*, vol. i, pp. 51–5.

35 *Textes*, pp. 148–51, 109–48.

36 *Textes*, pp. 151–2 and pp. 289–94.

37 Otto of St Blaise, *Chronicon, M. G. H. Scriptores in usum schol.,* ed. A. Hofmeister (1912), pp. 64–5. On Praepositinus, see the *Summa contra Haereticos ascribed to Prepositinus*, ed. J. N. Garvin and J. A. Corbett (Notre Dame, Indiana, 1958).

38 London, British Library, MS. Add. 19767, f.217, reproduced in *Textes*, pp. 24–5.

39 Baldwin, vol. i, pp. 3–11.

40 *Textes*, pp. 19–20.

41 Baldwin, vol. i, p. 6.

42 Baldwin, vol. i, pp. 44–5. Otto of Freising's *Chronicle*, with its date twenty years later unfortunately fits only Praepositinus' career.

43 PL 210.805B, 809B.

44 PL 210.630C, Rule 19, 'Cum enim nullum nomen Deo proprie conveniat'.

45 Rules 18–53.

46 PL 210.637C, Rule 34.

47 'Translatio nominis', PL 210.633C.

48 'Translatio rei', *ibid.*

49 'Definitio: solas voces...includat', PL 64.1187.

50 PL 210.633C–D, Rule 26.

51 That is, with the relationships between the Persons of the Trinity.

52 'Omni theologica predicatione ostenditur Deus esse quid, vel ad quid', PL 210.631C.

53 'Improprie dicitur esse', PL 210.630D, Rule 20.

54 'Et ita proprietas est in essendo, sed improprietas in dicendo', *ibid.*

55 'Omne simplex proprie est et improprie dicitur esse', *ibid.*

56 PL 210.630B, Rule 18.

57 N. M. Häring, 'A Treatise on the Trinity by Gilbert of Poitiers', *RTAM*, xxxix (1972), 15–16.

58 'A naturali facultati sunt translata nomina ad theologiam', N. M. Häring, 'A Latin Dialogue on the Doctrine of Gilbert of Poitiers', *Mediaeval Studies*, xv (1953), 267.

59 'Sunt etiam quedam translationes improprie. Sed ex similitudine quadam alie magis proprie.' F, f.16ᵛ.

60 'Nota quod omne verbum dicendum de Deo affirmative ponitur improprie, preter hoc verbum "esse", quod solum de Deo, et de solo Deo dicitur proprie, de quolibet alio translative.' F, f.16ᵛ.

61 'Deo proprie assignetur verbum essendi', F, f.16ᵛ.

62 'Eorum enim que sunt, alia subsistunt, alia insunt, alia assunt, alia prosunt, alia obsunt.'

63 F, f.16ᵛ, PL 210.635–6, Rules 30–1 on *concretivum*, Boethius *Contra Eutychen* III on Being, in *Theological Tractates*, ed. H. F. Stewart and E. K. Rand (rev. edn London, 1973).

64 *Quoniam Homines*, p. 11.

65 'Qui facit veritatem, venit ad lucem' (John 3.20); 'Non solum pro eo quod proprie dicitur facere, sed pro omni verbo.' *Anselmi Opera Omnia*, ed. F. S. Schmitt (6 vols., Rome/Edinburgh, 1938–68) vol. I.182 pp. 10–11.

66 *Ibid.*, I.182, p. 18.

67 PL 210.722B–C.

68 In an orthodox and traditional spirit, following Cassiodorus and Bede, Thomas of Salisbury explicitly calls metaphor an *impropria significatio*. See J. J. Murphy, *Rhetoric in the Middle Ages* (California, 1974), pp. 317–26 on Thomas of Salisbury. For a fuller explanation of the point, see *Quoniam Homines*, p. 199, para. 55.

69 'In sacra pagina periculosum est theologicorum nominum ignorare virtues.' PL 210.687B. Alan is echoing *Sophistici Elenchi*, I. 165ᵃ, pp. 15–16.

70 Thierry of Chartres, p. 237.68 and Gilbert of Poitiers, p. 277.68–74.

71 'Ut est sermo non loquitur', PL 210.687B.

72 'A propriis significationibus peregrinantur', PL 210.687B.

73 I am indebted to Dr D. P. Henry and Dr K. M. Fredborg for drawing some of the following parallels to my attention.

74 For a recent bibliography of the grammatical commentaries of the

twelfth century, see 'The Summa of Petrus Helias on Priscianus Minor', ed. J. E. Tolson, with an introduction by Margaret Gibson, *Cahiers*, XXVII and XXVIII (1978), 188–9. On Peter Helias' commentary as a standard work, see R. W. Hunt, 'The *Summa* of Petrus Helias on Priscianus Minor', *Historiographica Linguistica*, II.i (1975). On the evidence that Alan knew Peter Helias on rhetoric, see K. M. Fredborg, 'Petrus Helias on Rhetoric', *Cahiers*, XIII (1974), 31–41, and British Library, MS Harley 6324, f.61ra.

75 Book XVII.69–75.

76 'Quia pronomen significat substantiam sine respectu qualitatis', *Cahiers*, XXVII, p. 98.12.

77 *Ibid.*, p. 97.96.

78 'Ubi adiectiva substantivantur', PL 210.687B.

79 See D. P. Henry, *The Logic of St Anselm* (Oxford, 1967), p. 66.

80 *Cahiers*, XXVII, p. 72.98; 73.3. Cf. E. Jeauneau, 'Deux rédactions des gloses de Guillaume de Conches sur Priscian', *RTAM*, XXVII (1960), 213.

81 Rupert of Deutz, *De Victoria Verbi Dei*, ed. H. Haacke, MGH Quellen, V (1970), p. 56.7–13.

82 *Cahiers*, XXVII, p. 63.77; p. 66.69, cf. Boethius on the *De Interpretatione*, II, ed. C. Meiser (Leipzig, 1880), p. 56.16–18.

83 See Henry, *The Logic of St Anselm*, pp. 42–8 for the difference between *dicitur de* and *esse in*.

84 There are, however, relevant passages in Peter Helias which show that the notion was not confined to dialectic, *Cahiers*, XXVII, p. 33.64.

85 See *Logica Modernorum*, ed. L. M. de Rijk (2 vols., Assen, 1967), vol. II^1, p. 105 and *Petrus Abaelardus Dialectica*, ed. L. M. de Rijk (Assen, 1956), p. XXXVIII on inherence and identity theories. *Ibid.*, p. 105, De Rijk finds discrepancies in Abelard's own works.

86 'Faciat accidentia esse sine materiali subjecto', PL 210.360B. On transubstantiation, see *Contra Haereticos*, PL 210.359–63. On *materiale impositum* see *Logica Modernorum*, II^1, p. 231. Some play on words may be intended here.

87 'Ubi affirmatio impropria, negatio vera', PL 210.687C.

88 'Omnes affirmationes de Deo dictae incompactae, negationes vero verae'. PL 210.630A.

89 'Petrus est justus', PL 210.687C.

90 'Significare videtur compositionem iustitiae ad Petrum', *ibid.*

91 'Potius significatur esse iustitia, quam iustus', *ibid.*

92 'Negationes vero de Deo dictae, et verae et propriae sunt; secundum quae removetur a Dei quod ei per inhaerentiam non convenit', PL 210.630B.

93 'Ubi constructio non subiacet legibus Donati', PL 210.687C.

94 H. de Lubac discusses the history of this dictum in 'Saint Grégoire

et la grammaire', *Recherches de science réligieuse*, XLVIII (1960), 185–226, *sub regulis Donati*.

95 'Latina quidem locutio dissonat', PL 189.1570A.
96 'Congrua sensus aedificat', *ibid.*
97 'Tam voce quam sensu', *Cahiers*, XXVII, p. 1.
98 'Locutiones enim non fiunt nisi propter representandum intellectum', *Cahiers*, XXVII, p. 1.
99 *Cahiers*, XXVII, p. 1 *et al.*, and see Priscian, *Ars Minor*, ed. H. Keil, *Grammatici Latini*, vol. III (Leipzig, 1859), Books XVII–XVIII.
100 'Aliena a regulis Tullii', PL 210.687C.
101 Abelard, *Dialectica*, pp. 443–5.
102 'Ubi fides remota a rationis argumento', PL 210.688A.
103 *De Planctu Naturae*, PL 210.431, tr. D. Moffat (New York, 1908), p. 2.
104 PL 210.688B.
105 What Augustine would call *corporales imagines*. This is a favourite phrase of his in the *Confessions* and the Anti-Manichean writings.
106 *Textes*, p. 302, *Sermon on the Intelligible Sphere*.
107 *Ibid.*, and cf. *Quoniam Homines*, I.2, p. 122.
108 *Textes*, p. 242.
109 PL 210.329D.
110 PL 210.819C.
111 PL 210.922A–B.
112 'Ordinatissima republica', *ibid.*
113 'Ingenialis potentia', PL 210–922B.
114 'Potestas logistica', *ibid.*
115 PL 210.444A–B, *De Planctu Naturae*, tr. D. Moffat (New York, 1908), pp. 27–8.
116 *Textes*, pp. 243, 281; PL 210.18D, 224B.
117 'Celsa divinitatis', *Theological Tractates*, p. 4.23–4.
118 'Finis est constitutus', *ibid.*
119 L. M. de Rijk, *Logica Modernorum*, vol. II^{ii}, p. 702.15; cf. F. Giusberti, 'A treatise on Implicit Propositions from around the turn of the twelfth century', *Cahiers*, XXI (1977), p. 48.
120 'Scilicet nomen Dei essentiale', *Logica Modernorum*, II^{ii}, p. 684.1–2.
121 'Iuxta regulam grammaticorum', Simon of Tournai, *Disputationes*, XXXV.1, p. 203.15; cf. Priscian, *Ars Minor*, XVIII.36, ed. H. Keil, *Grammatici Latini*, vol. III (Leipzig, 1858), p. 130.24, and 'The Summa of Petrus Helias on Priscianus Minor', ed. J. E. Tolson, p 139.19ff., p. 151.44ff.
122 'Pro varietate affectuum', *ibid.*, p. 203.16–17.
123 'Subaudiendum est', *ibid.*, p. 103.203.
124 Simon of Tournai, *Disputationes*, XXXV.1.
125 'Philosophi per regulam humanarum artium non potuerunt aliquid

proprie discere de Deo', *Écrits théologiques de l'école d'Abélard*, ed. A. Landgraf, SSLov, xiv (1934), p. 6.

126 'Minus grammatice dicitur', *Sententie* of Peter of Poitiers, ed. P. S. Moore and M. Dulong (Notre Dame, Indiana, 1943), vol. i, Book I.3.175.

127 'Huius objectionis solutio pendet ex arte grammatica', *ibid.*, Book I.4.25.

128 'Cum nomina transferuntur ad theologica cuncta mutantur', *Quoniam Homines*, p. 200, para. 56; Boethius *De Trinitate* 4.

129 'Specialiter theologica, *Quoniam Homines*, p. 198, para. 55.

130 'Ex his colligitur regula', *ibid.*

131 'Essentiale quod idem significat et appellat', *ibid.*

132 *Ibid.*, p. 199, para. 55. On *significare* and *appellare*, see L. M. de Rijk, *Logica Modernorum*, vol. ii¹, pp. 177–263.

133 *Quoniam Homines*, p. 202, para. 58.

134 PL 210.621A–B.

135 Gilbert of Poitiers, pp. 189–90.

136 PL 210.621C.

137 'Ad limen theologie', *Textes*, p. 275.

138 'Ad ianuam celestis regine', *ibid.*

139 *Textes*, p. 275 'Relinquende sunt in pace', *Sermo de cleris ad theologiam non accedentibus*.

140 'Inanes et transitoriae scientiae', *Textes*, p. 274.

141 'A se institutas, a se ipso mirabiliter ordinatas', *Textes*, p. 275.

142 'Pedissecae theologie, ancillae celestis philosophiae', *Textes*, p. 275.

143 Rupert of Deutz, *De Trinitate et Operibus Eius*, ed. H. Haacke, CCCM xxiv, xi, viii. 3, pp. 2040–2.

144 *Ibid.*, p. 2048. 'Sed serio fideliterque quod expediebat de creatore loquerentur, bonumque ad honorem eius sermonem opere splendido texentes operarentur.'

145 'Theophania: the scientia angelica qua Deum intuetur angelus.' *Textes, Expositio Prosae de Angelis*, p. 227.

146 'Qua homo trinitatem intuetur', *Quoniam Homines*, p. 121.

147 'Fit homo deus, quia per hanc speculationem quodammodo deificatur', *Quoniam Homines*, p. 121.

148 'Ubi divina descendit excellentia ut humana ascendat intelligentia', PL 210.687B.

149 *Textes*, p 227.

150 'Offendit splendor oculos, mentemque stupore
Percussit rerum novitas, defecit in illis
Visus, et interior mens caligavit ad illas.' (*Anticlaudianus* vi.3–5)
On Alan's liking for the antithesis of earth and heaven (*solus* and *polus*), see *Textes*, pp. 241, 264, PL 210.172; Bossuat, pp. 128.166 and p. 130.243 on the *regina poli*. This identification of the Queen

of Heaven with Theology has been challenged, but it clearly accords with Alan's thinking here. On the *stupor* or *morbus communis* and its ancestry in Boethius' *De Consolatione*, see P. Dronke, 'Boethius, Alanus and Dante', *Romanische Forschungen*, LXXVIII (1966), 119–25.

151 Genesis 28.12.

152 *Ars Praedicandi*, Preface, PL 210.111 B.

153 'Que celestium spirituum, vel civium spondet doctrinam, *ibid.*

154 *Textes*, p. 195. Ralph Longchamps tells us where Alan found these terms in his Commentary on the *Anticlaudianus*, p. 42.3–5 (I.xxxi): John Scotus Eriugena, *Super Hierarchiam*, PL 122.1042.

155 'Sic altioribus theologie verbis intonuit,' *Textes*, p. 297.

156 *De Planctu Naturae,* PL 210.446B.

157 PL 210.621–2. For an alternative view of the *aenigmata,* see P. Dronke, *Fabula* (Leiden/Cologne, 1974), pp. 32–47.

158 *Anticlaudianus*, v.114, Bossuat, p. 126.

159 *Textes*, p. 277.

160 *Ibid.*

161 *Textes*, p. 83.

162 PL 210.621–2.

163 PL 210.577–80. This is a refrain recurring throughout these four columns.

164 *Quoniam Homines*, p. 119.

165 'Dum ad ineffabilia conscendunt, in varios errores ineffabiliter ruinosi descendunt'. *ibid.*

166 *Ibid.*

167 'Dum temptat divina loqui', *Anticlaudianus* v.120, Bossuat, p. 126.

168 *Anticlaudianus* v.121–2, Bossuat, p. 127.

169 On the manuals of the art of preaching, see J. J. Murphy, *Rhetoric in the Middle Ages* (California, 1974), pp. 317–26; on the *Liber Poenitentialis* and its novelty, see *Textes*, pp. 152–4; on the *Distinctiones*, see *Textes*, pp. 71–3.

170 *Quoniam Homines*, Prologue, p. 119.

171 'Verborum transpositiones in ordinem', Gilbert of Poitiers, p. 55.48.

172 'Novitates in regulam', *ibid.*

173 'Celsa divinitatis', PL 210.197B.

174 'Quod fit per spiritualem conjunctionem animae et Dei.' PL 210.197B.

175 *Asclepius*, ed. P. Thomas, *Apulei Opera*, vol. III (Leipzig, 1908) and ed. A. D. Nock and A. J. Festugière, Corpus Hermeticum, XIII–XVIII (2) *Les Belles Lettres* (Paris, 1945), Part 6, for Nock's introduction on the origins and history of this work, and see W. Gundel, *Neue astrologische Texte des Hermes Trismegistos* (Munich, 1936).

176 'Qualia veritas habet', Augustine, *De Civitate Dei* VIII.23, CCSL, XLVII, p. 302.

177 'Alios deos...a summo Deo factos, alios ab hominibus.' Augustine, *De Civitate Dei* VIII.23, *Asclepius*, 23, 24, 27.

178 Augustine, *Enarrationes in Psalmos*, CCSL, XXXVIII (1966), pp. 575–6. This passage will be discussed more fully later.

179 PL 42.1102–3.

180 'Dominus et omnium factor deorum secundum fecit dominum'.

181 See, too, Nock, Introduction, pp. 266–8 on the use of the *Asclepius* by Bernard Silvestris, John of Salisbury, Thierry of Chartres; Adelard of Bath knew the *Asclepius* too. His *De Eodem et Diverso* is edited by H. Willner, *Beiträge*, IV (1903), no. i, p. 10. For some borrowings from the *Asclepius* in Thierry of Chartres, see Thierry of Chartres, p. 97[n], p. 189[n], p. 270[n], p. 275[n], p. 287[n]. Peter Abelard, *Opera Theologica*, ed. E. M. Buytaert, CCCM, XI (1969), *Theologia Christiana* I.61, 64, 70; IV.101, *Theologia Scholarium* 114, 117, 123.

182 PL 210.404D.

183 Alan of Lille in particular: the *Summa Quoniam Homines* makes use of passages from *Asclepius*, 4, 8, 20, 23, 31, 33, 41.

184 *Asclepius*, 3.

185 *Asclepius*, 5.

186 'Species vero deorum, quas conformat humanitas', *ibid.*

187 *Asclepius*, 23.

188 'Spiritu et ratione', *Asclepius*, 10.

189 *Asclepius*, 10.

190 'Sed ex gratia deificatus', Gregory the Great, *Moralia in Job* XVIII.li.83, PL 76.88C.

191 *Letter* X.2, PL 33.74B–C.

192 'Deus deorum Dominus locutus est', CCSL, XXXVIII (1966), pp. 575–6.

193 *Quoniam Homines* II.i, p. 271.

194 'Assimilatur'; 'per similitudinem', *Hierarchia*, *Textes*, p. 223.

195 'Conformatur', *ibid.*

196 *Summa Quoniam Homines*, p. 271.

197 *Asclepius*, 23.

198 *Asclepius*, 6. This is something of a Neoplatonic commonplace. See Plotinus, *Ennead* III.

199 'A sua divinitate recedere', Bernard Silvestris (?) *Commentary on the Aeneid*, ed. E. W. Jones and E. F. Jones (Nebraska, 1977), pp. 28–30.

200 'Coniunctio deorum'; 'dignatio', *Asclepius*, 7.

201 *Textes*, p. 302.

202 'Optimum animal', *ibid.*
'In naturam ferae moresque beluarum', *ibid.*

203 'Sensualitas motus', *Asclepius* 7, and *De Planctu Naturae*, PL 210.443C.

204 'Rationis motus', PL 210.443C.

205 'In vitiorum occasum deducit'; 'in orientem virtutum ut oriatur invitat', PL 210.443C.

206 'Haec hominem in bestiam degenerando transmutat, ista hominem in deum potentialiter transfigurat', *ibid.*

207 'Disputare facit cum angelis', *ibid.*

208 'Liber Poenitentialis', PL 210.283C.

209 'Intellectualitas', *Textes*, p. 303.

210 'Fit anima deus', *ibid.*

211 *Textes*, p. 269 and PL 210.123A.

212 *Anticlaudianus* v.84.

213 PL 210.169 B–C. Chapter 29 of *The Art of Preaching*.

214 'Ad divinae rationis intellegentiam', *Asclepius*, 6.

215 'Quasi deificatio', PL 210.673D, *Regulae Theologicae*, 99.

216 PL 210.673C–4D, *Regulae Theologicae*, 99.

217 'Supra se', PL 210.674A.

218 'Se ipsa supra se utitur fitque etiam iuxta Mercurium deus', *Asclepius*, 6, cf. Thierry, pp. 70–1.

219 'Se humiliavit usque ad thesim nostrae naturae', PL 210.674A.

220 PL 210.674A.

221 *Anselmi Opera Omnia*, vol. II.59.27–8.

222 Thierry, p. 251.89–95, *Contra Eutychen*, 4.

223 Bonaventure, *Opera Omnia*, vol. v (1891), pp. 295–313.

224 'Iam nimis nostrae ratiocinationis series evagatur, quae ad ineffabile deitatis arcanum, tractatum audet attollere, ad cuius rei intelligentiam, nostrae mentis languescunt suspiria.' PL 210.444C–D.

225 PL 210.446A–B.

226 *Virtues and Vices*, p. 45.

227 'A vera sue rationis dignitate degeneres', *Quoniam Homines*, p. 119.

228 'Retento hominis nomine', *ibid.*

229 'Imaginatur figmenta', *ibid.*

230 'Theologiae facultatis derogant dignitati', *ibid.*

231 *Ibid.* On the idea that God gave man the liberal arts, see John Scotus Eriugena, *De Praedestinatione*, ed. G. Madec, CCCM, L (1978), p. 45.17–37.

2. THEOLOGIA RATIONALIS

1 *Textes*, pp. 68–9. See, in addition, J. Jolivet, 'Remarques sur les "Regulae Theologicae" d'Alain de Lille', AGJ, pp. 83–100.

2 Edited in Appendix to *Textes*. On the authorship of the *De Arte*, see further, Appendix I.

3 *De Naturae Philosophiae seu Platonis et Aristotelis Consensione* (Paris, 1560).

4 *Astrologia Gallica* (The Hague, 1661).

5 See Bodleian Library MS. Selden Supra 79, ff.vii–xxi, copied between 1620 and 1630 by B. Twyne.

6 The *Liber de Causis* is edited by A. Pattin (Louvain, 1966).

7 Proclus, *The Elements of Theology*, ed. and tr. E. R. Dodds (Oxford, 1963), p. xxx.

8 Ed. C. Baeumker, 'Das pseudo-hermetische Buch der vierundzwanzig Meister (*Liber XXIV Philosophorum*)', *Beiträge*, xxv (1927). Nicholas of Amiens had a copy of the *Liber*. See *Textes*, p. 319.

9 Ed. Baeumker, p. 207, and see *Textes*, p. 164 on Alan's introduction of *intelligibilis*.

10 *Textes*, p. 164.

11 PL 210.623D, 'Quidquid est, ideo est, quia unum numero est', cf. Dominicus Gundisalvi, *De Unitate et Uno*, ed. P. Corbens, *Beiträge*, I (1891), p. 17.

12 PL 210.654C–D, *Theological Tractates*, p. 42.

13 In Rule 1 there is a reference to *De Trinitate* III, in Rule 2 to *Consolatio Philosophiae* III.xi.29 and 39–41, in Rule 8 to *De Trinitate* IV and II, in Rule 10 to *De Trinitate* IV, in Rule 12 to *De Trinitate* III, in Rule 28 to *De Trinitate* IV, in Rule 12 to *Contra Eutychen* I, in Rule 43 to *De Trinitate* IV.

14 *Metalogicon* IV.6.

15 'Neque deduci ad imagines', Boethius, *De Trinitate* II.

16 *Textes*, p. 66; M. D. Chenu, 'Une théologie axiomatique au xiie siècle: Alain de Lille', *Cîteaux*, XI (1958), 137–42, and see V. Zoubov, 'Autour des *Quaestiones super Geometriam Euclidis* de Nicole Oresme', *Mediaeval and Renaissance Studies*, VI (1968), 150–71.

17 Boethius, *Theological Tractates*, p. 40.

18 *Ibid.*, p. 42.

19 Proclus, *In Primum Euclidis Elementorum Librum Commentarii*, ed. G. Friedlein (Leipzig, 1873), revised and translated G. R. Morrow (Princeton, 1970), Prologue I.i.3–4, cf. Boethius, *De Trinitate* II, *Theological Tractates*, p. 8.

20 *Ibid* II.viii.75, *De Hebdomadibus*, *Theological Tractates*, p.40.

21 *Posterior Analytics* I.x.76^{b}–77^{a}.

22 *Consolation of Philosophy* III.10, p. 270.

23 'Accedit ad ypothesim qua utitur ad ostendendum propositum', Thierry of Chartres, p. 424.12, *Theological Tractates*, p. 44.66–8, cf. Thierry, p. 60.29. For a passage in the field of logic, see Boethius *De Differentiis Topicis*, I, PL 64.1177.

24 *Life and Works of Clarembald of Arras*, ed. N. M. Häring (Toronto, 1965), p. 210.

25 Gilbert of Poitiers, p. 189.57.

26 Boethius, *De Institutione Arithmetica*, ed. G. Friedlein (Leipzig,

1867), includes the text of the pseudo-Boethian geometry, re-edited by M. Folkerts, *Boethius: Geometrie II* (Wiesbaden, 1970).

27 John the Scot and Remigius of Auxerre, *Commentaries on the Opuscula Sacra*, ed. E. K. Rand, Quellen und Untersuchungen zur lateinische Philologie des Mittelalters, 1 (1906), p. 51.

28 Thierry of Chartres, p. 119.31.

29 'Quoniam locali similitudine multa continent', Gilbert of Poitiers, p. 189.57–8.

30 PL 210.621A.

31 'In huiusmodi principiis stat omnium demonstrationum resolutio', Thomas Aquinas, *Opuscula Theologica*, vol. II, ed. R. Spiazzi (Rome, 1954), p. 393, *Lect.* 1.13 on Boethius' *De Hebdomadibus*.

32 *Ibid.*

33 Gilbert of Poitiers, pp. 189–90, Alan, PL 210.621A–B.

34 'Omnis scientia suis nititur regulis velut propriis fundamentis', PL 210.621A.

35 *Post. An.* 1.ix.75^b.

36 *Ibid.*, 1.ix.76^a.

37 Gilbert with a reference to *analectica* which may suggest that he had Aristotle's discussions in mind. Gilbert's list is as follows:

> Ut enim de positivis gramatice facultatis regulis taceamus, certum est quod et qui vocantur 'communes loci' rethorum et 'maxime propositiones' dialecticorum et 'theoremata' geometrarum et 'anxiomata' musicorum et 'generales sententie' ethicorum seu philosophorum continentur universalitate huius regule qua dicitur: 'communis animi conceptio est enuntiatio quam quisque probat auditam'. Gilbert of Poitiers, pp. 189–90.

38 Clarembald of Arras has: 'Regulae positivae grammaticae subserviunt facultati, loci communes oratoribus, maximae propositiones dialecticis, theoremata quadruvii probatur elementis. Harum igitur artium professores suarum diversitate utuntur conceptionum'. Clarembald of Arras, p. 194.

39 'Ut de grammatica taceamus, quae tota est in hominis beneplacito, et in voluntate, et de eius regulis, quae sunt in sola hominis positione; ceterae scientiae proprias habent regulas, quibus nituntur, ut dialectica regulae habet quas maximas vocat, rhetorica locos communes, ethica generales sententias, physica aphorismos, arithmetica porismata, id est regulas subtile...Sunt et anxiomata musicorum, quae sunt regulae artis musicae...Theoremata vero geometrarum regulae sunt.' PL 210.621A.

40 *Post. An.* 1.ix.76^a.

41 Gilbert of Poitiers, p. 295.

42 *Theological Tractates*, p. 38.

43 PL 210.621–2, cf. Gilbert of Poitiers, p. 186 on *dignitas*.

44 'Quasi intus in mente latentia', PL 210.622A.

45 'Internum intelligentiae splendorem', *ibid.*

46 Tota necessitate nutet', *ibid.*

47 'Consuetum naturae decursum', *ibid.*

48 'Puriore mentis acumine', *ibid.* cf. p. 000

49 'Immutabilem necessitatem', *ibid.*

50 'Gloriosam subtilitatem', PL 210.622A, cf. Clarembald of Arras, p. 83, on Boethius' statement in the Prologue to the *De Trinitate* that he is using *nova verba* for theological matters. Clarembald says that this is done deliberately, so as to keep the knowledge of high mysteries from the unworthy.

51 The *sphera intelligibilis* paradox is found in the *Liber XXIV Philosophorum*, a text probably composed in Alan's day, and containing the purported contributions of twenty-four philosophers who had met together to try to determine the nature of God. There the description is given of a *sphera infinita.* For the text, see, C. Baeumker, 'Das pseudo-hermetische Buch der vierundzwanzig Meister', *Beiträge*, xxv (1927), 194–214.

52 PL 210.623A.

53 *Theological Tractates*, p. 42.

54 Clarembald of Arras, p. 212.

55 Clarembald of Arras, p. 213, p. 217.

56 'Pro posse nostro', Clarembald of Arras, p. 220.

57 Clarembald of Arras, p. 220.

58 'Sed oportet esse prudentem qui velit ea propriis argumentis adaptare et convenientibus locis', Thierry, p. 416.66–7, *Abbreviatio Monacensis.*

59 Thierry, p. 417.74–5.

60 Gilbert of Poitiers, p. 208, p. 210, p. 212, p. 214, p. 219.

61 *Anselmi Opera Omnia* I.93.

62 'Descendit'; 'nascitur', PL 210.624C, 626C.

63 'Hae probat illam; iste praebet fidem illa', PL 210.627A, D.

64 'Monas est, qua quaelibet res est una', Alan describes Boethius' first Rule as the *generalissima maxima.* PL 210.623D, cf. Thierry, p. 555.75. *Tractatus de Sex Dierum Operibus.*

65 'Plena pluralitas', PL 210.624A.

66 'Multiplici varietate est obnoxium', *ibid.*

67 PL 210.623D–4C. On the debate over whether two is a number, see M. L. d'Ooge, *Nicomachus of Gerasa: Introduction to Arithmetic* (New York/London, 1926). For the *Hierarchia Alani*, see *Textes*, pp. 223–33.

68 PL 210.625D. For the *Liber*, see Baeumker, as above, note 51.

69 'Monas gignit monadem, et in se suum reflectit ardorem', PL 210.624C.

70 *De Doctrina Christiana* I.V.5, p. 19.4–6.

71 'Liquet ex antedicto', PL 210.625c.

72 'Haec maxima nascitur ex prima', PL 210.625c.

73 'Probat', PL 210.627A.

74 'Omne limitatum alpha et omega', PL 210.626B.

75 'Bonum ab alpha', PL 210.626c.

76 PL 210.627D.

77 'Deus est cui quidlibet quod est, est esse omne quod est', *ibid.*

78 'Omne simplex esse suum et id quod est, unum habet', PL 210.628D.

79 'Propositio theologica', PL 210.629A.

80 Thierry, p. 246.60, p. 309.23, p. 501.66.

81 'Considerandumque maxime quae ita accommodantur naturali facultati, quod non evagantur a theologica', PL 210.681c.

82 Gilbert of Poitiers, p. 61.27 on the *De Trinitate* and pp. 189–90 on the *De Hebdomadibus.*

83 'Humani locutionis usus', Gilbert of Poitiers, p. 120.

84 Gilbert of Poitiers, p. 120.

3. THEOLOGIA MORALIS

1 *Virtues and Vices*, p. 45.

2 Whether such denominatives refer to substance or quality is the opening question of Anselm's *De Grammatico*, but the special problems which arise when we use them of God are left out of account there. Anselm is engaged in a purely logical exercise. See D. P. Henry, *A Commentary on the De Grammatico* (Dordrecht, 1974) on this piece.

3 'Habitus mentis bene constitute', *Virtues and Vices*, p. 45.

4 *Virtues and Vices*, p. 47. We may include in this category the ability to walk and the ability to reason, *gressibilitas* and *rationalitas*.

5 'Aptus ad gradiendum', *ibid.*

6 'Aptus ad vitiis resistendum', *ibid.*

7 'Ab usu potentiarum quam potentias usuum', *ibid.*

8 *Ibid.*, p. 48.

9 *Ibid.*, p. 49.

10 *Ibid.*, p. 50.

11 'Debito fine privatus', *ibid.*, p. 68.

12 'Extraordinarium', *ibid.*

13 'Per negationem dicuntur', *ibid.*

14 *Ibid.*, p. 69.

15 Aquinas, *Summa Theologiae* II¹ Q.55, Q. 71.

16 *Virtues and Vices*, p. 66.

17 *Ibid.*, p. 68.

18 *Ibid.*, p. 85.
19 *Ibid.*, p. 86.
20 *Ibid.*, p. 91.
21 PL 210.119C–D.
22 PL 210.128C–D.
23 PL 210.139B–C.

4. EXPEDIMENTA

1 PL 210.111C. On contemporary preaching, see the survey in Baldwin, I, 36–42. C. Smyth, *The Art of Preaching: a Practical Survey of Preaching in the Church of England* (London, 1940), Chapters 2 and 3, and T. M. Charland, *Artes Praedicandi* (Paris, 1936), See, e.g. *Sermon for Advent*, PL 210.214. J. Longère, *Oeuvres oratoires de maîtres parisiens au xiie siècle* (2 vols., Paris, 1975).

2 *Memorials of St Anselm*, ed. R. W. Southern and F. S. Schmitt (London, 1969). Introduction, R. W. Southern, *St Anselm and his biographer* (Cambridge, 1963), p. 226.

3 PL 156.21–32.

4 PL 156.24C, cf. Augustine, *De Doctrina Christiana* IV.XV.32; IV.XXX.63.

5 PL 156.25B–C.

6 *Admonitoria*, PL 205.37D.

7 *Difficilia* or *expositoria*, *ibid.*

8 'Glossarum multitudine, lectionum superfluitate et prolixitate onerati sumus', *ibid.*

9 *Verbum Abbreviatum*, PL 205.37D and see Geoffrey of Auxerre, *Vita Sancti Bernardi* III.3, PL 185.307B.

10 M. and C. Dickson, 'Le Cardinal Robert de Courson: sa vie', *AHDLMA,* IX (1934), 76, 77, 82.

11 PL 205.27–370, esp. cols. 25ff and 104 (cf. *Textes*, p. 290).

12 On stories about masters see Baldwin, vol. I, Ch. 8.

13 Item legitur: *Si oculus tuus scandalizat te, erue eum et projice abs te* (Mt. 18.9). Oculus hic appellatur non materialis. Nemo enim in seipsum debet manum inicere, quamvis tamen prophetam quendam sibi oculos eruisse legamus, ut attentius prophetie vacaret. Similiter Abbas Clarevalensis cum in oculo pateretur, nullum medicamentum oculo adhiberi permisit, quo amisso dixit se unus ex inimicis suis amisisse. Sed dicimus quod oculus hic appellatur amicus nobis pernecessaria, qui nobis procurat necessaria, qui tamen si nos scandalizaverit prohiciendus est. Similiter si manus, ut per manum intelligamus quecunque nobis necessarium et auxiliatorum, a simile dicit magister. (Cambridge University Library, MS. G.4.17, f.13.)

14 See J. J. Murphy, *A Bibliography of Mediaeval Rhetoric,* on items in print, Roberts, p. 45 on M. de Sully, and C. A. Robson, *Maurice de Sully and the Mediaeval Vernacular Homily* (Oxford, 1952).

15 See Chapter 2 of the *Ars Praedicandi.*

16 Smalley, *The Study of the Bible in the Middle Ages,* pp. 253–4.

17 Cf. Roberts, p. 101.

18 C. *The Dream of the Rood,* ed. B. Dickens and A. Ross (London, 1963).

19 PL 210.113D.

20 PL 210.114C. The tag is not from Lucretius, an author little known in Alan's day. Alan presumably knew it from some *florilegium.*

21 F. Yates, *The art of memory* (London, 1969).

22 *Petrus Abaelardus, Dialectica,* ed. L. M. de Rijk, pp. 253–466.

23 PL 64.1039–1174.

24 PL 64.1173–1216.

25 *Dialectica,* pp. 414–66.

26 PL 64.1205C.

27 See M. Dickey, 'Some Commentaries on the *De Inventione* and the *Rhetorica ad Herennium* of the Eleventh and Twelfth Centuries', *Mediaeval and Renaissance Studies,* VI (1968), 1–41.

28 See P. S. Boskoff, 'Quintilian in the Late Middle Ages', *Speculum,* XXVII (1952), 71–8 and A. Mollard, 'La diffusion de l' *Institution Oratoire* au xii⁰ siecle', *Le Moyen Age,* XLIII (1934), 161–75 and XLIV (1935), 1–9.

29 The *ars dictaminis,* the *ars poetriae,* the *ars praedicandi.*

30 *Textes,* p. 109, n. 2.

31 PL 210.114D.

32 *Topica* II.7–8, ed. N. M. Hubbell (London, 1968).

33 There is no way of knowing at what stage the written text of the sermons which come down to us was established, whether the preacher actually preached from notes, or read a complete text.

34 PL 210.118B.

35 Statius, *Thebaid* 1.51.

36 PL 210.139C.

37 *Anselmi Opera* II.58, ed. Schmitt, *Cur Deus Homo* 1.7.

38 Ed. M. T. d'Alverny, 'Un sermon d'Alain de Lille sur la misère de l'homme', in *The Classical Tradition: Essays presented to H. Caplan* (Ithaca, 1966), p. 525, cf. *Ars Praedicandi,* Chapter 2.

39 PL 210.227B.

40 *Textes,* p. 268, *Sermon in Die Cinerum.*

41 *Ibid.*

42 *Textes,* p. 273.

43 PL 210.118B.

44 PL 210.200A–B.

45 Lucretius, *De Rerum Natura* IV.250–320; Seneca, *Naturales Quaestiones* 1.5.14, 1.5–7 passim.

46 PL 210.118B–C 'Un sermon', p. 525.

47 'Haec est una idololatriae filiae, cui deus venter est, quae latriam exhibet Baccho, unde et bacchilatria vocari potest, ficto vocabulo.' R. E. Latham has an instance of the use of *bacchilatria* in England c. 1200, *Revised Mediaeval Latin Word-List* (London, 1965), and see fascicle B of the *Mediaeval Latin Dictionary*.

48 PL 210.203B. *Nummilatria* is also in Latham, c. 1200.

49 PL 210.203B–C.

50 'O homo memorare quid fuisti sperma fluidum, quomodo sis vas stercoris, quomodo eris esca vermium.' PL 210.117A. Cf. *Liber Parabolarum*, line 594.

51 British Library MS. Vespasian D. XIII, f.66ʳ has *sesamum* for *fluidum*.

52 *Textes*, p. 272.

53 PL 210.172C.

54 'Corona soli et corona poli', *Textes*, p. 264.

55 *Lex poli* and *lex soli*, *Textes*, p. 241.

56 This occurred in 1179 and 1184 (*Textes*, p. 246).

57 *Textes*, p. 246 and see n. 1.

58 PL 210.180C.

59 *Textes*, pp. 274–8.

60 PL 210.112A.

61 Roberts, p. 21.

62 J. P. Bonnes, 'Un des plus grands prédicateurs du xiiᵉ siècle, Geoffroy Louroux dit Geoffroy Babion', *R. Bén.*, LVI (1945–6), 174–215.

63 PL 40.1233–1358.

64 Bonnes, 'Geoffroy Louroux', p. 177.

65 Cf. PL 210.128–9 and PL 40.1264–6; PL 210.143–7, and PL 40.1249–50; PL 210.151–3 and PL 40.155–8; PL 210.169–72, and PL 40.1253–5.

5. IMPEDIMENTA

1 M. D. Lambert, *Mediaeval Heresy* (London, 1977), p. 49. Lambert cites the most important of the many recent works on these developments. Compare R. I. Moore, *Origins of European Dissent* (London, 1977), Chapter 4, on early dualism for a more detailed account.

2 On these developments, see R. Brooke, *The coming of the Friars* (London, 1975).

3 Lambert, *Mediaeval Heresy*, p. 51.

4 S. Runciman, *The Mediaeval Manichee* (Cambridge, 1955), has traced the continuities and discontinuities in the transmission of dualist teaching from Manichean times.

5 Lambert, *Mediaeval Heresy*, p. 51.

6 See J. V. Fearns 'The *Contra Petrobrusianos* of Peter the Venerable', Ph.D. thesis, University of Liverpool, 1963, and *Archiv für Kulturgeschichte*, XLVIII (1966), 311–35. Fearns' edition of the text in CCCM (1968) does not include the introductory material, some of which is in *Archiv*.

7 Lambert gives a convenient summary of Tanchelm's life and teaching (pp. 55–7) and of that of Arnold of Breschia, Peter Abelard's pupil (pp. 58–9).

8 *Sermo 66 in Cantica Canticorum, Opera Omnia* II.178–88 and PL 183.1094. The outbreak of heresy at Cologne in 1143–4 was especially worrying to Bernard.

9 A number of papers by B. Hamilton are collected in *Monastic Reform, Catharism and the Crusades, 900–1300* (London, 1979).

10 On Valdès, see K. V. Selge, *Die Ersten Waldenser*: vol. I, 'Untersuchung und Darstellung'; vol. II, 'Der *Liber antiheresis* des Durandus von Osca' (Berlin, 1967), Chapter 3, and C. Thouzellier, *Hérésie et Hérétiques: Vaudois, cathares, patarins, albigeois*, Storia e Letteratura, 116 (Rome, 1969), pp. 81–188, and *Catharisme et Valdéisme en Languedoc à la fin du xiie et du début du xiiie siècle* (Paris, 1966, 2nd. ed. 1969).

11 Lambert, *Mediaeval Heresy*, p. 73.

12 *Ibid.*, p. 76.

13 *Ibid.*, p. 73.

14 Ed. A. Landgraf, *Écrits théologiques de l'école d'Abélard*, SSLov, XIV (1934), p. 25.

15 'Invisibilis gratiae visibilis forma'. See L. Antl, 'Stephen Langton's principle of determining the essence of a sacrament', *Franciscan Studies*, XIV (1954), 154, and D. Van den Eynde, *Les definitions des sacraments pendant la première periode de la théologie scolastique (1050–1240)* (Rome, 1950), pp. 68–96, and E. Dumoutet 'La théologie de l'Eucharistie à la fin du xiie siècle', *AHDLMA*, XIV (1943–4), 181–261.

16 'Signum sacrae rei'. Antl, 'Stephen Langton'.

17 'Sacramentum tantum', *ibid.*

18 'Sacramentum et res'. *ibid.*

19 'Res tantum', *ibid.*

20 *Missa bifaciata* or *Missa trifaciata*.

21 *Textes*, pp. 284–5.

22 Bodleian Library Oxford MS Canon Misc. 95, f.102, olim 108. See *Textes*, pp. 156–62 and N. M. Häring, 'Alan of Lille's *De Fide Catholica et contra Haereticos*', *An. Cist.*, XXXII (1976), 216–37, for discussions of the work.

23 J. de Montclos, *Lanfranc et Béréngar*, SSLov, xxxvii (1971), and
   M. T. Gibson, *Lanfranc of Bec* (Oxford, 1978).
24 Aquinas, *Summa contra Gentiles* iv.61.
25 Peter Lombard, *Sentences* iv.x.1–2, xi.1–2.
26 *De Sacramentis*, ed. Martin.
27 PL 210.308a–b.
28 Ambrose, *De Sacramentis*, i–vi, ed. O. Faller, CSEL, lxxiii (1955),
   pp. 13–85; Augustine, *Tr. in Johannem*, xxvi.15–9, CCSL, xxxvi
   (1954), pp. 267–9.
29 PL 149.1429a–b.
30 PL 149.1430a.
31 'Nihil omnino', *ibid*.
32 'Revera sed latenter contineri et impanari', *ibid*.
33 PL 210.359–60, Ch. 57.
34 'Ratiuncula', PL 149.1430a.
35 Gibson, *Lanfranc of Bec*, pp. 74–5.
36 PL 150.417a.
37 'Relictis sacris auctoritatibus a dialecticam confugium facis', PL
   150.416d.
38 British Library, MS Add. 8166, f.23.
39 PL 150.411c.
40 'Sola voce sic appellari', PL 149.1430a.
41 MS Add. 8166, f.22ᵛ.
42 Thierry, p. 447.86–8, cf. Peter Abelard, *Dialectica*, ed L. M. de
   Rijk, p. 432 and elsewhere.
43 PL 210.359, 361. On Boethius' contrast between *alteritas* and *aliud*
   see D. P. Henry, *A Commentary on the De Grammatico*, pp. 190–1.
44 'Per partium extensionem', PL 210.361a–b, cf. Gilbert of Poitiers,
   p. ff.256.85–6; Boethius, *Contra Eutychen* i.
45 'Per additionem', *ibid*.
46 'Incipiet', *ibid*.
47 'Fiet', *ibid*.
48 'Desinit esse', *ibid*.
49 'Corrumpitur', *ibid*.
50 'Per naturalem infirmationem', *ibid*.
51 'Per miraculum', *ibid*.
52 PL 210.362c, cf. William of St Thierry, *De Sacramento Altaris*,
   PL 180.353, 361–2.
53 PL 210.359b–c, PL 149.1433–4, cf. Lombard, *Sentences* iv.xii.2–4.
54 Cf. Alger of Liège, PL 180.809d, William of St Thierry, PL 180.343,
   349, and Peter Lombard, *Sentences* iv. xi.1.
55 PL 180.343c.
56 *Écrits théologiques*, ed. Landgraf, pp. 200–4; Peter Lombard,
   Sentences iv.xi.2.

57 PL 180.811A–B.

58 PL 210.112–13.

59 *Orator* 21.69.

60 *De Doctr. Chr.* IV.xii.27.

61 PL 210.111C.

62 'Quia in his specialiter resultat moralis instructio', PL 210.111.

63 PL 210.113A.

64 PL 210.111D.

65 Lamentations 4.3.

66 PL 210.113A.

67 *Variisque debacchantes erroribus, Quoniam Homines*, pp. 119–20. *Consolation of Philosophy* I. pr. 3.

68 PL 210.309C. C. Thouzellier, in her edition of the *Livre des deux principes* (Sources Chrétiennes), CXCVIII (1973), p. 55 discusses the possibility that the author may have been drawing on Alan. See, too, C. Thouzellier, *Catharisme et Valdéisme en Languedoc à la fin du xii*^e *et au début du xiii*^e *siècle* (Louvain, 1969), pp. 81–106 on the first two books of Alan's treatise, and p. 82 n. 9 on the inadequacies of the Migne text.

69 Matthew 7.18.

70 John 14.30.

71 Matthew 7.24.

72 PL 210.309–10, Ch. 4.

73 PL 210.309C, Ch. 3.

74 PL 210.310A.

75 PL 210.310B.

76 PL 210.308C.

77 PL 210.314–5, Ch. 8.

78 Matthew 15.24.

79 PL 210.321–2, Ch. 19.

80 PL 210.332 C–D.

81 PL 210.337C–D.

82 PL 210.357B–C.

83 PL 210.378.

84 PL 210.377D.

85 PL 210.377D.

86 PL 210.378D–80C.

87 PL 210.381–3.

88 PL 210.80D–81A.

89 PL 210.399A–403C.

90 PL 210.415C.

91 Gilbert's *Disputatio* is edited by B. Blumenkranz (Antwerp, 1956). On Alan's borrowings, see *Textes*, p. 161.

92 On the expansion of the abbey, see the introduction to the forthcoming edition of Gilbert Crispin's works in the *Auctores Britannici Medii Aevi*, ed. G. R. Evans and A. Abulafia (1983).

93 Hermannus Judaeus, *De Conversione Sua*, ed. G. Niemeyer, MGH Quellen, IV (1963).

94 See my *Old Arts and New Theology* (Oxford, 1980), pp. 137–66.

95 PL 210.421A–B.

96 PL 210.421C.

97 PL 210.428C.

98 R. W. Southern has discussed this problem in *Islam and the West* (Harvard, 1962).

99 M. T. d'Alverny, 'Deux traductions latines du Coran au Moyen Age', *AHDLMA*, XVI (1948), 69–131 and, on Peter's work in general, see P. Kritzeck, *Peter the Venerable and Islam*, pp. 51–68.

100 Peter the Venerable, *Contra Petrobrusianos*, ed. J. Fearns, CCCM, III, Hugh of Amiens, *Contra Haereticos*, PL 192.1255–1298; Gerhoch of Reichersberg, *Contra Haereses*, PL 194.1162–1188.

101 Although their structure presents some difficulties.

102 *Textes*, pp. 156–62; M. T. d'Alverny suggests that Alan may sometimes be confusing the Cathars with other sects, but it seems likely that on many occasions he has tried to arrange his material in such a way as to keep it in an easy-to-follow order. That would explain his inclusion of material on the Eucharist in the Cathar volume, which we have looked at above, *Textes*, p. 160.

103 *Contra Haereticos, Waldenses, Iudaeos et Paganos.*

104 PL 210.307A, Apostles' Creed, p. 16; Nicene Creed, p. 287.

105 'Non enim fugeremus malum nisi cognitum haberemus', *ibid.*

106 Apostles' Creed, p. 16.

107 'Christianis nominis retento caractere', *Two Questions*, p. 332.

108 *Two Questions*, p. 332, cf. *Quoniam Homines*, p. 119.

109 PL 210.307B, and Aquinas *Summa contra Gentiles* I.2.

110 'Una generalis haeresis', PL 210.308A.

111 PL 210.308A.

112 PL 210.307B.

113 PL 210.377C.

114 PL 210.421B.

115 PL 210.114C.

116 PL 210.211D.

117 *Textes*, p. 284.

118 'Nova secta', PL 210.377.

119 'Secta abominabilis', PL 210.421.

120 'In hoc tamen cum Judaeis conveniunt, quod in divina unitate trinitatem abnegant', PL 210.421C.

121 PL 210.421D.

122 PL 210.595A. On Nicholas' authorship of the *De Articulis*, see p. 64, and Appendix 1a.

123 'Partes tot sectarum corruptas', PL 210.595A.

124 Gilbert Crispin, *Disputatio*, ed. B. Blumenkranz (Antwerp, 1956), pp. 28–9.

125 R. W. Southern, *Medieval Humanism* (Oxford, 1970), p. 124 and MS Jesus College, Oxford, 38, f.82–102; f.86ᵛ, Col. 1.

126 PL 210.595A.

127 'De Trinitate in triviis disputare', 'Oppositiones contra Perfidiam Judaeorum', Jesus Coll. MS 38, f.70.

128 PL 210.307A.

129 Oxford, Bodleian Library, MS Canon. misc. lat. 95, ff.101–13.

130 *Summa contra Gentiles* 1.9.

6. MAKING MAN ANEW

1 The editors of Bernard Silvestris' *Commentary on the first six books of Virgil's Aeneid* doubt whether Bernardus is its author: E. W. Jones and E. F. Jones (Nebraska, 1977).

2 W. Wetherbee, tr. *Cosmographia* (Columbia, 1973), p. 3.

3 *De Mundi Universitate*, ed. C. Barach and J. Wrobel (Innsbruck, 1876); the *Mathematicus* is in PL 172.1365–80. See Wetherbee's Introduction to his translation, on Bernard's sources.

4 On this passage, see W. Wetherbee, *Platonism and Poetry in the Twelfth Century* (Princeton, 1972), p. 156; see, too, W. von den Steinen, 'Les sujets d'inspiration chez les poètes latins du xiiᵉ siècle', *Cahiers de civilisation médiévale*, IX (1966), 165–75 and 363–83, especially pp. 376ff. Von den Steinen points out that the hero has a name, a family and a situation, unlike Alan's hero.

5 Bernard of Clairvaux's *Parabolae* are edited among his 'Sentences' and sayings in *Opera Omnia* VI².

6 See H. de Lubac, *Exégèse Médiévale*, vol. 1 (Paris, 1959), on the way in which Origen's fourfold system of exegesis was transmitted to the Middle Ages, and B. Smalley, *The Study of the Bible in the Middle Ages*, Chapter 1.

7 M. Reeves, *The Influence of Prophecy in the Later Middle Ages* (Oxford, 1969), and, with B. Hirsch-Reich, *The Figurae of Joachim of Fiore* (Oxford, 1972).

8 Barach–Wrobel, *De Mundi Universitate*, p. 5.18.

9 *Ibid.*, p. 6.24–6.

10 *Ibid.*, p. 6.37–8.

11 'Literalis sensus', Bossuat, p. 56.

12 'Proficiens', *ibid.*

13 'Acutior allegoriae subtilitas perficientem acuet intellectum', *ibid.*

14 The 'theophani coelestis emblemata', *ibid.*

15 *Aeneid* VI.724–6. Thierry, pp. 566–7, Commentary on the *Aeneid*, p. 115 and *Textes*, p. 255.

16 See Bossuat, pp. 207–13, for an index of Alan's rare words.

17 *Anticlaudianus* III.53–7.

18 *Cosmographia*, tr. Wetherbee, *Microcosmos* XIII, pp. 118–22.

19 *Ibid.*, p. 118.

20 Bede, PL 90.187–277 and PL 90.277–293.

21 R. Roques, 'La notion dionysienne de hiérarchie', *AHDLMA*, XVI (1948), 183–222; *Dictionnaire de Spiritualité*, III (1954), 245–86; *L'univers dionysien* (Paris 1954). T. Klauser, *Reallexikon für Antike und Christentum*, III (1957), 1078–80.

22 Thierry of Chartres, pp. 555–75.

23 Macrobius, *Somnium Scipionis*, ed. J. Willis (Leipzig, 1964), p. 132.11–13.

24 Bernard Silvestris (?), *Commentary on the Aeneid*, p. 28.7–11.

25 For example: Romans 12.5; 1 Corinthians 7.20; 1 Corinthians 12.4ff. and 22; Ephesians 1.23.

26 John of Salisbury, *Policraticus*, ed. C. C. J. Webb, vol. 1, Bookv.ii, *passim*. On the likelihood that John of Salisbury invented the work, see J. Martin in *The World of John of Salisbury, Studies in Church History, Subsidia*, forthcoming.

27 W. Ullmann, *History of Political Thought* (London, 1965), p. 124.

28 W. Ullmann, *The individual and society* (Baltimore, 1966, London, 1967), p. 43; and see T. Struve, *Die Entwicklung der organologischen Staatsauffassung im M.A.* (Stuttgart, 1978), pp. 123–48.

29 Ullmann, *The Individual and Society*, p. 3.

30 Peter's *Verbum Abbreviatum* proves a mine of information in Baldwin's exploration of the world of the *Masters, princes and Merchants*.

31 Bernard of Clairvaux, *De Consideratione* I.x.13, *Bernardi Opera Omnia*, ed C. H. Talbot, J. Leclercq and H. Rochais, vol. III (Rome, 1963), p. 408.

32 On some of these general developments, see W. Wetherbee, Introduction to *Cosmographia*, p. 1.

33 *Cosmographia* II.xiv.116–18, p. 69.

34 See W. Ullmann, 'John of Salisbury's *Policraticus* in the later Middle Ages', *Geschichtsschreibung und geistiges Leben im Mittelalter: Festschrift für H. Löwe*, ed. K. Hauck and H. Mordek (Cologne/Vienna, 1978), p. 619.

35 *De Planctu Naturae*, Prose III, tr. D. Moffat, pp. 27–8.

36 Cf. Gregory, PL 76.94D, *Moralia in Job* XVIII.54.92, on 1 Corinthians 3.3–4: 'scriptura quippe sacra omnes carnalium sectatores, humanitatis nomina notare solet.'

37 *Ottonis Gesta Friderici*, MGH SS, 1.5.18.

38 'Individuum et singulare non sunt ad se convertentia, nam, omne individuum singulare, sed non omne singulare individuum.' *Ottonis Gesta Friderici*, 1.55.79.

39 PL64.97c.

40 Thomas Browne, *To a friend upon occasion of the death of his intimate friend.*

41 See, for example, W. A. Nitze, 'The so-called twelfth century renaissance' *Speculum*, XXIII (1948), 464–71; U. T. Holmes, 'The idea of the twelfth century renaissance', *Speculum*, XXVI (1951), 643–51; E. M. Sandford, 'The twelfth century: renaissance or proto-renaissance?', *Speculum*, XXVI (1951) 635–42, and W. Ullmann, *Mediaeval Foundations of Renaissance Humanism* (London, 1977). For a recent study, see P. G. Walsh, 'Alan of Lille as a Renaissance Figure', *Studies in Church History*, XIV (1977), 117–36. On humanism, see R. W. Southern, *Medieval Humanism* (Oxford, 1970), pp. 29–60. See, too, Colin Morris, *The Discovery of the individual* (London, 1972), p. 10, John of Salisbury, *Policraticus* III.1, ed. C. C. J. Webb (Oxford, 1909), p. 171 and cf. W. Ullmann, 'John of Salisbury's *Policraticus* in the later Middle Ages', cf. 17.34 above.

42 L. K. Born, 'The Perfect Prince', *Speculum*, III (1928), 470–504, surveys the literature. See, too, M. Wilks, 'Alan of Lille and the New Man', *Studies in Church History*, XIV (1977), 137–58.

43 *Essay on Man*, Ep. 1.ii.69–70.

44 R. Bossuat notes this in the introduction to his edition of Alan of Lille's *Anticlaudianus*, p. 35, and see Boethius, *Contra Eutychen*, in *Theological Tractates*, pp. 102–6.

45 Gilbert of Poitiers is the most obvious case in point. On his trial, see N. M. Häring's Introduction to his *Commentaries on Boethius* in Gilbert of Poitiers.

46 Cf. Cicero, *De Officiis* 1.20; Cassian, *Collationes* XX.2.1 and *Institutiones* 4.7; Augustine, *Sermo* 355.1.2.

47 'Omnes homines unit', Thierry, p. 166.18.

48 'Una...humanitas omnium hominum', Thierry, p. 175.12.

49 Thierry, p. 138.82.

50 Thierry, p. 170.45.

51 Gilbert of Poitiers, p. 118.

52 PL 171.1365–80, and see my *Old Arts and New Theology* (Oxford, 1980).

53 E.g., William, third abbot of Bec, 'Liberalibus artibus mirabiliter eruditus, litteris imbuendus', PL 150.743.

54 *Essay on Man*, Ep. 1.ii.71–2.

55 Bernard of Clairvaux, *De Diligendo Deo* X.33, *Opera Omnia*, vol. III (1963), p. 147.

56 Bossuat, Introduction, and see De Lage, *Textes*, and P. Ochsenbein, *Studien zum Anticlaudianus des Alanus ab Insulis* (Frankfurt, 1975), for a summary of recent views and a recent bibliography.

57 Walsh, 'Alan of Lille as a Renaissance Figure', p. 119.

58 *Ibid.*, pp. 133–5.

59 Ellebaut, *Anticlaudien*, ed. A. J. Creighton (Washington, 1944), p. 5.

60 *Ibid.*, p. 6, and cf. lines 1858–2167.

61 *Anticlaudianus* v.515–43.

62 *Contra Haereticos* I.19–20, PL 210.321–3.

63 In that he is careful not to make him Christ.

64 *Anticlaudianus* 1.338, II.62–3, V.215, VI.353, VII.34.

65 *Anticlaudianus* I¹.69–70.

66 'Natura quidem (ut ita loquar) universa facit, sed nulla perficit; procreat, sed non creat, nec replet: ad solum Spiritum Sanctum pertinet perficere, creare, replere.' PL 210.221D, *Sermo de Spiritu Sancto*.

67 Ochsenbein, *Studien zum Anticlaudianus*, pp. 132–6.

68 *Anselmi Opera Omnia*, vol. II.52.8–11.

69 'Oportuit enim ut sicut per hominem facta est humani generis perditio, ita per hominem fieret eiusdem redemptio...purus autem homo redimere non potuit; si enim purus homo esset, tabe humanae naturae infectus esset.' PL 210.323D, Book I.21.

70 *Anticlaudianus* VI.390–6, Ellebaut, lines 1818–93.

71 *Commentary on Romans*, ed. E. M. Buytaert, CCCM, XI (Turnholt, 1969), pp. 113–18. cf. Gregory, *Moralia in Job* I.xiii.17.

72 *Anticlaudianus* 1.243.

73 Genesis 1.25–7; Augustine, *De Trinitate*, Book X; Anselm 'Monologion', *Opera*, vol. I. pp. 77–8.

74 PL 210.118 B–C.

75 PL 210.579B.

76 *Anticlaudianus*, Prologue, p. 56.

77 E.g. Aquinas, *Summa Theologiae* II¹¹, Q. 183, Art. 4; Q. 184, *passim*.

78 'Perfectio naturae glorificatae', Peter Lombard, 'Sentences', *Spicilegium Bonaventurianum* IV (Rome, 1971), p. 350, II. Dist. IV.i, para. 6.

79 'Perfectio naturae increatae', *ibid.*

80 *Anticlaudianus* VIII.77.

81 *Summa Theologiae* II¹¹, Q. 184, Art. 1, reply.

82 'Imago et similitudo', Genesis 1.27.

83 'Corporea natura', *De Sacramentis* I.vi.2, PL 176.264.

84 'Similitudinem capere non potuit Divinitatis', *ibid.*

85 'In anima solo', *ibid.*

86 'Quod proprium est filiorum Dei', Rupert of Deutz, *De Trinitate*,

ed. H. Haacke, CCCM, xxi (Turnholt, 1971), *In Genesim* ii.3, p. 187.83–6.

87 In terris humanus erit, divinus in astris.
    Sic homo, sicque Deus fiet.
    Anticlaudianus i.238–41.

88 'Unum carni, alterum spiritui', p. 432, ii.xix, Chapter 6 (121), para. 1.

89 'Esse duplex hominis', *Anticlaudianus* i.364.

90 'Humane mentis ydea', *Anticlaudianus* vi. 420.

91 *Anticlaudianus* vi.429–44.

92 On the *Hexaemeron*, PL 172.258.

93 Dividit a tota, divisaque rursus in unum
    Colligit in summa commiscens, dumque futurum
    Sic prelibat opus, humani corpus aptat
    Materiam.
    Anticlaudianus vii.16–19.

94 Ni mea corporibus animas iunctura ligasset,
    Dedignans habitare casas, ergastula carnis,
    Spiritus egrediens proprios remearet in ortus.
    Anticlaudianus ii.253–5.

95 *Anticlaudianus* vii.56–8.

96 'Hoc duellum inter carnem et spiritum, ubi caro contra spiritum armatur', PL 210.141d, *Ars Praedicandi* xv.

97 'Commune nomen', *Commentary on Romans* ii, p. 158.169–70.

98 J. H. Newman, *Discourses to Mixed Congregations* (London, 1871), pp. 351–5.

99 *Anticlaudianus* v.510–14.

100 Genesis 2.15.

101 Peter Lombard, Book ii.xvii.4 (99), p. 413, Book ii.xix.1 (110), para. i, p. 421.

102 *Ibid.*

103 'Sine interventu mortis in angelorum consortium transferetur', PL 203.595, *De Salute Primi Hominis.*

104 'Propter maius meritum', PL 172.1118a.

105 PL 176.270a.

106 Hugh of St Victor, *De Sacramentis* i.vi.10, PL 176.269–70.

107 'Possibilitas est aptitudo recipiendi status diverso', Thierry, p. 74.96.

108 PL 210.443c–d.

109 Peter the Chanter, *Verbum Abbreviatum* PL 205.265b, Chapter 91.

110 'De Grandibus Humilitatis et Superbiae', *Opera Omnia*, vol. iii.

111 PL 172.1241–6.

112 PL 172.1229–47, *Scala Coelis Major; Scala Coeli Minor; De Gradibus Charitatis.*

113 *Anticlaudianus*, Book ix, Bossuat, pp. 185–201.

114 O. Lottin, *Psychologie et morale aux xiie et xiiie siècles*, vol. v
   (Gembloux, 1959), p. 36, para. 38; p. 123, para. 169; p. 124, para.
   170. On the inclusion of 'mortal' in the definition of man by
   Boethius and Anselm see D. P. Henry, *A Commentary on the De
   Grammatico*, pp. 152–3.

115 *Sententiae Petri Pictaviensis*, ed. P. S. Moore, J. N. Garvin, M.
   Dulong (Indiana, 1950), vol. ii, pp. 37–47.

116 Simon of Tournai, *Disputationes*, p. 145, *Disp.* xl, Q.6.

117 'Naturalia', *ibid.*

118 'Data sunt ei gratuita', *ibid.*

119 'Spoliatus gratuitis', *ibid.*

120 *Ibid.*, p. 144, Q.4.

121 Book ii, Dist. xvii, Chapter 4 (99), p. 413.

122 Thierry, p. 555.15–17.

123 Thierry, p. 563.24–5.

124 Thierry, p. 127.85–6.

125 Thierry, p. 555.18–19.

126 Thierry, p. 556.36–9.

127 On this classic question, see G. Bull, *The state of man before the
   Fall*, ed. E. Burton (Oxford, 1827), who assembles patristic statements on the point.

128 *The sermons and devotional writings of Gerard Manley Hopkins*,
   ed. C. Devlin (Oxford, 1959), Sunday Nov. 23, 1879.

129 PL 197.441C.

130 *Anticlaudianus* vii.11–36, cf. William of Conches, *Glosa super
   Platonem* 58, ed. E. Jeauneau (Paris, 1965), p. 128.

131 *Anticlaudianus*, p. 158.42–3.

132 'Hospicium, carnisque domum quam spiritus intret', *Anticlaudianus*
   vii.10.

133 PL 210.119–23.

134 PL 210.309–10, 321–3.

135 *Anticlaudianus* vii.100.

136 *Anticlaudianus* vii.119.

137 'Scurriles prohibet gestus nimiumque severos', *Anticlaudianus* vii.139.

138 *Anticlaudianus* vii.148–55.

139 *Anticlaudianus* vii.166–201.

140 *Anticlaudianus* vii.202–27.

141 *Anticlaudianus* vii.232–3: 'thesaurum mentis'.

142 'Omnes divicias animi'.

143 'Congruus', PL 176.270D.

144 Gunzo, *Epistola ad Augienses*, MGH Quellen, pp. 38.21–39.1.

145 *Textes*, pp. 207, para 3.–210, para. 3.

146 *Ibid.*, pp. 246–9, *Sermo in Dominica Palmarum*.

147 'Orbis terrarum', PL 210.222D.

148 PL 210.222D, *Sermo De Spiritu Sancto*.
149 'Imperatrix sapientia', PL 210.444A.
150 'Potestas logistica', PL 210.444A.
151 'Virtus praeteritorum recordativa', PL 210.444A.
152 *De Planctu Naturae*, PL 210.444A.
153 See W. Ullmann, 'Church and Law in the Earlier Middle Ages' (*Collected Studies*, vol. I, 1978), Chapter 13.
154 *The discovery of the individual*, pp. 11–12.
155   Possideat solus quicquid possedimus omnes;
     Omnis homo sic unus erit, sic omne quod unum:
     Unus in esse suo, sed erit in virtutibus omnis.
   Anticlaudianus II.50–2.
156 PL 210.246B.
157 'Ecclesia eleganter dicitur orbis terrarum', PL 210.272B.
158 'Vel orbis terrarum dicitur homo'. PL 210.272B.
159 PL 165. 943A–B, Book III, Chapter 1.
160 Ellebaut, *Anticlaudien*.

CONCLUSION

1 Roberts, p. 226.
2 *Ibid.*
3 *Ibid.*, p. 232.
4 *Textes*, p. 283.
5 PL 210.71, *Elucidatio in Cantica Canticorum*.
6 PL 210.55, *ibid.*
7 *Virtues and Vices*, p. 47.
8 PL 210.87, *Elucidatio in Cantica Canticorum*.
9 *Liber Poenitentialis*, PL 210.292.
10 *Doctor* means 'master' in this context.
11 P. G. Walsh, 'Alan of Lille as a Renaissance Figure', *Studies in Church History*, XIV (1977), 128. Walsh does allow the Christian complexion of the work, pp. 121ff.
12 *Ibid.*, p. 117.
13 M. Wilks, 'Alan of Lille and the New Man', *Studies in Church History*, XIV (1977), 143.
14 *Ibid.*, pp. 144–5.
15 *Anticlaudianus*, Prologue, p. 56.
16 *Textes*, p. 13, discusses the dedication of the *Contra Haereticos* to William VIII of Montpellier.
17 'Congrua dictionum ordinatio', Our Father, p. 159.
18 'Qui multociens excitatur per verba dum animus pigritatur', *ibid.*

APPENDIX I

1 *Textes*, p. 69 and pp. 319–22. The literature is listed in detail in *Textes*, pp. 68–9.

2 See, in particular P. Balić, 'Les anciens manuscrits de la bibliothèque métropolitaine de Zagreb', *Studia Medievalia in honorem R. J. Martin* (Louvain, 1948), pp. 462–6. The sixth book is edited by P. Balić in 'De Auctore Operis quod *Ars Fidei Catholicae* inscribitur', *Mélanges J. de Ghellinck*, vol. II (Paris, 1951), pp. 793–814.

3 P. Glorieux, 'L'Auteur de l'*Ars Fidei Catholicae*', *RTAM*, XXIII (1956), 118–22.

4 PL 210.596D.

5 PL 210.305–430.

6 *Textes*, pp. 156–62.

7 Rule 2, PL 210.623–4.

8 'Cadunt sub numero', PL 210.600C.

9 PL 210.600C, Book I, *Propositum* 12.

10 PL 210.621–3, cf. Gilbert of Poitiers, pp. 189–90.

11 'Generalissima maxima', PL 210.622B.

12 PL 210.622B. For a full discussion of this difference, see (b).

13 D'Alverny places it in the late 1170s, perhaps rather earlier, and suggests that it may have been composed while Alan was at Paris: *Textes*, p. 67.

14 Madrid, Bibliotheca nazionale 523.

15 PL 210.597B.

16 All six books are attributed to Nicholas in the Madrid MS, all six to Boethius in the Vatican MS.

17 E.g. MS. Royal 9 E XII; this text is set out as heading in the printed version of 1492.

18 'Quod non evagantur a theologia: que vero utrique facultati sunt communes', PL 210.681C.

19 *Textes*, p. 67.

20 Robert of Melun, *Sententie*, ed. R. M. Martin, SSLov, XXI (1947), p. 262.

21 PL 64.100.

22 *Logica Modernorum*, ed. L. M. de Rijk, II^{11}, p. 598.6–7, p. 676.23–4.

23 Thierry, *Treatise on the Work of the Six Days*.

24 Robert of Melun, *Sententie*, p. 262.

25 'Causa est per quam habet aliquid esse, quod dicitur creatum', PL 210.597C.

26 Omnis res habet esse per illud, quod causam eius perducit. Omnis causa prior et dignior est suo causato.
PL 210.598C–D.

27 *De Arte* I.x, xi, xii.

28 *De Arte* I.i, ix, cf. *Regulae*, Rules 58, 66–7.

29 PL 210.641, Rules 45–7.

30 Robert of Melun, *Sententie*, pp. 266–7.

31 PL 210.669C–D.

32 Proclus, *Elements*.

33 *Les Auctoritates Aristotelis*, Book II.3, ed. J. Hamesse, Philosophes
médiévaux, XVII (Louvain, 1974), p. 231, with an inaccurate reference
to *Liber de Causis* 1.16.57–8. It is also, incidentally, one of the
axioms of Morinus' seventeenth-century *Astrologia Gallica*.

34 *Auct. Arist.* 16.54.

35 *Ibid.*, 1.188; 1.211; 2.30; 3.39; 6.114; 6.121.

36 *Ibid.*, 1.44; 1.65; 35.118.

37 *Ibid.*, 1.43.

38 *Ibid.*, II.17, cf. *De Causis* XXI. 166.68–9.

39 Proclus, *Elements*, p. xxxi.

40 *Ibid.*, p. xlii.

41 See Balić, *Studia Med. in honorem R. J. Martin*, Appendix I(*a*), note 1.

42 'Collectio multorum principiorum, sive preceptorum, ad unum fidem
tendentium', *Logica Modernorum* II^{ii}, ed. L. M. de Rijk, p. 379.3–5,
cf. p. 357.14 (*Introductiones Parisienses*), p. 417.15–6 (*Logica cum sit
nostra*), cf. Domingo Gundisalvo, *De Scientiis*, ed. P. Alonso Alonso
(Madrid, 1954), pp. 59–62.

43 PL 210.597C.

44 'Explicat enim rerum diffinitiones', Bodleian Library, MS. Digby
174 f.99^r, and see M. Clagett, 'The Mediaeval Latin Translations
from the Arabic of the *Elements* of Euclid', *Isis*, XLIV (1953), 16–42,
33–4.

45 PL 210.601B.

46 'Propositiones artificioso successu propositum comprobantes'.

47 'Propositiones vero per indicitavum proposita per infinitum expli-
cantur', MS. Digby 174 f.99^r, Clagett, 'The Mediaeval Latin...
of the *Elements*', p. 36.

48 'Antecedit', Clagett, 'The Mediaeval Latin...of the *Elements*',
p.38.

49 'Ante expositionem', *ibid.*

50 Gilbert of Poitiers, p. 109.25.

51 Cicero, *Topica* II.8 deals with the distinction between intrinsic, or
artificial, and extrinsic, or inartificial, arguments.

52 Balić, *Studia Med. in honorem R. J. Martin*, p. 803; Book IV of the
De Arte contains a reference to: *definitione sive convertibili descrip-
tione*. See, too, PL 64.1187. *De Differentiis Topicis*, PL 64.166 (*In
Cat.*). For *descriptio* in the Euclid translations, see Bodleian Library,
MS. Auct. F.3.13, f.1^v, MS. Auct. F.5.28, f.ii^v, British Library MS.
Royal 15. A.27, f.2^r.

53 PL 210.597C, cf. *Theological Tractates*, p. 40.
54   Cuiuslibet compositionis causam componentem esse;
   nullius rei causam in infinitum ascendere;
   quae creatorum causis attribuimus, nec insunt per effectum, et
   causam illius attribui.
   PL 210.598C.
55 'Omnis res habet esse per illud, quod causam eius perducit ad esse;
   omnis causa prior et dignior est suo causato;
   nihil est prius, vel dignius, vel altius seipso.'
56 'Si aliquis maior possidet minorem se, minor se et ea, quae penes
   ipsum sunt, in honorem et voluntatem majoris tenetur convertere.
   iniuriosus tanto maiori dignus est poena, quanto maior est, cui
   infertur iniuria.'
57 'Iuxta dignitatem eius, contra quem peccatum est, debet satisfactio
   compensari.'
58 *Textes*, pp. 66–9.

APPENDIX 2

1 On *reportatio* see B. Smalley, *The Study of the Bible in the Middle
   Ages* (Oxford, 1952), pp. 200–6. *Verbum Abbreviatum*, PL 205.1–554.
   Peter the Chanter, *Summa de Sacramentis et Animae Consiliis*, ed.
   J. A. Dugauquier, Analecta Medievalia Namurcensia, IV, VII, XVI,
   XXI. P. S. Moore, *The Works of Peter of Poitiers* (Indiana, 1936).
2 Dugauquier (ed.), *Summa de Sacramentis*, III (1) 4.
3 Baldwin, vol. II, pp. 241–6.
4 Dugauquier, IV, p. 187, Baldwin, vol. II, p. 241.
5 Baldwin, vol. I, p. 14.
6 Baldwin, vol. I, pp. 14–15.
7 Baldwin, vol. II, pp. 247–65.
8 F. Stegmüller, *Repertorium Biblicum Medii Aevi* (7 vols., Madrid,
   1950–61), vol. IV, pp. 6452–3.

Manuscripts cited

Avranches, Bibliothèque municipale 28
Bern, Stadtbibliothek, AA 90 nr. 20
Cambridge, St John's College, B.8
„   Corpus Christi College, 217
„   Jesus College, Q.G.18
„   Trinity College, R.14.40
„   University Library, Gg.4.17
„   „   Ii.1.24
„   „   Kk.1.28
London, British Library, Add. 8166
„   „   Add. 19767
„   „   Harley 3596
„   „   Royal 9 E XII
„   „   „ 12 F XII
„   „   „ 15 A 27
„   „   Vespasian D XIII
„   Lambeth Palace, 122
Orleans, Bibliothèque municipale, 199
Oxford, Bodleian Library, Auct. F., 3.13
„   „   Canon Misc. Lat., 95
„   „   Digby 174
„   „   Rawlinson C 161
„   „   Selden Supra 79
„   Jesus College, 38
„   St John's College, 31
Paris, Bibliothèque Mazarine 298
„   „   891
„   Bibliothèque Nationale, Lat. 3487 A
„   „   1444 S
„   „   14892
Rein, Stiftsbibliothek, 61
Salisbury, Cathedral Library, 171
Troyes, Bibliothèque municipale, 398
„   „   789

Manuscripts cited

Vatican, Regina Lat. 1283
Worcester, Cathedral Library, F 61
Zürich, Zentralbibliothek, C 97, ii

Bibliography

I STUDIES ON ALAN OF LILLE

Details of editions of Alan's writings will be found in the Table of Alan's Writings on pp. 14–19.

Alverny, M. T. d' 'Note sur deux oeuvres théologiques du xiie siècle: Alain de Lille, *Expositio Prosae de Angelis*; Achard de Saint-Victor, *De Trinitate*', *Bibliothèque de l'École des Chartes*, CXII, 1954, 247–50.

'Alain de Lille et la *Theologia*', *Théologie*, LVII, 1964, 111–28.

Textes inédits, Paris, 1965.

'Alain de Lille: problèmes d'attribution', AGJ, pp. 27–46.

Barbera, C. 'La teologia del sacramento della penitenzia in Alano di Lilla', *Studia patavina*, VIII, 1961, 442–99.

Baumgartner, M. *Die Philosophie des Alanus de Insulis in Zusammenhange mit den Anschauungen des 12 Jahrhunderts*, Beiträge, II.4, Münster, 1896.

Betti, H. 'Animadversiones in Summam "Totus homo"', *Antonianum*, XXVII, 1952, 333–48.

'L'edizione critica dell'anonima "Summa Totus homo" e il maestro Alano di Lilla', *Divus Thomas*, LVIII, 1955, 423–9.

Bossuat, R. 'Quelques personnages cités par Alain de Lille', *Mélanges Louis Halphen*, Paris, 1956, pp. 33–42.

Châtillon, J. 'La méthode théologique d'Alain de Lille', AGJ, pp. 47–60.

Chenu, M. D. 'Une théologie axiomatique au xiie siècle: Alain de Lille', *Cîteaux*, IX, 1958, 137–42.

'A la mémoire renouvelée du docteur universel Alain de Lille', *Cîteaux*, XIII, 1962, 67–70.

Cilento, V. *Alano di Lille, poeta e teologo del secolo xii*, Naples, 1958.

Ciotti, A. 'Alano e Dante', *Convivium*, XXVIII, 1960, 257–88.

Curtius, E. R. 'Dante und Alanus ab Insulis', *Romanische Forschungen*, LXII, 1950, 28–31.

Delhaye, P. 'Pour la "fiche" Alain de Lille', *Mélanges de science religieuse*, XX, 1963, 39–51.

Donovan, M. J. 'The *Anticlaudian* and three passages in *The Franklin's Tale*', *Journal of English and Germanic Philology*, LVI, 1957, 52–9.

Dronke, P. 'Boethius, Alanus and Dante', *Romanische Forschungen*, LXXVIII, 1966, 119–25.

Engelhardt, G. J. 'An emendation in *Anticlaudianus*', *Speculum*, XXIII, 1948, 110–111.

Evans, G. R. '"The Book of Experience": Alan of Lille's use of the classical rhetorical topos in his pastoral writings', *An. Cist.*, XXXII, 1976, 113–21.

'Boethian and Euclidean axiomatic method in the theology of the later twelfth century', *Archives internationales d'histoire des sciences*, CIII, 1980, 13–29.

'Alan of Lille and the threshold of theology', *An. Cist.* XXXVI, 1980, 129–47.

'Alan of Lille's *Distinctiones* and the problem of theological language'. *Sacris Erudiri*, XXIV, 1980, 67–86.

(tr.) *The Art of Preaching*. Cistercian Fathers, Michigan, 1981.

'*Perfectus Homo*: Alan of Lille's new creation', *Paideia* (in press).

Gandillac, M. de 'La nature chez Alain de Lille', AGJ, pp. 61–76.

Garzia, A. '*Integritas carnis* et *virginitas mentis* in Alano di Lilla', *Marianum*, XVI, 1954, 125–49.

Glorieux, P. *Répertoire des maîtres en théologie de Paris au xiii*e*s.*, Paris, 1933, vol. I.

'Le *Moralium dogma philosophorum* et son auteur', *RTAM*, XV, 1948, 360–6.

'L'auter de la Somme "*Quoniam Homines*"', *RTAM*, XVII, 1950, 29–45.

'Alain de Lille docteur de l'Assomption', *Mélanges de science religieus*, VIII, 1951, 5–18.

'Le prétendu *Liber Sententiarum et dictorum memorabilium* d'Alain de Lille', *RTAM*, XX, 1953, 229–64.

'L'auteur de l'*Ars fidei catholicae*'. *RTAM*, XII, 1956, 118–22.

'Alain de Lille, le moine et l'abbaye du Bec', *RTAM*, XXXIX, 1972, 51–62.

'Alain de Lille: problèmes de l'édition', AGJ, pp. 77–82.

Green, B. H. 'Alan of Lille's *De Planctu Naturae*', *Speculum*, XXXI, 1956, 649–74.

Gregory, T. 'L'idea di natura', *Congresso: La filosofia della natura nel medioevo*, Milan, 1966.

Häring, N. M. 'Alan of Lille's *De Fide Catholica et contra Haereticos*', *An. Cist.*, XXXII, 1976, 216–37.

'Die Rolle des hl. Schrift in der Auseinandersetzung des Alanus de Insulis mit dem Neu-Manichäismus', *Die Mächte des Guten und Bösen*, Miscellanea Mediävalia, XI, Berlin, 1977, pp. 315–43.

Huizinga, J. 'Über die Verknüpfung des Poetischen mit dem

Theologischen bei Alanus de Insulis', *Verzamelde Werke,* vol. IV, Harlem, 1949.

Javelet, R. *Image et ressemblance de S. Anselme à Alain de Lille,* 2 vols., Strasbourg, 1967.

Jolivet, J. 'Remarques sur les "Regulae Theologicae" d'Alain de Lille', AGJ, pp. 83–100.

Lebeau, M. 'La découverte du tombeau du bienheureux Alain de Lille', *Coll.,* XXIII, 1961, 254–60.

Longère, J. 'Alain de Lille, théologien de la pénitence', AGJ, pp. 101–2.

Lottin, O. 'Un traité sur les vertues, les vices et les dons restitué à Alain de Lille', *RTAM,* XVI, 1949, 161–4.

'Alain de Lille, une des sources des *Disputationes* de Simon de Tournai', *RTAM,* XVII, 1950, 175–86.

Michel, A. 'Rhétorique, poétique et nature chez Alain de Lille', AGJ, pp. 113–24.

Michaud-Quantin, P. 'Le *Liber poenitentialis* d'Alain de Lille. Le témoignage des manuscrits belges et français', *Cîteaux,* X, 1959, 93–106.

Moffat, D. (tr.) *Alan of Lille: The Complaint of Nature,* Yale Studies in English, XXXVI, New York, 1908.

Ochsenbein, P. *Studien zum Anticlaudianus des Alanus ab Insulis,* Frankfurt, 1975.

Payen, J. C. 'L'utopie du contrat social dans l'*Anticlaudianus*', AGJ, pp. 125–34.

Poirion, D. 'Alain de Lille et Jean de Meung', AGJ, pp. 135–52.

Raynaud de Lage, G. *Alain de Lille, poète du xiie siècle,* Montreal/Paris, 1951.

Rossi, G. F. 'Alano di Lilla, autore della Summa "*Totus homo*"', *Divus Thomas,* LVIII, 1955, 430–40.

'L'edizione critica della Summa *De Sacramentis* magistri Alani ab Insulis e il mancato riconoscimento della sua paternita', *Divus Thomas,* LVIII, 1955, 330–9.

'Dom Lottin nega in vano che Alano di Lilla sia l'autore della Summa *Totus homo*', *Divus Thomas,* LIX, 1956, 372–88.

Sheridan, J. J. 'The seven liberal arts in Alan of Lille and Peter of Compostella', *Mediaeval Studies,* XXXV, 1973, 27–37.

(tr.) *Anticlaudianus, or The Good and Perfect Man,* Toronto, 1973.

(tr.) *Plaint of Nature,* Toronto, 1980.

Szöverffy, J. 'Alain de Lille et la tradition tchèque. Notes Hymnologiques', *Études d'histoire littéraire et doctrinale,* XVII, Montreal/Paris, 1962. pp. 239–58.

Trout, J. M. 'Alan the Missionary' *Cîteaux,* XXVI, 1975, 146–54.

'The monastic vocation of Alan of Lille', *An. Cist.,* XXX, 1974, 46–53.

Tuve, R. 'Notes on the Virtues and Vices', *Journal of the Warburg and Courtauld Institutes*, XXVI, 1963, 295–303.

Vasoli, C. 'Studi recenti su Alano di Lilla', *Bollettino dell' Istituto storico italiano ed Archivio Muratoriano*, LXXII, 1960, 35–89.

'Il *Contra Haereticos* di Alano di Lilla', *ibid.*, LXXV, 1963, 123–72.

'Le idee filosofiche di Alano di Lilla nel *De Planctu* e nell' *Anticlaudianus*', *Giornale critico della filosofia italiana*, XL, 1961, 462–98.

'La *"Theologia apotheca"* di Alano di Lilla', *Rivista critica di storia della filosofia*, XVI, 1961, 153–87, 278–314.

Viarre, S. 'La description du palais de la nature dans l'*Anticlaudianus* d'Alain de Lille: 1.55–206', AGJ, pp. 133–70.

Walsh, P. G. 'Alan of Lille as a renaissance figure', *Studies in Church History*, XIV, 1977, 117–36.

Wetherbee, W. 'The function of poetry in the *De Planctu Naturae* of Alan of Lille', *Traditio*, XXV, 1969, 87–125.

Wilks, M. 'Alan of Lille and the New Man', *Studies in Church History*, XIV, 1977, 137–57.

Zink, M. 'La rhétorique honteuse et la convention du sermon *ad status* à travers la *summa de arte praedicatoria* d'Alain de Lille', AGJ, pp. 133–70.

2 SOURCES

Abelard, Peter *Opera Theologica*, ed. E. M. Buytaert, CCCM, XI, 1969.

Logica ingredientibus, ed. B. Geyer, Beiträge, XXI, Munster, 1919–27.

Dialectica, ed. L. M. de Rijk, Assen, 1956.

School of *Écrits théologiques de l'école d'Abélard*, ed. A. Landgraf, SSLov, XIV, 1934.

Adam de la Bassée *Ludus super Anticlaudianum*, ed. P. Bayaert, Tourcoing, 1930.

Adelard of Bath *De Eodem et Diverso*, ed. H. Willner, Beiträge, IV, 1903.

Alberic of Trois Fontaines *Chronica*, MGH SS, XXIII, pp. 631–950.

Alger of Liège *De Sacramentis Corporis et Sanguinis Domini*, PL 180. 727–853.

Ambrose of Milan *De Sacramentis*, ed. O. Faller, CSEL, LXXIII, 1955, pp. 13–85.

Anonymous of Affligem 'Der Literaturkatalog von Affligem', ed. N. M. Häring, *R. Bén.*, LXXXI, 1970, 80–2.

Anselm of Canterbury *Opera Omnia*, ed. F. S. Schmitt, Rome/Edinburgh, 6 vols., 1938–68.

Memorials of St Anselm, ed. F. S. Schmitt and R. W. Southern, London, 1969.

Apuleius, see Hermes Trismegistus, Ps.

Aquinas, Thomas '*Lectiones* on Boethius *De Hebdomadibus*', *Opuscula Theologica*, vol. II, ed. R. Spiazzi, Rome, 1954.

Summa Theologiae, ed. P. Caramello, Turin, 3 vols., 1962–3.

Summa Contra Gentiles, ed. P. Marc, Rome, 2 vols., 1961–7.

Aristotle *Analytica Posteriora*, ed. W. Ross, Oxford, 1949, repr. 1965.

Sophistic Elenchi, ed. E. S. Forster, London, 1955, 2nd edn, 1965.

Ps. *Liber de Causis*, ed. A. Pattin, Louvain, 1966.

Les Auctoritates Aristotelis, ed. J. Hamesse, Philosophes médiévaux, XVII, Louvain, 1974.

Arnaud, Abbot *Opera*, PL 189.1507–1733.

Augustine *Tractatus in Iohannem*, CCSL, XXXVI, 1954.

Sermones de Veteri Testamento, ed. C. Lambot, CCSL, XLI, Turnholt, 1961.

De Doctrina Christiana, CCSL, XIII, 1962.

Enarrationes in Psalmos, CCSL, XXXVIII, 1966.

Confessions, ed. M. Skutella, Stuttgart, 1969.

De Civitate Dei, CCSL, XLVII–VIII, 1968.

Bede *De Schematibus et Tropis*, PL 90.175–86.

De Temporibus, PL 90.187–277.

De Natura Rerum, PL 90.277–93.

Bernard of Clairvaux *Opera Omnia*, ed. J. Leclercq, C. H. Talbot and H. Rochais, 8 vols., Rome, 1957–78.

De Diligendo Deo, ibid., pp. 119–54.

Bernard Silvestris *De Mundi Universitate*, ed. C. S. Barach and J. Wrobel, Innsbruck, 1876, repr. Frankfurt, 1964.

Cosmographia, tr. W. Wetherbee, Columbia, 1973.

(?) *Commentary on the first six books of Virgil's Aeneid*, ed. E. W. and E. F. Jones, Nebraska, 1977.

Boethius *Opera*, PL 63–4.

De Institutione Arithmetica and *De Musica*, ed. G. Friedlein, Leipzig, 1867, repr. Frankfurt, 1966.

De Interpretatione, ed. C. Meiser, Leipzig, 1877–80.

Consolation of Philosophy and Theological Tractates, ed. H. F. Stewart and E. K. Rand, London, 1918 and revised by S. J. Tester, London, 1973.

(Ps.) *Geometrie II*, ed. M. Folkerts, Wiesbaden, 1970.

Bonaventure *Opera Omnia*, 10 vols., Quarrachi, 1882–1902.

Browne, Thomas *Works*, 2nd edn, ed. G. Keynes, London, 1964.

Bull, G. 'The state of man before the Fall', *Opera Omnia* (first edn, 1703), ed. E. Burton, 8 vols., Oxford, 1827.

Cassian *Collationes*, ed. M. Petschenig, CSEL, XIII, Vienna, 1886.

Institutiones, ed. M. Petschenig, CSEL, XVII, Vienna, 1888.

Institutiones, ed. R. A. B. Mynors, Oxford, 1937.

Cassiodorus *In Psalmos*, CCSL, XCVII–XCVIII, 1968.

Cicero *De Officiis*, ed. W. Miller, London, 1947.

Orator, ed. P. Reis, Stuttgart, 1963.

Topica, ed. H. M. Hubbell, London, 1968.

Clarembald of Arras *Life and Works*, ed. N. M. Häring, Toronto, 1965.

Dante *Divina Commedia*, ed. G. L. Bickersteth, Oxford, 1972.

Dionysius (Ps.) *De Ecclesiastica Hierarchia*, ed. J. Parker, London, 1899.

De Caelesti Hierarchia, ed. R. Roques, G. Heil, M. de Gandillac, Sources chrétiennes, LVIII, Paris, 1958.

De Divinis Nominibus, PG 3.586–995.

Distinctiones ed. J. B. Pitra, Spicilegium Solesmense, II Paris, 1855.

Dream of the Rood, The ed. B. Dickens and A. Ross, London, 1963.

Durandus of Troarn *De Corpore et Sanguine Domini*, PL 149.1375–1423.

Eadmer *Vita Anselmi*, ed. R. W. Southern, Oxford, 1963.

Ellebaut *Anticlaudien*, ed. A. J. Creighton, Washington, 1944.

Eriugena, John Scouts *De Praedestinatione*, ed. G. Madec, CCCM, L, 1978.

Geoffrey of Auxerre *Libellus*, PL 185.587–613.

Vita Sancti Bernardi, PL 185.1162–87.

Geoffrey of Monmouth *Historia Regum Britanniae*, ed. J. Hammer, Cambridge, Mass., 1951.

Gerhoch of Reichersberg *Liber contra Duas Haereses*, PL 194.1162–87.

Gilbert Crispin *Disputatio Judei et Christiani*, ed. B. Blumenkranz, Antwerp, 1956.

Gilbert of Poitiers *Commentaries on Boethius*, ed. N. M. Häring, Toronto, 1966.

Gregory the Great *Moralia in Job*, PL 75–6.

Guibert of Nogent *Quo Ordine Sermo Fieri Debeat*, PL 156.21–32.

Guimund of Aversa *De Corpore et Sanguine Domini*, PL 149.1427–95.

Gundisalvi, Domingo *De Unitate et Uno*, ed. P. Corbens, Beiträge, I, 1891.

De Scientiis, ed. P. Alonso Alonso, Madrid, 1954.

Gunzo *Epistola ad Augienses*, ed. K. Manitius, MGH Quellen, II, Weimar, 1958.

Hermes Trismegistus, Ps. 'Asclepius', ed. P. Thomas, *Apulei Opera*, vol. III, Leipzig, 1908.

'Das pseudo-hermetische Buch der vierundzwanzig Meister', ed. C. Baeumker, *Beiträge*, XXV, 1927, 194–214.

Hildegard *Opera*, PL 197.

Hopkins, G. M. *The sermons and devotional writings*, ed. C. Devlin, Oxford, 1959.

Honorius Augustodunensis *Speculum Ecclesiae*, PL 172.807–1106.

Hugh of Amiens *Contra Haereticos*, PL 92.1255–99.

John of Garland *De Triumphis Ecclesiae*, ed. T. Wright, London, 1965.

John of Salisbury *Policraticus*, ed. C. C. J. Webb, 2 vols., Oxford, 1909.

Metalogicon, ed. C. C. J. Webb, Oxford, 1929.

Sources

John the Scot and Remigius of Auxerre *Commentaries on the Opuscula Sacra*, ed. E. K. Rand, Quellen und Untersuchungen zur lateiniche Philologie des Mittelalters, 1 Munich, 1906.

Lanfranc *De Corpore et Sanguine Domini*, PL 150.407–42.

Logica Modernorum ed. L. M. de Rijk, 2 vols., Assen, 1967.

Lucretius *De Rerum Natura*, ed. J. Martin, Leipzig, 1963.

Macrobius *In Somnium Scipionis*, ed. J. R. Willis, Leipzig, 1964.

Martianus Capella *De Nuptiis Philologiae et Mercurii*, ed. A. Dick, Leipzig, 1925, repr. with additions by J. Préaux, 1969.

Morinus, Johannes Baptistus *Astrologia Gallica*, The Hague, 1661.

Morzillus, Sebastianus Foxius *De Natura Philosophiae seu Platonis et Aristotelis Consensione*, Paris, 1560.

Newman, John Henry *Discourses to Mixed Congregations*, London, 1871.

Nicholas of Amiens *De Articulis Catholicae Fidei*, PL 210.593–617.

Nicomachus of Gerasa *Introduction to Arithmetic*, tr. M. L. d'Ooge, New York/London, 1926.

Otto of Freising *Gesta Friderici*, 3rd edn, G. Waitz, MGH SS, Leipzig, 1912.

Otto of St Blaise *Continuatio Sanblasiana*, ed. R. Wilmans, MGH SS, xx.

Peter the Chanter *Verbum Abbreviatum*, PL 205.21–554.

Summa de Sacramentis et Animae Consiliis, ed. J. A. Dugauquier, Analecta Medievalia Namurcensia, vols. IV, VII, XVI, XXI, 1954–62.

Peter Helias 'The Summa of Petrus Helias on Priscianus Minor', ed. J. E. Tolson, *Cahiers*, XXVII–XXVIII, 1978.

Peter Lombard 'Libri Quatuor Sententiarum', Books I, II, *Spicilegium Bonaventurianum*, 2 vols., Rome, 1971; Books III, IV, PL 192.453–965.

Commentary on the Pauline Epistles, PL 191.1297–1695.

Peter of Poitiers *Sententie*, ed. P. S. Moore and M. Dulong, Notre Dame, Indiana, 2 vols., 1943, 1950.

Peter the Venerable *Contra Petrobrusianos*, ed. J. Fearns, CCCM, x, 1968.

Plato (Latinus) *Timaeus a Calcidio Translatus*, ed. P. Jensen and J. Waszink, London/Leiden, 1962; 2nd edn, 1975.

Pope, Alexander *Essay on Man*, 1733.

Praepositinus *The 'Summa contra Haereticos' ascribed to Praepositinus*, ed. J. N. Garvin and J. A. Corbett, Notre Dame, Indiana, 1958.

Priscian *Ars Grammatica*, ed. H. Keil, Grammatici Latini, II–III, Leipzig, 1855–9.

Proclus *In Primum Euclidis Elementorum Librum Commentarii*, ed. G. Friedlein, Leipzig, 1873; rev. and tr. G. R. Morrow, Princeton, 1970.

Ralph of Longchamps *In Anticlaudianum Alani Commentum*, ed. J. Sulowski, Warsaw, 1972.

Remigius of Auxerre, see John the Scot.

Robert of Melun *Sententie*, ed. R. Martin, SSLov, XXI, 1947.

Bibliography

Rupert of Deutz *De Trinitate et Operibus Eius*, ed. H. Haacke, CCCM, XXII–IV, 1971–2.
De Victoria Verbi Dei, ed. H. Haacke, MGH Quellen, v, 1970.
Seneca *Naturales Quaestiones*, ed. T. H. Corcoram, 2 vols., London, 1971–2.
Simon of Tournai *Disputationes*, ed. J. Wariches, SSLov, XII, 1932.
Statius *Thebaid*, ed. H. W. Garrod, Oxford, 1965.
Thierry of Chartres *Commentaries on Boethius by Thierry of Chartres and his School*, ed. N. M. Häring, Toronto, 1971.
Twenty-Four Philosophers, See Hermes Trismegistus, Ps.
William of Conches *Glosa super Platonem*, ed. E. Jeauneau, Paris, 1965.
William of St Thierry *De Sacramento Altaris*, PL 180.341–63.

3 STUDIES

Alverny, M. T. d'. 'Le cosmos symbolique du xii⁰ siècle', *AHDLMA*, xx, 1953, 31–81.
Antl, L. 'Stephen Langton's principle of determining the essence of a sacrament', *Franciscan Studies*, XIV, 1954, 151–75.
Baldwin, J. W. 'A debate at Paris over Thomas Becket', *Studia Gratiana*, XI, 1967, 119–32.
Masters, princes and merchants, 2 vols., Princeton, 1970.
Balić, P. 'Bemerkungen zur Verwendung mathematischer Beweise und zu den Theoremata bei den scholastischen Schriftstellern', *Wissenschaft und Weisheit*, III, 1936, 206.
'Les anciens manuscrits de la bibliothèque metropolitaine de Zagreb', *Studia Medievalia in honorem R. J. Martin*, Louvain, 1948, pp. 462–6.
'De Auctore Operis quod *Ars Fidei Catholicae* inscribitur', *Mélanges J. de Ghellinck*, vol. II, Paris, 1951, pp. 793–814.
Birkenmajer, A. *Le rôle joué par les médicins et les naturalistes dans la réception d'Aristote aux xii⁰ et xiii⁰ siècles*, Warsaw, 1930.
Bloomfield, M. W. 'Preliminary list of incipits of Latin works on the Virtues and Vices', *Traditio*, XI, 1955, 259–379.
Bonnes, J. P. 'Un des plus grands prédicateurs du xii⁰ siècle, Geoffroy Louroux, dit Geoffrey Babion', *R. Bén.*, LVI, 1945–6, 174–215.
Born, L. K. 'The perfect prince', *Speculum*, III, 1928, 470–504.
Boskoff, P. S. 'Quintilian in the late Middle Ages', *Speculum*, XXVII, 1952, 71–8.
Brooke, R. *The coming of the friars*, London, 1975.
Callus, D. A. 'The contribution to the study of the Fathers made by the thirteenth century Oxford School', *Journal of Ecclesiastical History*, v, 1954, 139–48.
Charland, T. M. *Artes Praedicandi*, Paris, 1936.

240

Chenu, M. D. 'Un essai de méthode théologique au xii⁰ siècle', *Revue des sciences philosophiques et théologiques*, xxiv, 1935, 259–67.

'Grammaire et théologie aux xii⁰ et xiii⁰ siècles', *AHDLMA*, x, 1935–6, 5–28.

'Platon à Cîteaux', *AHDLMA*, xxi, 1954, 99–106.

La théologie au xii⁰ siècle, Paris, 1957.

'Erigène à Cîteaux, la philosophie et ses problèmes', *Recueil d'études et de doctrine et d'histoire offert à R. Jolivet*, Lyon, 1960, pp. 99–107.

Clagett, M. 'The mediaeval Latin translations from the Arabic of the *Elements* of Euclid', *Isis*, xliv, 1953, 16–42.

Clerval, A. *Les écoles de Chartres au Moyen-Age*, Chartres, 1895.

Courcelle, P. *Les lettres grecques en occident, de Macrobe à Cassidore*, Paris, 1943, 2nd edn, 1948. Eng. tr. H. E. Wedeck, 1969.

'Traditions néo-platoniciennes et traditions chrétiennes de la région de dissemblance', *AHDLMA*, xxiv, 1957, 5–33.

'Témoins nouveaux de la "région de dissemblance"', *Bibliothèque de l'Ecole des Chartes*, cviii, 1960.

'*Nosce teipsum*, du Bas-Empire au Haut Moyen-Age', *Settimane di studi del centro italiano di studi sull'alto Medioevo*, vol. xi, Spoleto, 1961.

Connais-tu toi même, 3 vols., Paris, 1974.

Delhaye, P. 'L'organisation scolaire au xii⁰s.', *Traditio*, v, 1947, 211.

Dickey, M. 'Some commentaries on the *De Inventione* and the *Rhetorica ad Herennium* of the eleventh and twelfth centuries', *Mediaeval and Renaissance Studies*, vi, 1968, 1–41.

Dickson, M. and C. 'Le Cardinal Robert de Courson: sa vie', *AHDLMA*, ix, 1934, 53–142.

Dondaine, A. 'Aux origines du valdéisme. Une profession de foi de Valdès', *Archivum Fratrum Praedicatorum*, xvi, 1946, 191–235.

'Cinq citations de Jean Scot chez Simon de Tournai', *RTAM*, xvii, 1950, 303–11.

Le corpus dionysien de l'Université de Paris au xiii⁰s., Rome, 1952.

'Ecrits de la "petit école" porrétaine', *Conférence Albert le Grand*, Montreal/Paris, 1962.

Dronke, P. *Fabula*, Leiden/Cologne, 1974.

Dumoutet, E. 'La théologie de l'Eucharistie à la fin du xii⁰ siècle', *AHDLMA*, xiv, 1943–4, 181–261.

Evans, G. *Old Arts and New Theology*, Oxford, 1980.

'Peter the Chanter's *De Tropis Loquendi*: the problem of the text', *New Scholasticism*, lv, i, 1981, 95–103.

Faral, E. *Les arts poétiques du xii⁰ et du xiii⁰ siècle*, Paris, 1923.

Fearns, J. V. 'The *Contra Petrobrusianos* of Peter the Venerable', University of Liverpool Ph.D. thesis, 1963.

Fredborg, K. M. 'Petrus Helias on Rhetoric', *Cahiers*, xiii, 1974, 31–41.

Gandillac, M. de *La Philosophie de Nicholas de Cues*, Paris, 1941.

'Sur la sphère infinie de Pascal', *Revue d'histoire de la philosophie et d'histoire générale de la civilisation*, XXXIII, 1943, 32–44.

Garvin, J. N. 'Peter of Poitiers and Simon of Tournai on the Trinity', *RTAM*, XVI, 1949, 314–16.

and Corbett, J. A. *The Summa contra Haereticos ascribed to Praepositinus of Cremona*, Notre Dame, 1958.

Ghellinck, J. de 'Nani et gigantes', *Archivum Latinitatis Medii Aevi*, XVIII, 1945, 25–9.

L'essor de la littérature latine au xiie siècle, Brussels/Paris, 1948.

Le mouvement théologique du xiie siècle, Brussels/Paris, 1948.

Gibson, M. T. *Lanfranc of Bec*, Oxford, 1978.

Gilson, E. 'Le platonisme de Bernard de Chartres', *Revue néo-scolastique de philosophie*, XXV, 1923, 5–19.

'La cosmogonie de Bernardus Silvestris', *AHDLMA*, III, 1928, 5–24.

Giusberti, F. *Materials for a Study on Twelfth Century Scholasticism*, Naples, 1983.

Glorieux, P. 'L'auteur de l'*Ars Fidei Catholicae*, *RTAM*, XXIII, 1956, 118–22.

Gregory, T. *Anima Mundi: La filosofia di Guglielmo di Conches e la scuola di Chartres*, Florence, 1955.

Platonismo medievale, Rome, 1958.

Gundel, W. *Neue astrologische Texte des Hermes Trismegistos*, Munich, 1936.

Hamilton, B. *Monastic Reform, Catharism and the Crusades, 900–1300*, London, 1979.

Häring, N. M. 'A Latin Dialogue on the Doctrine of Gilbert of Poitiers', *Mediaeval Studies*, XV, 1953, 243–89.

'A Treatise on the Trinity by Gilbert of Poitiers', *RTAM*, XXXIX, 1972, 14–50.

Haskins, C. *Studies in the History of Mediaeval Science*, Cambridge, Mass., 1927.

The renaissance of the twelfth century, Cambridge, Mass., 1927.

Hauréau, B. *Notices et extraits de manuscrits de la bibliothèque nationale*, vols. I–VI, Paris, 1891–3.

Henry, D. P. *The Logic of St Anselm*, Oxford, 1967.

A Commentary on the De Grammatico, Dordrecht, 1974.

Holmes, U. T. 'The idea of the twelfth century renaissance', *Speculum*, XXVI, 1951, 635–42.

Hunt, R. W. 'English learning in the late twelfth century', *Transactions of the Royal Historical Society*, XIX, 1934.

'The introduction to the Artes in the 12th century', *Studia Medievalia in honorem R. J. Martin*, Louvain, 1949, pp. 85–112.

reprinted in *Essays in Mediaeval History*, ed. R. W. Southern, London, 1968, pp. 119–30.

'The Summa of Petrum Helias on Priscianus Minor', *Historiographia Linguistica*, ii (i), 1975, 1–23.

Huygens, R. B. C. *Accessus ad Auctores*, Leiden, 1970.

Jeauneau, E. 'L'usage de la notion d'*integumentum* à travers les gloses de Guillaume de Conches', *AHDLMA*, lxxix, 1957, 35–100.

'Macrobe, source du platonisme chartrain', *Studi Medievali*, i, 1960, 3–24.

'Deux redactions des gloses de Guillaume de Conches sur Priscian', *RTAM*, xxvii, 1960, 212–47.

Kennedy, V. L. 'The handbook of Master Peter, Chancellor of Chartres', *Mediaeval Studies*, v, 1943, 1–38.

Klauser, T., ed. *Reallexikon für Antike und Christentum*, vol. iii, Stuttgart, 1957, pp. ff.1075–1121 (R. Roques).

Klibansky, R. *The continuity of the Platonic tradition during the Middle Ages*, London, 1950.

'The School of Chartres', *Twelfth century Europe and the foundations of modern society*, ed. M. Clagett, G. Post, R. Reynolds, Madison, Wisconsin, 1961, pp. 3–14.

Kritzeck, J. *Peter the Venerable and Islam*, Princeton, 1964.

Lambert, M. D. *Mediaeval Heresy*, London, 1977.

Landgraf, A. M. 'Peter of Capua', *New Scholasticism*, xiv, 1940, 57–74. and see under *Sources*, Abelard, school of.

Latham, R. E. *Revised mediaeval Latin word-list*, London, 1965.

Lawn, B. *The Salernitan questions: an introduction to the history of mediaeval and renaissance problem literature*, Oxford, 1963.

Lefèvre, Y. *L'Elucidarium et les lucidaires*, Paris, 1954.

Longère, J. *Oeuvres oratoires des maîtres Parisiens du xiie siècle*, 2 vols., Études Augustiniennes, 1975.

Lottin, O. *Psychologie et morale aux xiie et xiiie siècles*, 6 vols., Gembloux, 1957–60.

Lubac, H. de 'Saint Grégoire et la grammaire', *Recherches de science religieuse*, xlviii, 1960, 185–226.

Exégèse médiévale. Les quatre sens de l'Écriture, 2 vols., Paris, 1959–61.

Michaud-Quantin, P. 'La classification des puissances de l'âme au xiie siècle', *Revue du Moyen Age latin*, v, 1949, 15–34.

Sommes de casuistique et manuels de confession au Moyen Âge, Analecta Medievalia Namurcensia, xiii, Louvain, 1962.

Mollard, A. 'La diffusion de l'*Institution Oratoire* au xiie siècle', *Le Moyen Age*, xliii, 1934, 161–75 and xliv, 1935, 1–9.

Montclos, J. de *Lanfranc et Bérengar*, SSLov, xxxvii, 1971.

Moore, P. S. *The Works of Peter of Poitiers*, Notre Dame, Indiana, 1936.

Morris, C. *The discovery of the individual*, London, 1972.

Murphy, J. J. *Rhetoric in the Middle Ages*, California, 1974.

A bibliography of mediaeval Rhetoric, Toronto, 1971.

Nitze, W. A. 'The so-called twelfth century renaissance', *Speculum*, XXIII, 1948, 464–71.

Nock, A. D. *Asclepius*, 'Introduction', Corpus Hermeticum, XIII–XVIII (2). *Les Belles Lettres*, Paris, 1945.

Pitra, J. B. See Sources, *Distinctiones*.

Poole, R. L. 'The masters of the Schools of Paris and Chartres in John of Salisbury's time', *English Historical Review*, XXXV, 1920, 321–42.

Reeves, M. *The influence of prophecy in the later Middle Ages*, Oxford, 1969.

Roberts, P. B. *Studies in the Sermons of Stephen Langton*, Toronto, 1968.

Robson, C. A. *Maurice de Sully and the mediaeval vernacular homily*, Oxford, 1952.

Roques, R. *L'univers dionysien*, Paris, 1954.

(and see Klauser, T.)

'La notion dionysienne de hiérarchie', *AHDLMA*, XVI, 1948, 183–222.

Rouse, R. H. and M. A. 'The verbal concordance to the Scriptures', *Archivum Fratrum Praedicatorum*, XLIV, 1974.

'Biblical *Distinctiones* in the thirteenth century', *AHDLMA*, XLI, 1974, 27–37.

Runciman, S. *The Mediaeval Manichee*, Cambridge, 1955.

Sandford, E. M. 'The twelfth century: renaissance or proto-renaissance?', *Speculum*, XXVI, 1951, 635–42.

Schneyer, J. B. *Repertorium der Lateinischen Sermones des Mittelalters*, A–D, Münster, 1969.

Selge, K. V. *Die Ersten Waldenser*, 2 vols., Berlin, 1967.

Silverstein, T. 'The fabulous cosmogony of Bernardus Silvestris', *Modern Philology*, XLVI, 1948, 92–116.

Smalley, B. *The study of the Bible in the Middle Ages*, Oxford, 1949, 2nd edn, 1952.

Smyth, C. *The art of preaching: a practical survey of preaching in the Church of England*, London, 1940.

Southern, R. W. *St Anselm and his biographer*, Cambridge, 1963.

Medieval Humanism, Oxford, 1970.

Stegmüller, F. *Repertorium Biblicum Medii Aevi*, 7 vols., Madrid, 1950–61.

Steinen, W. von den 'Les sujets d'inspiration chez les poètes latins du xiie siècle', *Cahiers de civilisation médiévale*, IX, 1966, 165–75 and 363–83.

Stock, B. *Myth and science in the twelfth century*, Princeton, 1972.

Struve, T. *Die Entwicklung der organologischen Staatsauffassung im M.A.*, Stuttgart, 1978.

Thorndike, L. '*Quaestiones Alani*', *Isis*, LI, 1960, 181–5.

Thouzellier, C. *Liber contra Manicheos*, SSLov, XXXII, 1964.

Hérésie et hérétiques: Vaudois, cathares, patarins, albigeois, Storia e Letteratura, CXVI, Rome, 1966, 2nd edn, 1969.

Catharisme et Valdéisme en Languedoc à la fin du xiiᵉ et au début du xiiiᵉ siècle, 2nd edn, Louvain/Paris, 1969.

Livre des Deux Principes, Sources chrétiennes, CXCVIII, Paris, 1973.

Tuve, R. 'Notes on the Virtues and Vices', *Journal of the Warburg and Courtauld Institutes*, XXVI, 1963, 295–303.

Uhlfelder, M. L. *De Proprietate Sermonum vel Rerum*, Papers and monographs of the American Academy in Rome, XV, Rome, 1954.

Ullmann, W. *A history of political thought*, London, 1965.

The individual and society, Baltimore, 1966, London, 1967.

'Church and Law in the Earlier Middle Ages', *Collected Studies*, vol. I, London, 1978.

'John of Salisbury's *Policraticus* in the later Middle Ages', *Geschichtsschreibung und geistiges Leben im Mittelalter: Festschrift für H. Löwe*, ed. K. Hauck and H. Mordek, Cologne/Vienna, 1978, pp. 619–46.

Van den Eynde, D. 'Deux sources de la Somme théologique de Simon de Tournai', *Antonianum*, XXIV, 1949, 19–42.

Les définitions des sacrements pendant la première période de la théologie scholastique (1050–1240), Rome, 1950.

Vicaire, M. H. 'Les Porrétains et l'Avicennisme avant 1215'. *Revue des sciences philosophiques et théologiques*, XXVI, 1937, 449–82.

Warichez, J. *Etienne de Tournai et son temps*, Paris, 1937.

Wetherbee, W. *Platonism and poetry in the twelfth century*, Princeton, 1972.

Wolsey, R. B. 'Bernard Silvester and the Hermetic Asclepius', *Traditio*, VI, 1948, 340–4.

Yates, F. *The art of memory*, London, 1969.

Zubov, V. 'Autour des *Questiones super Geometriam Euclidis* de Nicholas Oresme', *Mediaeval and Renaissance Studies*, VI, 1968, 150–71.

Index